POEMS AND POETS

POEMS

David Aloian

Headmaster, Concord Academy

AND POETS

Foreword by John Crowe Ransom

WEBSTER DIVISION
MCGRAW-HILL BOOK COMPANY
St. Louis   New York
San Francisco
Dallas   Toronto   London

Mr. David Aloian, a graduate of Harvard College, has his Master's degree in English from Boston University. In fourteen years of teaching, he has taught all grades of English from 5 to 12, principally at the Belmont Hill School, Belmont, Massachusetts. Mr. Aloian has spoken to various conventions of the National Council of the Teachers of English. He has written articles on poetry for various magazines, and he is the author of the introduction to Walden *in the Modern Classics edition.*

34567VB9876

01397

ACKNOWLEDGMENTS

The editors wish to thank the following for granting permission to reprint material included in this book.

CONRAD AIKEN "Frostbite."
ROBERT BELOOF
"A Spring Night." Reprinted by permission of Robert Beloof and *Saturday Review.*
BRANDT & BRANDT
"Does It Matter?" by Siegfried Sassoon. From COUNTER ATTACK. Publisher: E. P. Dutton & Co., Inc. Copyright 1940 by Siegfried Sassoon.
CONSTABLE & COMPANY LTD.
"Heat," by Hilda Doolittle.
J. M. DENT & SONS LTD.
From TYPHOON, Joseph Conrad.
DODD, MEAD & COMPANY
"The Soldier," from THE COLLECTED POEMS OF RUPERT BROOKE. Copyright, 1915, by Dodd, Mead & Company. Copyright 1943 by Edward Marsh; "The Skater of Ghost Lake," by William Rose Benét, from GOLDEN FLEECE. Copyright, 1933, 1935 by Dodd, Mead & Company. "The World State," by G. K. Chesterton, from THE COLLECTED POEMS OF G. K. CHESTERTON. Copyright 1932 by Dodd, Mead & Co., Inc. All reprinted by permission of Dodd, Mead & Co.
DOUBLEDAY & COMPANY, INC.
"Ballad of East and West," "Danny Deever," "Gunga Din," all by Rudyard Kipling, from RUDYARD KIPLING'S VERSE: Definitive Edition. Reprinted by permission of Mrs. George Bambridge, and Doubleday & Company, Inc.; "The Honey Bee": 4 lines from "Certain Maxims of Archy," from the book ARCHY AND MEHITABEL by Don Marquis. Copyright 1927 by Doubleday & Company, Inc.; "Elegy for Jane," copyright, 1950 by Theodore Roethke, from THE WAKING by Theodore Roethke; "The Sloth," copyright, 1950 by Theodore Roethke from WORDS FOR THE WIND by Theodore Roethke. All by permission of Doubleday & Company, Inc.
E. P. DUTTON & COMPANY, INC.
"The Donkey," from the book THE WILD KNIGHT AND OTHER POEMS by G. K. Chesterton. "On the Vanity of Earthly Greatness," from the book GAILY THE TROUBADOUR by Arthur Guiterman. Copyright 1936 by E. P. Dutton & Company, Inc. "Sky-Writer," from the book AUTOLYCUS IN LIMBO by

Vincent Starrett. Copyright 1943 by Vincent Starrett. All published by E. P. Dutton & Company, Inc. and reprinted by their permission.
MAX EASTMAN "At the Aquarium."
NORMA MILLAY ELLIS
"Lament," by Edna St. Vincent Millay. Reprinted from COLLECTED POEMS, Harper & Row. Copyright 1921, 1923, 1928, 1948, 1951, 1955 by Edna St. Vincent Millay and Norma Millay Ellis. By permission of Norma Millay Ellis.
HARCOURT, BRACE & WORLD, INC.
"Next to of Course God," by E. E. Cummings. Copyright, 1926, by Horace Liveright; renewed, 1954, by E. E. Cummings. Reprinted from POEMS 1923–1954 by E. E. Cummings; "Journey of the Magi," "Preludes I and II," and 8 lines from "The Love Song of J. Alfred Prufrock," all from COLLECTED POEMS OF T. S. ELIOT. Copyright, 1914, by Harcourt, Brace & World, Inc., renewed, 1942, by Louis Untermeyer. Reprinted from his volume, LONG FEUD, by permission of the publishers. Excerpts from "Gerontion" and "The Waste Land," by T. S. Eliot, from COLLECTED POEMS 1909–1962; "King Juke," from AFTERNOON OF A PAWNBROKER, copyright 1943, by Kenneth Fearing; "Salem," by Robert Lowell from LORD WEARY'S CASTLE, copyright 1944, 1946, by Robert Lowell; "The Hammer," from COMPLETE POEMS, copyright, 1950, by Carl Sandburg; "Caliban in the Coal Mines," from LONG FEUD by Louis Untermeyer; "Immortal Love," from THE ROAMER by George E. Woodberry. All reprinted by permission of Harcourt, Brace & World, Inc.
HARVARD UNIVERSITY PRESS
"The Day." Reprinted by permission of the publishers from Theodore Spencer, POEMS 1940–1947. Cambridge, Mass.: Harvard University Press, copyright, 1944, 1948 by The President and Fellows of Harvard College.
HOLT, RINEHART AND WINSTON, INC.
"The Golf Links." From PORTRAITS AND PROTESTS by Sarah N. Cleghorn. All rights reserved; "Exit," "From 'Irradiations,'" from SELECTED POEMS by John Gould Fletcher. Copyright 1938 by John Gould Fletcher; "Nothing Gold Can Stay," "Design," "Once by the Pacific," "Fire and Ice,"

FOREWORD

UNTIL THE publication of this book, most high school students have had to go to college to discover what poetry really is, unless by some prodigious natural talent they have discovered it at an early age by themselves.

Poetry is not much more difficult than music or painting; but it suffers in popularity because it has not been exhibited in the schools so intimately and lovingly as have those other admirable arts.

It is an honor to be making a small general introduction to this textbook. But I do not mean to infringe upon the author's good talk, which will be meaningful to students in its own right. I wish to look into their futures for a moment, for the sake of a bold forecast. Mr. Aloian's text is going to send them to college prepared for advanced reading. I predict that many of them will manage to read with confidence even our rather difficult poetry of this century; some will conceive a lifelong passion for understanding the whole poetic art intuitively, that is, by the sense of it which comes with much experience; and some may even come to understand it philosophically. In this foreword, I would like to discuss with you two major poetic principles.

First principle: The well-furnished and well-turned and perfect poem will always be fabulous. Poetry begins that way for us in our childhood, the season when imagination runs without restriction and, in our innocence, we believe firmly in magic.

> Hey, diddle, diddle,
> The cat and the fiddle,
> The cow jumped over the moon;
> The little dog laughed
> To see such sport,
> And the dish ran away with the spoon.

Nothing could be more childish, irresponsible, and agreeable. But it is strictly according to the laws of poetry that we should always love the weather, the hills and dales, the nicer creatures, and even the homely objects around us, and to assume that they love us too. We confer upon nature an intelligence like our own. Let us say that Mother Goose is for children aged about four to nine, even though her rhymes and fantasies get into our blood so that we never stop recalling them with pleasure.

But there is Browning's poem about Pippa, the Italian girl who is matured enough to work in the silk mills. Now she is on holiday, and rises and goes out very early to marvel at the fine morning that is spread out before her. She sings:

The year's at the spring,
And day's at the morn;
Morning's at seven;
The hillside's dew-pearled;
The lark's on the wing;
The snail's on the thorn;
God's in His heaven—
All's right with the world.

The poem does not in strictness require the next-to-last line. It is sufficient if nature appears in the beauty of ordered appointments everywhere, and how that should be is not ordinarily in question. The rightness of the world is natural and fabulous too. That is all we need to
know.

The poetic imagination tends to make the natural effects more
perfect than the fact (as in the "dew-pearled" hillside), and to leave
out some effects which are hateful. In any event, nature is very change-
ful, and the beauty of a poem is the luck of a moment, and highly
precarious. That is why it is almost a truism to say that every poem
must be in its time new in its effects and even in its style. If a poetry
merely imitates another poetry in either respect, its author seems to
us a poor poet. But if new poets and new poems continue to appear,
it proves that the poetic faith is persistent, like any vital compulsion.

Second principle: A poem is musical. It builds a structure of
formal or informal rhythms which repeat themselves. The music is
oral, not instrumental, consisting in like combinations of stressed and
high-pitched syllables with unstressed and low-pitched syllables. In
measured or metrical verse there are standard or uniform lines made
of standard or uniform feet, with only slight and permissive variations.
But in the 19th century the best ear for the music of verse belonged
to Tennyson, and here is a small passage from his poem "Ulysses":

The long day wanes: the slow moon climbs: the deep

Moans round with many voices. Come, my friends,
'Tis not too late to seek a newer world.
Push off, and sitting well in order smite
The sounding furrows.

I have marked the stressed syllables of the first two lines; the lines are
iambic pentameters. It is possible to figure that the strong adjective
long and the verb *wanes*, between them, define the subject *day* suffi-
ciently, and are capable of taking its stress away from it, making it all
the easier for *slow* and *climb* likewise to steal the stress away from
moon, which they indicate pretty well anyhow. Therefore, forgetting
for a moment the standard foot-rhythm structure, suppose we arrange
these logical phrases independently to show them off more spec-
tacularly:

The lóng dáy wánes;

The slów móon clímbs:

The déep móans róund . . . .

Here is a new and odd rhythm chiming perfectly three times as a new
rhythm suddenly attempted in the midst of the foot-rhythms: one
unstressed syllable followed by three stressed syllables each time. It
is impossible to get into the standard rhythm of the piece unless, as
we have calculated, the second stressed syllable is taken as less important than its two companions and sounded a little less strongly.

In Tennyson's poem the phrase-rhythm occurs three times to
establish itself so well that we cannot ignore it. Yet it harmonizes with
the standard foot-rhythm if we suppress slightly the stress on the third
syllable, as we have marked it in scanning the two long lines. Then
we are conscious of two musics at once, without the sacrifice of either.
The musical name of this sort of thing is counterpoint; the most familiar example in our musical experience is hearing a song sung by four
voices at once, as in a barbershop quartet; one of them carrying the
main air or melody, the others carrying other airs, going three different
ways, though not one of the three nor all three together dominate
over the main melody but all three harmonize with it. Such is the
wonderful footwork that Tennyson achieves. Such wonders are possible if the poet is able to make perfect meanings and perfect music
out of the same words.

But, when we look at our revolutionary modern poetry, that is
only half of the story. Free verse has come; it is the staple of some
important poets. It seems to keep no metrical or standard rhythm
throughout, but only to pick its own unmusical way trying to supply
the exact sense of the given situation; as if afraid the meters would
meddle with its exactitude of meaning and make it silly. So it would,
so it does, if they are poor poets. And we think to ourselves, much as
we may admire their meaningful achievements: How good it would
be if at least every now and then they might set up some loose or
informal rhythm and repeat it, over several phrases. But that very
thing happens many times in free verse. Perhaps the best ear among
our modern poets is T. S. Eliot's. In honor of the "traditional new-
ness" of all poetry, and the difficulty nowadays of using the old meters
otherwise than tritely, he came after many experiments to a kind of
free verse line. The first poem in which he expresses his mastery is
thought to be "Gerontion," about the old man who lived in his solitude
and disillusionment, with a sneezing woman keeping the kitchen, and
meditated on his loss of religious faith. After much rumination and
distress the old man sums up at the end the result of seventy-five lines
of careful free verse:

Tenants of the house,
Thoughts of a dry brain in a dry season.

But we could write them like this:

> Tenants of the house,
> Thoughts of a dry
> Brain in a dry
> Season.

The phrases printed that way would make a good Mother Goose rhythm—or a miniature ballad. The norm of the lines of this poem as they are actually printed is a sort of free yet pentameter line, with great adaptability in the individual phrases. We cannot study this line-and-a-half without making possible rhythms of it, though loose ones. It is musical.

Or consider the opening lines of *The Waste Land:*

> April is the cruellest month, breeding
> Lilacs out of the dead land, mixing
> Memory and desire, stirring
> Dull roots with spring rain.
> Winter kept us warm, covering
> Earth in forgetful snow, feeding
> A little life with dried tubers.

Here in free verse is rhythm realized first in a sentence of four lines, of which the first three have -*ing* participial endings and the concluding line drops the rhythm; then in a similar sentence where the rhythm occurs in two lines and is dropped in the conclusion. This poet is tirelessly inventive in seeding his free verse with rhythms. Even while we mourn the passing of music from much of the verse of our time, suddenly the sound of music comes to us out of the free verse itself and is more impressive there than it could be otherwise.

I have no more poetic principles to declare, but only a curious riddling question to leave in my readers' minds, if they care to hold it and solve it when they may. Among literary critics there is scarcely one, according to my impression, who does not remark that the aim of the poem is to give pleasure to the reader. Yet there must be only a handful of literary critics who care to define the kind or the cause of the pleasure. Perhaps they mean at least that the poem brings joy or happiness, which is quite a different and better thing; or means, like a tonic, to restore our vital sense of health and being. But how could that be? The riddle is a philosophical one. Yet Mr. Aloian's book often speaks of enjoying poems; that is, Finding Joy in Poetry. Aristotle said in his *Poetics* that we like poetry because we like to learn something; presumably, something from our betters. The theory of the arts in general goes by the Greek name of aesthetics, which means the theory of feeling; of the feeling of pleasure and pain, undoubtedly. But I should like to ask of Aristotle, "Learning what?" And of the aestheticians, "Feeling what sort of pleasure?"

JOHN CROWE RANSOM

CHRISTMAS, 1963

PREFACE

POEMS AND POETS is dedicated to the idea that reading poems is the best means of learning how to read. Of all the forms of literature, poetry presents the most concise, the most brilliant, and the most dramatic use of language. For this reason, the practice of reading poetry is one of the surest ways to develop reading skills. All the resources of language—its image-making powers, its sounds and rhythms, its implications and inferences, its puns and understatements—are employed most intensely in poetry. In a short space a poem can illustrate and demonstrate principles of organization and unity. Beginning, middle, and end are closely related. Each metaphor, each line, is part of a tightly unified structure. For this reason, experience in reading poetry is the best training to develop more intelligent and capable readers.

The first part of *Poems and Poets* is divided into nine chapters. "Poetry and Prose," the first chapter, introduces students to the experience of poetry by first demonstrating its similarities to literary prose and then drawing attention to those characteristics that make poetry a distinctive, and important, form of literature. Of the remaining chapters, four deal with specific properties of poetry and with the language devices a poet uses to communicate his ideas and feelings to the reader. Among these devices and properties are rhyme, rhythm, tone, sound effects, symbol, and metaphor. The last of these chapters on the language of poetry, "The Whole Poem: Statement and Meaning," investigates the way in which numerous poetic devices combine to reveal and enrich the meaning of a poem. Every aspect of poetry discussed in these chapters is clearly illustrated by quotations ranging in length from single lines to whole poems. Each chapter contains useful and imaginative exercises through which students may evaluate their understanding of poems and sharpen their reading skills.

The remaining four chapters of Part One are devoted to four major poets: Edgar Allan Poe, Robert Frost, A. E. Housman, and William Butler Yeats. Each chapter on a major poet follows a chapter in which the poetic devices discussed are particularly appropriate to that poet. Thus, the chapter on Poe follows the chapter on rhythm, rhyme, and sound effects; and the chapter on Housman follows the chapter on tone. All four chapters present generous selections from the poets' works. The poets are presented in an order determined by the increasing complexity of their work. In these chapters, students can cultivate those lifelong enthusiasms for a writer which are the richest reward of reading and the measure of intellectual growth.

Part Two of *Poems and Poets* consists of an anthology of well over three hundred poems. Rather than arrange this anthology by any one system, a combination of principles was used to achieve a wider range and to give a greater variety of interest. Thus poems are presented by types (as in "Ballads and Narrative Poetry" and "Free Verse"), by themes (as in "Great Themes in Poetry"), and by subject matter (as in "Character Poems"). The last section of the anthology is devoted to a treasury of poems ranging in date of composition from the work of the medieval ballad writers to that of such contemporary poets as T. S. Eliot, Marianne Moore, Robert Lowell, and the Russian Khodasevich.

Great care has been taken in selecting the poems for this anthology. More than twenty teachers of high school English were consulted in its preparation. They were asked to list poems which they thought suitable for the high school classroom. In every case, the final decision for or against inclusion was determined by the answers to two questions: Is it a good poem? Is it a meaningful poem for high school readers? Poets of all ages have written great poems that can be comprehended readily by high school readers. The problem was to search out these poems.

Part One of this book, "A Guide to Reading Poetry," is a preparation for Part Two, "An Anthology of Poems." Once a student has come to understand the nature of poetry and to develop his own taste for it—as Part One should lead him to do—he should then be encouraged to exercise that taste and understanding. In the second part of *Poems and Poets,* students and teachers alike will find an anthology whose substance and variety will meet any demands of taste and ability.

It is important for students to understand why poets are the most highly esteemed of writers. The reason is that poetry is one of the very best means of enriching and deepening our experience as human beings. Every serious poem is not merely a presentation of life but a commentary on it. What is the poet saying? What is his view of the individual? Of society? Of God? Poetry stands at the very center of the humanities curriculum. From the beginning, it has recorded through the medium of language man's deepest insights about the meaning of human experience and has made them readily and widely accessible to all who would read. The experience of reading good poems of all kinds broadens and deepens our ethical, intellectual, and emotional lives.

DAVID ALOIAN

CONTENTS

xvii

LIGHT AND HUMOROUS VERSE   220

Part One

A GUIDE

TO READING

POETRY

ONE

POETRY AND PROSE

POETS carry on a dialogue with the world. A poet does not have to travel in order to make new and surprising discoveries; everywhere about him, in his house and in his city, is an endless store of material. Millions of people awake each morning and thoughtlessly wind their watches; the poet wonders who winds the universal watch. The poet watches birds migrating south and wonders what forces are guiding him through life. Or he sees his neighbor's fence and wonders about all the kinds of fences and barriers which separate people. Or he watches the animals in a zoo and makes up rhymes to describe their humorous characteristics. The poet finds the surprising and unusual in the ordinary. Because he is sensitive to sights and sounds and smells and to events of all kinds, because he is imaginative in his use of language, his words become memorable.

But the poet is only one half of the dialogue; the reader or listener makes up the other half. The poet expresses his thoughts and feelings in words—from his words the reader must strive to understand and re-create those thoughts and feelings. When the reader can associate the poet's experience with his own, then the communication of ideas and of emotion is successful, and the dialogue is complete. The poet does the recording; the reader does the responding.

Expository prose and literary prose

If poetry is nothing more or less than a dialogue, in what way is it any different from prose? For the prose writer, too, is speaking to the reader. Before trying to answer that question, consider the differences between two kinds of prose: expository prose and literary prose. Study the following two samples:

A

The West Suburban chapter of the Massachusetts Mothers of Twins Assn. will meet Monday at 8:15 P.M. at the Cole School.

A panel discussion by five sets of adult twins will be moderated by Mrs. Booth. Among the participants will be Mrs. Henry Allen, Mrs. Robert Dwyer, and Joan Graham, all of Boston.

All mothers and grandmothers of twins are invited to attend and ask questions. Refreshments will be served by the hospitality committee after the meeting.

B

During the whole of a dull, dark, and soundless day in the autumn of the year, when clouds hung oppressively low in the heavens, I had been passing alone, on horseback, through a singularly dreary tract of country; and at length found myself, as the shades of evening drew on, within view of the melancholy House of Usher.

Which of the samples is trying to present information in an orderly, concise way? Which is seeking to describe a

4

scene and set up a mood? The samples have different purposes. Sample A is expository prose, and sample B is literary prose.

Expository prose is the prose of textbooks, newspapers, news magazines, and technical reports. It is factual; it relates events without elaborating or commenting on them. Expository writing sets out to inform the reader or to explain something to him in a step-by-step order. It might deal with the results of an election or the importance of international trade, or the operation of some machine or instrument.

Literary prose, on the other hand, is never merely factual. It is the prose of novels, short stories, plays. Although it uses facts, the facts are not most important in themselves. More important are the author's interpretation and mood, his ideas and the way he presents them, his comparisons and contrasts. Literary prose seeks to captivate the reader's imagination, to delight and to excite him. Even a hasty look at sample B will show that the author is setting up a mysterious and foreboding scene. The reader is being prepared for dark events. The day is *dull* and *dark;* it is *autumn* with darker evenings and dying leaves; the clouds are *oppressively low,* hinting at the burdens the characters labor under; the narrator is *alone;* the country is very *dreary;* the *shades,* with suggestions of night and ghostliness, are falling; the isolated house is called *melancholy.* Each detail of sample B, which is the first sentence of Edgar Allen Poe's short story "The Fall of the House of Usher," adds to the developing mystery and horror.

Poetry resembles literary prose in this respect: All elements contribute to the unity of impression or feeling that the writer is attempting to achieve. Each detail plays a part in the whole work. Nothing is included which does not add to the total effect. Poetry, like literary prose, seeks to stir the reader's emotions.

Poetry and literary prose: similarities

Despite the differences, there is no sharp line that will always separate poetry from literary prose. Some writers emphasize the differences; William Wordsworth, a great English poet, emphasized the similarities. He claimed:

> It may be safely affirmed that there neither is nor can be any *essential* difference between the language of prose and poetry . . . the same human blood circulates through the veins of them both.

How can you test the rightness of Wordsworth's point of view? Look at a portion of a prose composition from Herman Melville's great sea novel *Moby Dick*. In Chapter 37, entitled "Sunset," Captain Ahab, alone in his cabin, stands at the window watching the ship's wake. Here is a paragraph of Melville's prose rearranged in the form of a poem. The punctuation is exactly as Melville wrote it.

I leave a wide and turbid wake;
Pale water, paler cheeks, where'er I sail.
The envious billows sidelong swell
To whelm my track; let them; but first I pass.
Yonder, by the ever brimming goblet's rim,
The warm waves blush like wine.
The gold brow plumbs the blue.
The diver sun—slow dived from noon—
Goes down; my soul mounts up!

In your opinion, can this piece of literary prose stand as a reasonably authentic poem? To decide this question, you might ask the following: Is there a rhythm to the lines? Do they evoke vivid pictures? Are Captain Ahab's thoughts charged with strong feeling?

Just as prose can sometimes stand as poetry, so too some poetry is like prose. The following poem by Walt

Whitman describes the family of a Civil War soldier as they receive a letter. Why is it like a short story in many ways?

Come Up From the Fields Father

WALT WHITMAN

Come up from the fields father, here's a letter from our Pete,
And come to the front door mother, here's a letter from thy
dear son.

Lo, 'tis autumn,
Lo, where the trees, deeper green, yellower and redder,
Cool and sweeten Ohio's villages with leaves fluttering in the
moderate wind,
Where apples ripe in the orchard hang and grapes on the
trellis' vines,
(Smell you the smell of grapes on the vines?
Smell you the buckwheat where the bees were lately buzz-
ing?)
Above all, lo, the sky so calm, so transparent after the rain,
and with wondrous clouds,
Below too, all calm, all vital and beautiful, and the farm
prospers well.
Down in the fields all prospers well,
But now from the fields come father, come at the daughter's
call,
And come to the entry mother, to the front door come right
away.

Fast as she can she hurries, something ominous, her steps
trembling,
She does not tarry to smooth her hair nor adjust her cap.

Open the envelope quickly,
O this is not our son's writing, yet his name is sign'd,
O a strange hand writes for our dear son, O stricken mother's
soul!

All swims before her eyes, flashes with black, she catches
    the main words only,
Sentences broken, *gunshot wound in the breast, cavalry
    skirmish, taken to hospital!*
At present low, but will soon be better.

Ah now the single figure to me,
Amid all teeming and wealthy Ohio with all its cities and
    farms,
Sickly white in the face and dull in the head, very faint,
By the jamb of a door leans.

Grieve not so, dear mother, (the just grown daughter speaks
    through her sobs,
The little sisters huddle around speechless and dismay'd)
See, dearest mother, the letter says Pete will soon be better.

Alas poor boy, he will never be better, (nor may be needs to
    be better, that brave and simple soul,)

While they stand at home at the door he is dead already,
The only son is dead.

But the mother needs to be better,
She with thin form presently drest in black,
By day her meals untouch'd, then at night fitfully sleeping,
    often waking,
In the midnight waking, weeping, longing with one deep
    longing,
O that she might withdraw unnoticed, silent from life
    escape and withdraw,
To follow, to seek, to be with her dear dead son.

Written in prose paragraphs, "Come Up From the Fields
Father" would be a powerful short story. Like a short story,
it has character, setting, and plot. It is a moving account of
how a great war affects one family.

Although "Come Up From the Fields Father" is a poem and Captain Ahab's thoughts are prose, both pieces have a number of things in common. The words in each are strongly felt: Ahab's words are moody and restless, and Whitman's poem has many exclamations and outbursts of feeling. Both are eloquent; that is, they are expressed in language that precisely fits the feeling. While neither of them has any rigid, patterned rhythm, they are rhythmical in their natural pauses and in certain emphasized words. Both are vividly written; that is, the words present a scene which the imagination can see. Poetry begins when language becomes strong with emotion, eloquent, rhythmical, and vividly appealing to the imagination.

Poetry and literary prose: differences

Although there are no *essential* differences between the language of poetry and the language of literary prose, still certain differences do exist. Poetry and prose are not very often as easily interchangeable as the two examples above might suggest. Here are the first four lines of Browning's poem "How They Brought the Good News From Ghent to Aix."

> I sprang to the stirrup, and Joris, and he;
> I gallop'd, Dirck gallop'd, we gallop'd all three;
> "Good speed!" cried the watch, as the gate-bolts undrew;
> "Speed!" echoed the wall to us galloping through;

Exactly the same information that these lines convey might be written in a prose version. Such a version could read: "Joris, Dirck and I galloped off. The watch wished us well as we galloped through the gates. The wall echoed his words." Now this is not a clumsy, ungrammatical, or incorrect series of sentences. Yet, compared to the poetry, how flat and dull it is! Why the difference? Both versions communicate exactly the same facts; nothing different has been said. Whatever makes one poetry and the other prose has nothing to do with content. The difference lies in one word: *music*. The poem is musical—it has rhythm, rhyme, and sound effects, qualities that the prose lacks. In this poem which describes the swift riding of three horsemen, the music produces excitement and gives something of the urgency the riders must have felt.

The next chapter will discuss at length the importance of rhythm, rhyme, and sound in poetry. However, reread now the four lines from Browning's poem and notice several things about them. Notice first the strong, natural beat in the lines. Does the beat in any way seem suitable to the subject of galloping horses? Notice also two things about the word *gallop'd*. It is used four times and it has a sound roughly similar to that made by horses' hooves on pavement. The repetition and the sound of the word, as well as the rhythm, admirably suit the subject. Prose conveys information in a quick, orderly way; but in poetry, rhythm and sound reinforce the information. All details in the four lines contribute to the effect of galloping horses.

To conclude then, poetry and prose are not always easily separable, yet there are important differences between them. Perhaps the most important difference is that poetry is musical: it has a higher degree of organized sound and rhythm. Although music alone does not make a poem, it is one of the essential elements. Generally speaking, the truth can be summed up in the following lines:

> But mere indentations
> And Capitalizations
> or lack of capitalizations
> And all the tricks of ingenious printers
> And, in addition,

The matter and mood of poetry
Cannot make such a sentence
As this
Into a poem
    without
RHYTHM.

What poetry is not

There are other qualities besides rhythm in poetry which distinguish it from prose. Before considering some of these, it might be well to pause and state certain things that poetry is not.

First of all, poetry is not just a collection of words mechanically arranged to produce certain rhythms and sound effects, however musical and clever such arrangements might be. If poetry were merely rhyme, rhythm, and sound, the following lines would not be the obvious nonsense they are.

Hoity-toity, hoi-polloi,
The book's on the bed of the bitter boy.
Namby-pamby, shipmates ahoy,
The bed's on a billow by the buoy.

Music is very important to poetry because it helps the poet communicate his ideas and feelings in an exciting, memorable way. But music alone is meaningless. When sound is fused together with meaning, when sound brings out and emphasizes meaning, when sound and sense are one, then we have poetry.

Secondly, poetry is never merely flowery or pretty language, crowded with big or decorative words. Unfortunately, some students have the idea that poems are forever describing "whispering leaves," "babbling brooks," "twinkling stars," "chirping squirrels," and that poets favor fancy words like *celestial, exquisite,* and *iridescent.* Nothing could be farther from the truth. Poets do not deal in prettiness, nor is their language namby-pamby. As the hundreds of poems in this book demonstrate, poetic language is forceful, exact, and stirring.

Thirdly, poetry is not impractical. If poetry is impractical, then most of our thoughts, most of everything we see, read, or hear would also be impractical. Some students may wonder why a poet cannot merely relate facts, in much the same way that a scientist might. But, except in science, practical facts by themselves form only one part of what we say. In recounting the events and sights of a vacation trip or in describing the details of an athletic contest, who presents or wants to hear facts and facts alone? A completely factual description of a football game would sound like this:

> At the end of the first period the Blues were ahead 20–14; at the end of the half they were ahead 30–21; at the end of the third period they were ahead 38–34; at the end of the game they were behind 45–46.

Such a description of the game would be dull, uninformative, and exasperating. No one communicates in such a lifeless way. Rather, by tone of voice, by facial expressions, by exclamatory words and phrases, by hand and body gestures, someone recounting the game would convey his attitudes, his reactions, and his opinions about the game. The opinions and reactions are easily as important as the period-by-period statistics, and they tell more about the game than statistics can. Poetry begins as individuals respond to the experiences around them. In a sense, all beings who have felt love and joy and sadness, who have been moved by a beautiful country landscape or been awed by the skyscrapers of a large city, who have formed ideas and opinions based on their experiences, all such human beings are poets, though they may lack the poet's gift of expression.

Fourthly, poetry is not a big-game hunt with the reader, armed with a magnifying glass (or a book like this), setting out to find the "hidden meaning" cleverly concealed in a jungle of words by a crafty poet. *Poets do not hide meanings.* They do not seek to confuse and baffle. On the contrary, they want to show, to make clear, to dramatize some thought or feeling so that others can understand it. Put it out of your mind that poetry is hide-and-seek. Robert Frost defined poetry as a "clarification of life . . . a momentary stay against confusion." It is true that some poetry, like some prose, or some algebra, is not easy; but none of it is impossible. Any student can learn to read, understand, and enjoy it.

Another point ought to be made about the meaning, and it is that poetry should not be read for its meaning alone. What a poem says is important, of course, but poetry is not simply a fancy way of communicating an idea or thought. Reading a poem for its meaning or "message" only is like experiencing a song by hearing the words only. The melody, the rhythm, the tone, the tempo, the mood, the harmony, the particular instruments used and emphasized—all of these are as much a part of the song as the words. In a similar way, meaning is only part of the whole poem.

Finally, poetry is not necessarily the lofty statement of beautiful or inspiring ideas, nor does it have to be deep or philosophical. Poetry can deal with any human experience and with any human reaction to it. As William Wordsworth said, ". . . the honorable character of poetry is that its materials are to be found in every subject which can interest the human mind." Ambition, laziness, pride, humility, birth, death, love, anger, greed, jealousy, faith, kindness, cruelty, joy, humor, melancholy—these are only some of the materials

of poetry. The following few poems may suggest the variety
of feeling and subject matter that poems communicate.

Song of the Open Road

OGDEN NASH

> I think that I shall never see
> A billboard lovely as a tree.
> Perhaps, unless the billboards fall,
> I'll never see a tree at all.

Lord Randal

ANONYMOUS

> "O where have you been, Lord Randal, my son?
> O where have you been, my handsome young man?"—
> "I have been to the wild wood; mother, make my bed soon,
> For I'm weary with hunting, and fain would lie doon."

> "Who gave you your dinner, Lord Randal, my son?
> Who gave you your dinner, my handsome young man?"—
> "I dined with my sweetheart; mother, make my bed soon,
> For I'm weary with hunting, and fain would lie doon."

> "What had you for dinner, Lord Randal, my son?
> What had you for dinner, my handsome young man?"
> "I had eels boiled in broth; mother, make my bed soon,
> For I'm weary with hunting, and fain would lie doon."

> "And where are your bloodhounds, Lord Randal, my son?
> And where are your bloodhounds, my handsome young
>   man?"—
> "O they swelled and they died; mother, make my bed soon,
> For I'm weary with hunting, and fain would lie doon."

> "O I fear you are poisoned, Lord Randal, my son!
> O I fear you are poisoned, my handsome young man!"—
> "O yea! I am poisoned; mother, make my bed soon,
> For I'm sick at the heart, and I fain would lie doon."

LORD RANDAL: *doon* = down

Meeting at Night

ROBERT BROWNING

> The gray sea and the long black land;
> And the yellow half-moon large and low;
> And the startled little waves that leap
> In fiery ringlets from their sleep,
> As I gain the cove with pushing prow,
> And quench its speed i' the slushy sand.
>
> Then a mile of warm sea-scented beach;
> Three fields to cross till a farm appears;
> A tap at the pane, the quick sharp scratch
> And blue spurt of a lighted match,
> And a voice less loud, through its joys and fears,
> Than the two hearts beating each to each!

Invictus

WILLIAM ERNEST HENLEY

> Out of the night that covers me,
> Black as the Pit from pole to pole,
> I thank whatever gods may be
> For my unconquerable soul.
>
> In the fell clutch of circumstance
> I have not winced nor cried aloud.
> Under the bludgeonings of chance
> My head is bloody, but unbowed.
>
> Beyond this place of wrath and tears
> Looms but the horror of the shade,
> And yet the menace of the years
> Finds, and shall find me, unafraid.
>
> It matters not how strait the gate,
> How charged with punishments the scroll,
> I am the master of my fate:
> I am the captain of my soul.

INVICTUS: *Invictus* = unconquerable, unconquered

WHAT POETRY IS NOT

What poetry is

No definition of poetry will completely sum up and describe its infinite variety. However, some important characteristics of poetry have emerged as poetry has been contrasted with prose. It would be well at this point to list a number of these characteristics. Any one or more of them will from time to time apply to prose, but never in the complete and unqualified way that they apply to poetry.

First and foremost, in its broadest sense, poetry is one person talking to another about some human experience. It is a dialogue between the poet and his reader. From the poet there is always the communication of some new experience, a fresh understanding of the familiar, or the expression of something everyone has felt but never put into words. For the reader there is pleasure and enlightenment in listening to and responding to the poet's words.

Poetry is musical. The rhythm, rhyme, and sound effects of poetry serve many purposes. Word music goes along with word meaning; the sound of the words echoes the sense of the words. When he describes galloping horses, the poet's lines are swift and exciting, and there is the sound of clomping on paving stones. When the poet describes the wash of salty seas at the stern of a ship, the reader can almost hear the hiss of the water. Rhythms are slow and meditative for some subjects, strong and emphatic for other subjects, broken and irregular for still others. The poet's word sounds are fused to his meaning. His word music is to poetry what melody is to a song.

Poetry is compact. In a relatively few, well-chosen, exact words, poetry says and suggests a great deal. Poems are tightly organized so that every detail—from individual words and sounds to the figures of speech and the structure of the lines—contributes in some way to the central effect or purpose of the whole. Nothing is superfluous or accidental.

In all poetry the ideas are set forth in a minimum of words, the emotions are intensely felt, the images are closely clustered. A poem is a small, tightly packed suitcase which carries much feeling and thought.

Poetry is dramatic. It is vivid and imaginative, full of expressive statements, unexpected observations, striking contrasts and comparisons, and surprising, sudden shifts of thought. One writer has said that poetry consists of the best words in the best order. The poet's language is never flat and dull. His descriptions are vigorous and lively. Compare the following examples of poetic language with their prose counterparts.

Poetry	*Prose*
Shoe the steed with silver.	Put a silver shoe on the horse.
Oh the bells, bells, bells! What a tale their terror tells Of despair! How they clang, and clash, and roar.	The bells tell a terrible story of fear and trouble. Listen to their troubled noises.
A buck leaped out and took the tide With jewels flowing past each side.	The buck, racing out of the woods, jumped into the water and swam across.

What in each pair of examples is similar? What is different? Why is the language of poetry more colorful and dramatic?

Poetry is important. Poems are not a special interest; they speak to everyone. Throughout history, poets have been, in Shelley's phrase, "the legislators for mankind."

WHAT POETRY IS

Study the highest ideals of men—justice, freedom, equality —and you will find that they were born in the imaginations of poets. The ancient Hebrew writers of the Old Testament were often poets; the ideals and beliefs of many of the world's great religions were first advanced by poets. When tyranny, injustice, and cruelty reigned, the poets were among the first to speak out their indignation; the words of poets have inspired many of the laws that have passed through the world's parliaments.

Poetry is important not only in history but in one's daily life. Poems can make people more thoughtful because poets are constantly seeing life in new ways and constantly asking important questions. Poems also provide entertainment and humor; they add to the joy of living. Like good music, plays, and movies, they enrich leisure hours.

Today, thanks to the phonograph, the tape recorder, television, and public readings, the words of poets can reach millions of people. Poetry is more popular and more available than ever before. Through television, the words of Robert Frost and Carl Sandburg have been heard all over America. The verse plays of Eliot and MacLeish have been successful on Broadway and elsewhere. Poets like Auden, Cummings, Thomas, and others have traveled to many American colleges to recite and discuss their poems. The poet's words continue to be important. The poet inspires thought and he inspires laughter; he fires the imagination; he gives meaning to the experience of living. Poetry, especially for the students still in school, is a vital part of education. All the student has to do is to reach out, to read, and to listen.

Exercise: Identifying Poems

Here are five selections. Although they are printed as prose, four of them were written and published as poems. Read all selections thoughtfully, identify the four which you think are the poems, and tell why you think so in each case.

1. When I was one-and-twenty I heard a wise man say, "Give crowns and pounds and guineas but not your heart away; give pearls away and rubies but keep your fancy free." But I was one-and-twenty, no use to talk to me. When I was one-and-twenty I heard him say again, "The heart out of the bosom was never given in vain; 'tis paid with sighs a plenty and sold for endless rue." And I am two-and-twenty, and, oh, 'tis true, 'tis true.

2. Cliff Klingenhagen had me in to dine with him one day; and after soup and meat, and all the other things there were to eat, Cliff took two glasses and filled one with wine and one with wormwood. Then, without a sign for me to choose at all, he took the draught of bitterness himself, and lightly quaffed it off, and said the other one was mine. And when I asked him what the deuce he meant by doing that, he only looked at me and smiled, and said it was a way of his. And though I know the fellow, I have spent a long time a-wondering when I shall be as happy as Cliff Klingenhagen is.

3. Only a man harrowing clods in a slow silent walk with an old horse that stumbles and nods half asleep as they stalk. Only thin smoke without flame from the heaps of couch-grass; yet this will go onward the same though Dynasties pass. Yonder a maid and her wight come whispering by: war's annals will fade into night ere their story die.

4. A faint burst of lightning quivered all round, as if flashed into a cavern—into a black and secret chamber of the sea, with a floor of foaming crests. It unveiled for a sinister, fluttering moment a ragged mass of clouds hanging low, the lurch of the long outlines of the ship, the black figures of the men caught on the bridge, heads forward, as if petrified into the act of butting. The darkness palpitated down upon all this, and then the real thing came at last. It was something formidable and swift, like the sudden smashing of a vial of wrath. It seemed to explode all around the ship with an overpowering concussion and a rush of waters, as if an immense dam had been blown up to windward. In an instant the men lost touch of each other. This is the disintegrating power of a great wind: it isolates one from one's kind.

5. This I beheld, or dreamed it in a dream: there spread a cloud of dust along a plain; and underneath the cloud, or in it, raged a furious battle, and men yelled, and swords shocked upon swords and shields. A prince's banner wavered, then staggered backward, hemmed by foes. A craven hung along the battle's edge, and thought, "Had I a sword of keener steel—that blue blade that the king's son bears,—but this blunt thing—!" He snapt and flung it from his hand, and lowering crept away and left the field. Then came the king's son, wounded, sore bestead, and weaponless, and saw the broken sword, hilt-buried in the dry and trodden sand, and ran and snatched it, and with battle-shout lifted afresh he hewed his enemy down, and saved a great cause that heroic day.

TWO

RHYTHM, RHYME AND
SOUND EFFECTS

RHYTHM is a natural and instinctive part of life. Rhythms are everywhere about us. Day follows night in a set rhythm, seasons follow each other in another rhythm, the tides rise and fall in rhythm, the moon waxes and wanes in a definite and predictable rhythm, the human heart beats in a steady rhythm. Rhythms are so dominant and natural in our living and thinking that men are constantly searching for them where none may exist. Thus, some historians see a more or less definite rhythmic pattern in the rise and fall of nations. Some economists are convinced that booms and busts follow each other in certain rhythms. Astronomers try to discover the rhythm in which sun spots appear.

It is, therefore, not surprising that languages have rhythm too. English is a stress language; that is, *some English words and syllables receive more stress than others. Stress may be defined as the weight or emphasis a word or syllable receives.* Look at the following three-syllable words:

  wonderful   columbine   colorful

Careful pronunciation of these words will show that the syllables in each word are not equally stressed. One syllable in each receives the heaviest emphasis. With a slanted line, a stress mark, indicating this syllable, the words may be written as follows:

wónderful   cólumbine   cólorful

Although the words taken together convey little meaning, they do reveal a series of stressed and unstressed syllables which form a rhythm. It is a regular *ONE*twothree, *ONE*twothree, *ONE*twothree. Such a pattern is more regular than spoken language, written prose, and, for that matter, more regular than most poetry. But it is important to realize that such patterns are everywhere in our language. Individual words have their own rhythm, and groups of words like the sentences you are now reading have their rhythm. Language rhythms may fall into a strict, regular pattern, into a loose pattern, or—rarely—into no pattern at all. Speech, prose, and poetry all have rhythm. The difference is that *poetry uses rhythm more purposely than speech or prose.*

Patterns of rhythm

When the chain of stressed and unstressed syllables forms a fixed and highly regular arrangement, that arrangement is called meter. In describing the meter of a line of poetry, the reader should mention two items: first, the kind of stress pattern that the line follows, and second, the quantity, or length, of the line. Consider first the stress pattern of the line.

There are at least two dozen patterns of stress in the English language, each with a name of its own. Most of these, however, are variations or combinations of six basic patterns.

Read over as naturally as possible the following two lines. Try not to sing-song the words.

The curfew tolls the knell of parting day,
The lowing herd wind slowly o'er the lea.

As you read the lines, which syllables did you stress? Most of you will agree that *Cur-*, *tolls*, *knell*, *par-*, and *day* in the first line and *low-*, *herd*, *slow-*, *o'er*, and *lea* in the second line are the stressed syllables. In both lines the pattern is unstressed-stressed, unstressed-stressed. This pattern is the most natural and the most used meter in English poetry. It is called *IAMBIC*.

Now read over the following two lines:

Rafael made a century of sonnets,
Made and wrote them in a certain volume.

Over which syllables would you place the stress mark? Do you see that the meter here is a sequence of stressed-unstressed syllables? Using the slant line to indicate stressed syllables and a small U-shaped notation to indicate unstressed syllables, you could mark the lines as follows.

Ráfael máde ă céntŭry ŏf sónnets

This pattern, stressed-unstressed, is the reverse of the iambic meter. It is called *TROCHAIC*. It may seem odd to separate the *iambic* (unstress-stress) from the *trochaic* (stress-unstress), but you will see that iambic puts emphasis on the last syllable of the line and trochaic emphasizes the beginning of the line. This difference can be important.

A third meter is used in the following line:

Oút, oút, brief cándlĕ.

Here every syllable except the last receives a stress. A pattern of stressed syllables is called a *SPONDAIC* meter. The *spondaic* meter is rarely used by itself. It is most often mixed with other meters, generally to express heavy emphasis or to show strong emotion, as in the following line:

Ó, dárk, dárk, dárk, ămíd thĕ bláze ŏf noón.

Another meter that is rarely used by itself is the *PYRRHIC*, a pattern of two unstressed syllables. Poets use it to give a line of poetry a light, airy feeling, or to make it move very quickly, like the following lines which describe the movements of a little girl.

There wăs sŭch spéed ĭn hĕr líttlĕ bŏdy
Ănd sŭch líghtnĕss ĭn hĕr fóotfăll.

A fifth basic meter may be seen in the famous opening lines of Henry Wadsworth Longfellow's *Evangeline:*

Thís ĭs thĕ fórest prĭmévăl. Thĕ múrmŭrĭng pínĕs ănd thĕ hémlŏcks

The pattern which is composed of a stressed syllable followed by two unstressed syllables is called *DACTYLIC* meter. It is not an easy meter to write consistently. Even in this line by Longfellow you can see a break. When it is consistently written, *dactylic* often tends toward monotony.

Just as trochaic meter (´ ˘) is the reverse of iambic (˘ ´), the sixth basic meter, *ANAPESTIC*, is the reverse of dactyllic (´ ˘ ˘). *Anapestic* meter may be seen in the following lines from Lord Byron's "The Destruction of Sennacherib."

Thĕ Ăssýrĭăn cáme dówn lĭke thĕ wólf ŏn thĕ fóld
Ănd hĭs cóhŏrts wĕre gléamĭng ĭn púrplĕ ănd góld.

The *anapestic* meter, as these lines indicate, is a pattern of two unstressed syllables followed by one stressed syllable. Like *dactylic* meter, the anapestic (˘ ˘ ´) is almost never used without variation in English poetry.

So much for the stress pattern of the line. It is also necessary to know the length, or quantity, of the line. The length of a line of poetry is measured in *feet*. But these are not, of course, the feet used, with inches and yards, to measure distances. In poetry, a *foot* is *one unit of the stress pattern*. In iambic meter, for instance, one foot consists of an unstressed syllable and a stressed syllable in that order, as in the word *deny* (dĕný). The word *foreign* taken by itself forms a trochaic foot (fóreĭgn). Similarly, a series of one stressed and two unstressed syllables, as in the word *yesterday* (yésterdăy), makes one foot of dactylic meter. In a line of poetry, of course, the feet never fall regularly into a string of separate words. Since meter is determined by the accents on syllables, a foot may begin or end in the middle of a word, depending on the stressed or unstressed nature of the syllables in the word. Thus, in the following lines of iambic meter, several of the breaks between one foot and the next come inside a word. These breaks may be marked by drawing a vertical line between the feet.

Nŏt már|blĕ, nór|thĕ gíl|dĕd món|umĕnts
Ŏf prínc|ĕs, shall|oŭtlíve|thĭs pówĕr|fŭl ríme;

A line with two feet is called *dimeter*, from the prefix *di-*, meaning "two." One with three feet is called *trimeter;* a four foot line is called *tetrameter;* a five foot line is called *pentameter;* a six foot line is known as *hexameter,* and so on.

Thus the meter of a line of poetry is described by telling its stress pattern (iambic, trochaic, spondaic, pyrrhic, dactylic, or anapestic) and its quantity or length in feet (dimeter, trimeter, tetrameter, pentameter, hexameter). Below are some sample lines divided into feet and marked according to pattern.

Iambic dimeter: Wĭth ráv|ĭshĕd eárs

Trochaic trimeter: Mórtăl|mán ănd|wómăn

Dactylic tetrameter: Júst|fŏr ă|hándful ŏf|sílvĕr hĕ|léft ŭs

Iambic pentameter: The Cúr|few tŏlls|the knéll|ŏf pár|tĭng dáy

Anapestic trimeter: Ŏ wéll|fŏr the físh|ĕrmăn's bóy

The following exercise will give you more practice in identifying the meter of a line of poetry.

Exercise: Discovering Meter

The following are individual lines of poetry. Copy them down on your paper. Then read them over carefully and mark them for stress pattern and number of feet. Use the slant bar for stressed syllables and the U-mark for unstressed syllables. Divide the feet with a vertical line, and then give a name to the meter in each case. If you have difficulty identifying the stressed and unstressed syllables at the beginning of the line, look at those in the middle. Note that relatively unimportant words like *an, a, the, and,* and so forth, are usually unstressed.

1. How sleep the Brave who sink to rest

2. All that web of pain

3. That he shouts with his sister at play

4. Though the moonshine mostly keep us

5. So all day long the noise of battle rolled

6. To be or not to be; that is the question

7. Just for a riband to stick in his coat

8. The dew was falling fast, the stars began to blink

9. And its pleasures in all their bright lustre begin

10. The long light shakes

11. Something there is that doesn't love a wall

12. Where he could find the strongest oak

Free verse and blank verse

Does all poetry, in order to be poetry, have a definite stress pattern that can be measured in feet? The answer to this question is *No.* Strict, regular patterns of stress are not absolutely necessary to poetry. Many poems have loose, irregular rhythms. Such poems come under the heading of *free verse. Free verse does not follow any fixed pattern;* it has no rhyme, no fixed stanza form, and no fixed meter. The following short poem by Stephen Crane is an example of free verse.

> Many workmen
> Built a huge ball of masonry
> Upon a mountain top.
> Then they went to the valley below,
> And turned to behold their work.
> "It is grand," they said;
> They loved the thing.
>
> Of a sudden, it moved:
> It came upon them swiftly;
> It crushed them all to blood.
> But some had opportunity to squeal.

Free verse is sometimes confused with blank verse, a kind of poetry that is far from free. For *blank verse is poetry of iambic pentameter without rhyme.* Shakespeare's plays and Milton's epic *Paradise Lost,* towering works of literature, are written in blank verse. In Shakespeare's *Hamlet,* for instance, the hero speaks in blank verse in his famous soliloquy:

> To be, or not to be—that is the question:
> Whether 'tis nobler in the mind to suffer
> The slings and arrows of outrageous fortune
> Or to take arms against a sea of troubles.

Common errors concerning rhythm

There are several common errors concerning rhythm that ought to be mentioned. One of the commonest errors is to sing-song all poetry. Generally speaking, it is better not to stress regular rhythms; read the lines naturally for their meaning and the rhythm will assert itself. The rhythm is in the words; it will be heard without trying to put any special emphasis on it.

A second common error is thinking that the more regular meters make better poems. Robert Frost, perhaps the finest of recent American poets, has said that there are really only two patterns in English poetry: strict iambic and loose iambic. Many fine poems have a looseness in their meter. As a matter of fact, Frost and many other poets have said that appropriate and even surprising changes and shifts in meter are marks of a poet's excellence. Poets purposely vary their meters.

A third common error is to suppose that knowing the pattern and the length of a line of poetry is knowing all there is on the subject of rhythm. Knowing that a line is iambic pentameter or dactylic hexameter or that a poem is written in blank verse or free verse is very helpful. But it is not an end in itself. Knowing the meter of a line is not so important as knowing how that meter and its variations contribute to the poem as a whole—in short, how the meter makes the communication between poet and reader more effective. A poet uses rhythm more carefully than a prose writer uses it. He is not just giving his words a jingle to be read by; he uses rhythm to bring out his meaning more dramatically.

Uses of rhythm in poetry

What purpose does the poet have for the careful use of rhythm? What does rhythm do for the poem? The major purposes of rhythm can be expressed in four general ideas:

it helps the memory, excites the imagination, creates a hypnotic mood, and emphasizes meaning.

RHYTHM HELPS THE MEMORY

Rhythm is a device for making us remember more easily what the poet wants to tell us. It makes words memorable. Jingles, limericks, proverbs, and musical recitations stick in the mind. Children in the kindergarten and first grade often learn the alphabet by singing the letters in rhythm. Everyone remembers the familiar counting song:

> One, two
> Buckle a shoe;
> Three, four
> Shut the door;
> Five, six
> Pick up sticks;
> Seven, eight
> Lay them straight;
> Nine, ten
> A big red hen.

Adults as well as children remember by, and learn through, rhythms. Sailors and fishermen have their weather sayings:

> Red sky at night,
> Sailors delight.
> Red sky in the morning,
> Sailors take warning.

In Shakespeare's time, each occupation and trade had its particular slogan or catchword to help sell its products. Many of these slogans had rhythm and rhyme. For example, broom makers were known to sing variations of this rhythmic bit of advertising:

New brooms, new brooms, will you buy any?
Maidens come quickly; they're only a penny.

Advertising today, whether on television, on the radio, or in magazines and newspapers, still uses rhythm and rhyme in its slogans. How many can you think of?

RHYTHM EXCITES THE IMAGINATION

A poem's rhythm may stimulate and excite or retard and sadden the emotions of the reader. Louis Untermeyer, poet and anthologist, describes this idea in the following paragraph. He says:

> It seems that the rhythms which affect us most deeply are the so-called "regular rhythms," those which most nearly approximate the beat of the human heart. Those poems which run at a more rapid tempo than the heart tend to excite and exhilarate us, while those which move at a slower tempo than the pulse tend to retard, and sometimes, to depress us.

John Philip Sousa, the famous composer of marches, is said to have written and arranged all his music to be played at a tempo slightly faster than the human heart. The American playwright Eugene O'Neill began his play *The Emperor Jones* with tom-toms beating at the same rate as the human heartbeat. As the play went along, the tom-toms beat faster and faster, reaching their peak at the exciting climax, when, he hoped, the hearts of the audience would be beating faster than normal. In poetry, as well as in parades, stage plays, and musical compositions, the tempo of the rhythm affects the emotional response of the listener or reader.

RHYTHM CREATES A HYPNOTIC MOOD

The regular beat of a rhythm puts the reader at ease and makes him more ready to be swayed by the poet's thought and feeling. Rhythm in a poem is like hypnosis; it puts the reader into a receptive mood. The mood is not a dull, sleepy one; it is a state in which his resistance is put to rest while his imagination is entirely free to react to the poet's suggestions. Once the main rhythm is established, the variations and departures from it help the reader to notice words and phrases to which the poet is giving special emphasis. Edgar Allan Poe's poem "The Raven" (p. 46) can be read as a poem with a hypnotic rhythm that works a kind of spell on the reader's imagination.

RHYTHM EMPHASIZES MEANING

The rhythm of a poem reinforces its meanings. In his "An Essay on Criticism," written in the 1700s, Alexander Pope put it this way:

> The sound must seem an echo to the sense.
> Soft is the strain when Zephyr gently blows,
> And the smooth stream in smoother numbers flows;
> But when loud surges lash the sounding shore,
> The hoarse, rough verse should like the torrent roar;
> When Ajax strives some rock's vast weight to throw,
> The line too labors, and the words move slow;
> Not so, when swift Camilla scours the plain,
> Flies o'er th' unbending corn, and skims along the main.

The rhythm should correspond to the meaning. If the line of poetry describes Ajax's labors to throw a huge stone, the rhythm of the line should be slow and laborious. The line that begins *When Ajax* cannot properly be read in a fast rhythm; it must be read slowly. But notice how swiftly the last line can be read.

Exercise: *How Rhythm Emphasizes Meaning*

A study of one brief poem will show how effectively rhythm helps to make the poet's meaning more emphatic. Read the following poem and then turn to the questions below.

Stopping by Woods on a Snowy Evening
ROBERT FROST

> Whose woods these are I think I know.
> His house is in the village though;
> He will not see me stopping here
> To watch his woods fill up with snow.
>
> My little horse must think it queer
> To stop without a farmhouse near
> Between the woods and frozen lake
> The darkest evening of the year.
>
> He gives his harness bells a shake
> To ask if there is some mistake.
> The only other sound's the sweep
> Of easy wind and downy flake.
>
> The woods are lovely, dark and deep,
> But I have promises to keep,
> And miles to go before I sleep,
> And miles to go before I sleep.

1. Copy the first stanza. Place stress marks on the lines and divide the lines into feet with a vertical stroke.

2. What are the stress pattern and length of each line? What is the name for this meter?

3. The man in the poem is momentarily entranced with the beauty of the snowfall in the woods. What one word reminds him that he must be on his way?

4. All the words in this poem are either one- or two-syllable words, with one exception. What is the only word in the poem which receives three stress marks?

5. State the meaning of the poem in your own words. Then tell how the one word that breaks the pattern of rhythm and word length emphasizes this meaning.

Rhyme

Any repetition of identical, similar, or related sounds in poetry is called rhyme. The most obvious rhymes are those that come at the end of a line, but the repeated sounds may also come in the center of the line, at the beginning of a word, in the center of a word, or at the end of a word. Rhyme has several purposes in a poem. Like rhythm, it makes poetry more memorable and more pleasurable to read. It also emphasizes and reinforces a poet's meaning in a way similar to the way that rhythm does. The poet generally rhymes important idea words; that is, his rhymes link together words whose meanings are also linked together in the poem. Rhyme has another important use: it helps to organize the poem and bind ideas into lines and stanzas.

END RHYME

As you have seen, rhythm sets up a regularity of pattern which the reader anticipates. Rhyme works in a similar way. It is patterned into *rhyme schemes*. The rhyme scheme of a poem is determined by looking at the *end rhymes*, which appear in the last words of each line. To discover the pattern, a letter from the alphabet is assigned to each final word. The letter is repeated for each word that repeats the sound of another. Thus, if the final words of four lines of poetry are

woe, slow, grief, and *leaf,* the rhyme scheme of those lines
is said to be *aabb.* If a new sound is introduced, the next letter of the alphabet is given to it. If the final words in six
lines are *fly, find, last, past, mind,* and *sky,* the rhyme
scheme would be *abccba.* Rhyme schemes help a poet
organize his ideas into line and stanza units, which are to a
poet what sentences and paragraphs are to the prose writer.

There is a great variety of rhyme schemes in English
poetry. A study of the following examples will show you how
the poets have used end rhymes to bind lines into stanzas,
and rhyme schemes to tie stanzas together.

1. When I remember *all*   a
   The friends so link'd *together*   b
   I've seen around me *fall*   a
   Like leaves in wintry *weather*   b

2. I told my love, I told my *love,*   a
   I told her all my *heart,*   b
   Trembling, cold, in ghastly *move.*   a
   Ah! she did *depart!*   b

3. It was a tall young oysterman lived by the river-side,   a
   His shop was just upon the bank, his boat was on the tide;   a
   The daughter of a fisherman, that was so straight and slim,   b
   Lived over on the other bank, right opposite to him.   b

4. Ask me no more where Jove bestows   a
   When June is past, the fading rose;   a
   For in your beauties' orient deep   b
   These flowers as in their causes sleep.   b

5. Follow her, while yet her glory shineth!   a
   There comes a luckless night   b
   That will dim all her light;   b
   And this the black unhappy shade divineth.   a

6. Cromwell, our chief of men, who through a cloud   *a*
   Not of war only, but detractions rude   *b*
   Guided by faith and matchless fortitude,   *b*
   To peace and truth thy glorious way hast plough'd.   *a*

7. And furthermore, her brethren wondered much   *a*
   Why she sat drooping by the basil green,   *b*
   And why it flourished, as by magic touch;   *a*
   Greatly they wondered what the thing might mean: *b*
   They could not surely give belief, that such   *a*
   A very nothing would have power to wean   *b*
   From her own fair youth, and pleasures gay,   *c*
   And even remembrance of her love's delay.   *c*

OTHER KINDS OF RHYME

Do not think that rhyme applies only to the repetition of the last word in each line. True, this is the most familiar kind of rhyme, but there are other kinds of identical or related sounds.

Internal Rhyme: Internal rhyme links a word in the middle of the line with the word at the end of the line. Read the following three separate lines, all of them taken from "The Rhyme of the Ancient Mariner" by Samuel Taylor Coleridge.

> This hermit good lives in that wood
>
>   .   .   .   .   .
>
> And the bay was white with silent light
>
>   .   .   .   .   .
>
> Farewell, farewell; but this I tell

In each of these three examples, the word at the end of the line repeats a similar sound in the middle of the line: *good* and *wood; white* and *light; farewell* and *tell*. Such a rhyme is called internal rhyme. Notice that internal rhyme emphasizes the important idea-words and links them together.

Alliteration. From end rhyme and internal rhyme it is but a step to alliteration. Alliteration is the repetition of the initial consonant sound of two or more consecutive words or words that are near each other in the sentence. Here are some samples of alliteration:

> While I *w*andered *w*eak and *w*eary

> • • • • •

> *m*erry *m*instrel *m*usic

Alliteration is an ancient kind of rhyme; in fact, it precedes every other kind of rhyme in the English language. One of the earliest poems of English literature is called "The Seafarer." This poem is thought to have been written in the fifth or sixth century, about 1500 years ago. The translation below of the first four lines preserves the rich alliteration of the original Anglo-Saxon:

> O, wildly my heart
> Beats in my breast and bids me to try
> The tumble and surge of seas tumultuous,
> Breeze and brine and the breakers' roar.

Alliteration, carefully used, gives a line rich sound and links together for emphasis the alliterated words.

Similar to alliteration is *consonance,* the repetition of consonant sounds in the middle of words, rather than at the beginning. Notice the consonance of *t* in the following line:

> Drawn with a team of li*tt*le a*t*omies.

Assonance. Repetition of vowel sounds in two or more words, when the consonant sounds preceding or following these vowel sounds are different, is called *assonance.* Some examples of assonance are the following:

> The s*ea*s did s*ee*the
> Fair t*a*les of sh*a*de, the poplar t*a*ll

Assonance acts in the same way that alliteration, and indeed all rhyme, does; it binds together words for greater unity and emphasis. Notice that in the line *The seas did seethe* the poet connects the idea of an angry sea with the hissing sound of tossing water.

SUMMARY OF RHYME

This entire section on rhyme may be summed up by examining a stanza of Tennyson's "The Charge of the Light Brigade." There are a number of examples of end rhyme, alliteration, consonance, and assonance, some of which have been noted in the margin.

		rhyme scheme
Notice:	Flashed all their sabres bare,	*a*
assonance of a	Flashed as they turned in air,	*a*
	Sabring the gunners there,	*a*
	Charging an army, while	*b*
alliteration of w	All the world wondered:	*c*
	Plunged in the battery-smoke,	*d*
	Right through the line they broke;	*d*
	Cossack and Russian	*e*
	Reeled from the sabre-stroke,	*d*
consonance of r	Shattered and sundered.	*c*
	Then they rode back, but not,	*f*
	Not the six hundred.	*c*

Rhyme makes poetry more memorable and more enjoyable; it emphasizes meaning; and it helps to organize and bind ideas into lines and stanzas. Stanzas themselves may be long or short, they may have one stress pattern or another, and they may have one rhyme scheme or another. But the stanza is the principal large unit within a poem, and both the poem's meaning and its form are revealed to the reader by the many kinds of rhyme.

Exercise: Hearing Rhythm and Rhyme

One line has been omitted from each of the following short portions of poems. Below each selection three possible choices are presented, one of which is the correct line. By determining the rhythm and rhyme of the given three lines, select the alternate line that you think is correct.

1. Farewell, ye milk-white dove, farewell
   This parting gives me pain;
   To think, perhaps, I ne'er shall see

   a) Thee strolling happily down the lane
   b) Thy gentle form again
   c) Thee standing up to chant

2. What is this life, if full of care,
   We have no time to stand and stare.
   And stare as long as sheep or cows.

   a) No leisure to sit around, here and now
   b) No leisure to wonder, that I vow,
   c) No time to stand beneath the boughs

3. In summer I'm disposed to shirk,
   As summer is no time to work.
   In winter inspiration dies

   a) There are no gay, fluttering butterflies
   b) Hard work my spirit denies
   c) For lack of outdoor exercise

4. Of all the fruits I ever pluck
   To try to feed my fill,
   The plum I leave upon the bough

   a) Remains the sweetest still.
   b) Will the best aroma distill
   c) Inspires and gives the deepest thrill

5. Out of the woods my Master went,
   And he was well content.
   Out of the woods my Master came,

   a) Content with death and shame
   b) Blissfully happy with blame and shame
   c) Death and shame were no worse than fame.

Other sound effects

Aside from rhythm and rhyme, a poet has several other sound effects at his disposal to make his communication with the reader more exciting and effective. Two of these in particular, refrain and onomatopoeia, are quite commonly used.

REFRAIN

A refrain is a word or a group of words repeated at intervals, usually at the end of a stanza, which sums up or carries along some important idea in a poem. Edgar Allan Poe's poem "The Raven" (p. 46) uses refrain, as you shall see. The poem below also uses it.

Boot and Saddle

>   Boot, saddle, to horse, and away!
>   Rescue my castle before the hot day
>   Brightens to blue from its silvery gray,
>   CHORUS: *Boot, saddle, to horse, and away!*
>
>   Ride past the suburbs, asleep as you'd say;
>   Many's the friend there, will listen and pray,
>   "God's luck to gallants that strike up the lay—
>   CHORUS: *Boot, saddle, to horse, and away!*"
>
>   Forty miles off, like a roebuck at bay,
>   Flouts Castle Brancepeth the Roundheads' array;

BOOT AND SADDLE: *Roundheads'* = name given the followers of Oliver Cromwell, intended as ridicule; *fay* = faith

OTHER SOUND EFFECTS

Who laughs, "Good fellows ere this, by my fay,
CHORUS: *Boot, saddle, to horse, and away!*"

Who? My wife Gertrude; that, honest and gay,
Laughs when you talk of surrendering, "Nay!
I've better counselors; what counsel they?
CHORUS: *Boot, saddle, to horse, and away!*"

In this poem the refrain is not merely a flat repetition at the end of a group of lines. Although the words are the same, the meaning of the refrain varies according to the ideas which immediately precede it. The refrain is a call to battle in the first stanza, a prayer in the second, a laugh in the third, and a cry of encouragement in the fourth.

ONOMATOPOEIA

When a word or group of words imitates the sounds the words are describing, the effect is called onomatopoeia. Many words in English are onomatopoeic; that is, their sounds actually correspond to, or resemble, the meaning of the word. A partial list of onomatopoeic words would include the following common examples: *buzz, boom, bang, crash, hiss.* As the buzz-saw operates, its sound is much like the sound of the word *buzz.* The line *the seas did seethe,* which is a good example of assonance, is also an example of onomatopoeia. The words sound like the boiling hiss of water on a beach. Another onomatopoeic line is

And the silken, sad, uncertain rustling of each purple curtain.

Its sound, read aloud, resembles the swish of a silk curtain's being rustled. Onomatopoeia echoes the sense of the poem at the same time that it tries to re-create, as much as language can, the actual sound it is describing.

Conclusions

The English language contains rhythms, rhymes, and certain sound effects which the poet uses to say what he means as memorably, as imaginatively, and as dramatically as he can. *What* the poet says is, of course, most important; yet *how* he says it is important too. Many students ask, "Did the poet really intend all those things in the poem?" The answer to this question is *Yes*. Poems are very carefully, very methodically written. Manuscripts at Harvard University by the modern poet Dylan Thomas show that he used forty-seven work sheets, sixty-five written sides of paper, for one sixty-line poem.

Yet it must be emphasized that analyzing a poem for its sound is not necessarily understanding and enjoying the poem. Analysis is not a goal in itself—it is valuable only if it leads to an improved reading and appreciation of poetry. Because poetry is the richest and the most complete use of language, the improved reading of poems must inevitably lead to improved reading of all writing.

Exercise: *The Sound of a Poem*

A. "To _____" by Percy Bysshe Shelley is a very brief poem, but it is a good example of how rhythm, rhyme, and sound effects work together with the meaning to make a memorable and effective poem. Read it through once and answer the questions that follow.

> To ——
>
>   Music, when soft voices die,
>   Vibrates in the memory—
>   Odors, when sweet violets sicken,
>   Live within the sense they quicken.
>   Rose leaves, when the rose is dead,
>   Are heaped for the beloved's bed;
>   And so thy thoughts when thou art gone,
>   Love itself shall slumber on.

1. What is the rhyme scheme of the poem?

2. What is the stress pattern of the first two lines? Of the last two?

3. Find several examples of alliteration.

4. What examples of assonance are there in the poem?

5. What consonance is there in the last line?

B. Now read the poem a second time and consider how the meaning of the poem is related to your answers to questions 1 through 5. In other words, how is the sound related to the sense? Once you have studied the poem further, answer the following questions.

1. Are the words that are rhymed important to the ideas of the poem? In what way?

2. Where does the rhythmic stress emphasize important words?

3. Does the alliteration in the poem emphasize ideas? Does it link ideas? Contrast ideas?

4. How do assonance and consonance contribute to the poem?

5. The climactic idea in a poem often comes at the end of the poem. In your own words, what is the climax idea of this poem?

6. How do rhythm and sound focus attention on the important word or words in the last line?

C. Using any one of the following poems as an example, write a composition on *How Sound Aids Sense*.

"How They Brought the Good News from Ghent to Aix" (p. 195)

The Bells (p. 57)

Binsey Poplars (p. 374)

Sea Fever (p. 103)

THREE

EDGAR ALLAN POE
The Creation of Beauty

PROBABLY more than any other American writer, Edgar Allan Poe—in his life as well as in his poems and stories—has appealed to the young imagination. His unstable life, his unhappy marriage, his difficulties with his guardian, his mistakes at the University of Virginia and later at West Point, his struggles as an artist, and his mysterious death, all these have been the sources of a great deal of interest and speculation. His stories have been read and enjoyed by generations of young Americans. In recent times a number of these stories have been made into movies and performed on television. Poe's views on how a short story should be constructed are today almost universally followed by professional story writers. He is often called the Father of the Short Story. His poems, far more influential today than they were in his own time, have been included in thousands of anthologies of great poetry, and several of them are among the most famous poems ever written by an American.

Edgar Allan Poe was born in Boston in 1809, the son of traveling theatrical parents, both of whom died before Poe was two years old. After their deaths Poe became the ward of, but was never legally adopted by, John Allan, a well-to-do citizen of Richmond, Virginia. Spoiled, temperamental, adventurous, Poe grew up into a trouble-filled young manhood. There was much friction between him and his foster father; he was withdrawn from the University of Virginia after less than a year's attendance there because of gambling debts. There followed a relatively successful period of service in the U.S. Army from 1827 to 1829. Then came a completely unsuccessful period at West Point Military Academy, where, in 1831, he was court-martialed and discharged for neglecting his duties. In 1832, when he was just twenty-three years old, Poe made a final break with Mr. Allan.

But before the break, Poe had already published three slim volumes of poetry, none of which attracted much attention or earned any money. Forced to make his own living, Poe began to write short stories. He was successful almost from the start when one of his first stories, "The MS Found in a Bottle," won a one-hundred-dollar prize. Later stories won him popular acclaim. Working as both an editor and a contributor to some of the best magazines of the time, Poe showed that he was a brilliant critic and craftsman. He saw that short tales of horror were very popular—even in the ladies' magazines—and he worked out a formula for writing them. But his temperament worked against any sustained happiness.

Before and after 1832, when he broke with his guardian, Poe spent much time with Mrs. Maria Clemm, mother of his cousin, Virginia, in a home wracked by debt, poverty, and disease. In 1835 Poe married his thirteen-year-old cousin Virginia, a sickly girl who remained on the threshold of death for many years before she died at the age of twenty-six. Such a home, such a marriage, did not bring to Poe the stability he needed. Periods of creative work were followed

EDGAR ALLAN POE

by drunken sprees and subsequent self-pity and guilt. Though he had won a large popular success, he never seemed to earn enough money. The grinding life of his home and the frustrating life of a writer left Poe bitter about the world. More and more he drank to escape its sorrows. Yet, in 1845, near the end of his life, he published a collection entitled *The Raven and Other Poems,* which was an immediate popular success, but a financial failure. A collection of short stories brought out at the same time met with a similar fate; it earned many rave reviews but few dollars. In 1848 his wife died, and in the following year Poe himself died, at the age of forty, in very mysterious circumstances.

Poe's definition of poetry

In the essay "The Poetic Principle" Poe set forth many of his theories of poetry. A poem, he said, should be neither too short nor too long; it should be capable of being read in one sitting. If it required more than one sitting, the affairs of the world would interrupt and distract the reader's attention. But if the poem were too short, it would fail to build up an emotional effect. Because the poem was a unity and sought to create a single impression on the reader, length was an important consideration.

Poe's next, and perhaps most important, point was that no poem deserved to be called a poem unless it *excited and elevated the soul.* Poe wrote that nothing elevated the soul so much as *Beauty;* he wrote that a sense of the Beautiful was an immortal instinct within the spirit of man. This instinct is like the desire of the moth for the star, he claimed. In his own words, poetry is "but a wild effort to reach the Beauty above; it is the struggle to apprehend 'supernal Loveliness.'"

Poe also made the following distinction between poetry and prose. In his opinion, the poem was not to deal with moral truths, nor was it to teach lessons or make comments on living. Poe thought that Truth should be presented in "Words simple, precise and terse, cool, calm, and unimpassioned." Such words, he felt, were far more appropriate to prose than to poetry. Truth appealed to the Moral Sense and was best presented in the language of prose; Beauty appealed to the Soul and was best presented in the language of poetry.

About Music—meter, rhythm, and rhyme—Poe was very clear: no poet could afford to ignore it. The great purpose of poetry—to show supernal, or sublime, Beauty—was most effectively attained, Poe said, when poetic words were charged with music. The union of poetry and music was absolutely essential if the Soul were to be elevated by Beauty. As Poe wrote in the essay, "I would define, in brief, the Poetry of words as *The Rhythmical Creation of Beauty.*"

The composition of "The Raven"

Perhaps Poe's best-known poem is "The Raven." In another of his essays, "The Philosophy of Composition," he presents an account of the way this famous poem came to be written. This essay methodically explains the entire process of composition from the first idea to the last.

The Raven

Once upon a midnight dreary, while I pondered, weak and
weary,
Over many a quaint and curious volume of forgotten lore,
While I nodded, nearly napping, suddenly there came a
tapping,
As of someone gently rapping, rapping at my chamber door.
" 'Tis some visitor," I muttered, "tapping at my chamber
door—
Only this, and nothing more."

THE RAVEN: *Plutonian* = infernal; *Gilead* = a region of Jordan, prominent in Biblical history; *Pallas* = Pallas Athene, Greek goddess of wisdom

EDGAR ALLAN POE

Ah, distinctly I remember it was in the bleak December,
And each separate dying ember wrought its ghost upon the
floor.
Eagerly I wished the morrow;—vainly I had sought to bor-
row
From my books surcease of sorrow—sorrow for the lost
Lenore—
For the rare and radiant maiden whom the angels name
Lenore—
Nameless here for evermore.

And the silken, sad, uncertain rustling of each purple curtain
Thrilled me—filled me with fantastic terrors never felt be-
fore;
So that now, to still the beating of my heart, I stood repeat-
ing,
" 'Tis some visitor entreating entrance at my chamber
door;—
Some late visitor entreating entrance at my chamber door—
This it is and nothing more."

Presently my soul grew stronger; hesitating then no longer,
"Sir," said I, "or Madam, truly your forgiveness I implore;
But the fact is I was napping, and so gently you came rap-
ping,
And so faintly you came tapping, tapping at my chamber
door;—
That I scarce was sure I heard you"—here I opened wide
the door;—
Darkness there, and nothing more.

Deep into that darkness peering, long I stood there wondering, fearing,
Doubting, dreaming dreams no mortal ever dared to dream
before;
But the silence was unbroken, and the stillness gave no
token,

THE COMPOSITION OF "THE RAVEN"

And the only word there spoken was the whispered word,
"Lenore!"
This I whispered, and an echo murmured back the word,
"Lenore!"
Merely this and nothing more.

Back into the chamber turning, all my soul within me burn-
ing,
Soon I heard again a tapping somewhat louder than before.
"Surely," said I, "surely that is something at my window lat-
tice;
Let me see, then, what thereat is, and this mystery ex-
plore;—
Let my heart be still a moment and this mystery explore—
'Tis the wind and nothing more!"

Open here I flung the shutter, when, with many a flirt and
flutter,
In there stepped a stately raven of the saintly days of yore;
Not the least obeisance made he; not an instant stopped or
stayed he;
But, with mien of lord or lady, perched above my chamber
door—
Perched upon a bust of Pallas just above my chamber
door—
Perched, and sat, and nothing more.

Then this ebony bird beguiling my sad fancy into smiling,
By the grave and stern decorum of the countenance it wore,
"Though thy crest be shorn and shaven, thou," I said, "art
sure no craven
Ghastly grim and ancient raven wandering from the Nightly
shore—
Tell me what thy lordly name is on the Night's Plutonian
shore!"
Quoth the raven, "Nevermore."

Much I marveled this ungainly fowl to hear discourse so
plainly,
Though its answer little meaning—little relevancy bore;
For we cannot help agreeing that no living human being
Ever yet was blessed with seeing bird above his chamber
door—
Bird or beast upon the sculptured bust above his chamber
door,
With such a name as "Nevermore."

But the raven, sitting lonely on the placid bust, spoke only
That one word, as if his soul in that one word he did out-
pour.
Nothing farther then he uttered—not a feather then he flut-
tered—
Till I scarcely more than muttered "Other friends have
flown before—
On the morrow he will leave me, as my hopes have flown
before."
Then the bird said, "Nevermore."

Startled at the stillness broken by reply so aptly spoken,
"Doubtless," said I, "what it utters is its only stock and store
Caught from some unhappy master whom unmerciful Dis-
aster
Followed fast and followed faster till his songs one burden
bore—
Till the dirges of his hope that melancholy burden bore
Of 'Never—nevermore.'"

But the raven still beguiling all my sad soul into smiling,
Straight I wheeled a cushioned seat in front of bird and bust
and door;
Then, upon the velvet sinking, I betook myself to linking
Fancy unto fancy, thinking what this ominous bird of yore—
What this grim, ungainly, ghastly, gaunt, and ominous bird
of yore
Meant in croaking "Nevermore."

This I sat engaged in guessing, but no syllable expressing
To the fowl whose fiery eyes now burned into my bosom's
     core;
This and more I sat divining, with my head at ease reclining
On the cushion's velvet lining that the lamplight gloated
     o'er,
But whose velvet violet lining with the lamplight gloating
     o'er,
          She shall press, ah, nevermore!

Then, methought, the air grew denser, perfumed from an
     unseen censer
Swung by angels whose faint foot-falls tinkled on the tufted
     floor.
"Wretch," I cried, "thy God hath lent thee—by these angels
     he hath sent thee
Respite—respite and nepenthe from thy memories of Le-
     nore!
Quaff, oh quaff this kind nepenthe and forget this lost Le-
     nore!"
          Quoth the raven, "Nevermore."

"Prophet!" said I, "thing of evil—prophet still, if bird or
     devil!—
Whether Tempter sent, or whether tempest tossed thee here
     ashore,
Desolate yet all undaunted, on this desert land enchanted—
On this home by Horror haunted—tell me truly, I implore—
Is there—is there balm in Gilead?—tell me—tell me, I im-
     plore!"
          Quoth the raven, "Nevermore."

"Prophet!" said I, "thing of evil—prophet still, if bird or
     devil!
By that Heaven that bends above us—by that God we both
     adore—
Tell this soul with sorrow laden if, within the distant Aidenn,

EDGAR ALLAN POE

It shall clasp a sainted maiden whom the angels name Le-
nore—
Clasp a rare and radiant maiden whom the angels name
Lenore!"
Quoth the raven, "Nevermore."

"Be that word our sign of parting, bird or fiend!" I shrieked,
upstarting—
"Get thee back into the tempest and the Night's Plutonian
shore!
Leave no black plume as a token of that lie thy soul has
spoken!
Leave my loneliness unbroken!—quit the bust above my
door!
Take thy beak from out my heart, and take thy form from off
my door!"
Quoth the raven, "Nevermore."

And the raven, never flitting, still is sitting, still is sitting
On the pallid bust of Pallas just above my chamber door;
And his eyes have all the seeming of a demon's that is
dreaming,
And the lamplight o'er him streaming throws his shadow on
the floor;
And my soul from out that shadow that lies floating on the
floor
Shall be lifted—nevermore!

the grief of Lenores death has come to accept

The composition of this poem, Poe said, proceeded step
by step to its completion with the precision and rigidness of
a mathematical problem. The following paragraphs are sum-
maries of each step Poe took in writing "The Raven."

STEP 1

The first concern was that of length. The poem must be read
in one sitting. Too long a poem defeats itself by allowing

interruptions, just as a poem that is too short defeats itself because it does not build up an effect. The length depends on the intensity of the effect the poet is trying to achieve. With these considerations in mind, Poe decided on a poem of about 100 lines. "The Raven" is actually 108 lines long.

STEP 2

Next Poe had to decide on the province, or subject area, of the poem. He felt that the poem should be universally appreciable and that people of all ages and places should be able to understand and enjoy it. He decided on beauty as the province of the poem because contemplation of the Beautiful gives the most intense, the most elevating, and the most universal pleasure. And since he further believed that beauty, of whatever kind, at its highest pitch always excites the soul to sadness, he chose *melancholy* as the best tone for the poem.

STEP 3

The *length*, the *province*, and the *tone* of the poem having been selected, Poe then proceeded to consider its construction. In searching for some keynote for constructing the poem, some pivotal idea, he hit upon the device of the refrain, the repetition of a word, or a small group of words which are alike in sound and thought. Poe decided to keep the same sound in the refrain throughout the poem, but to change the meaning of the sound each time it was used. The refrain would have to be brief—a single word would be best—and it would have to be repeated in a changing situation in order to have a different meaning each time. The word itself should have a rich sound and it should be capable of heavy, emphatic pronunciation. Poe thought of the letter *o* as rich and sonorous and of the letter *r* as capable of heavy emphasis. What word combined both letters that would contribute to a melancholy tone? The very first word Poe thought of, according to his essay, was *nevermore*.

Once he had chosen *nevermore* as the word of the refrain, he had to devise an excuse for repeating it again and again in the poem. A reasoning human being in the poem could not very conveniently utter the same word over and over; a non-reasoning creature that could talk would be far more logical. Poe first thought of the colorful parrot, but then settled on the dark raven as more in keeping with the melancholy tone of the poem.

STEP 4

Up to this point he had settled on a poem of about 100 lines, decided its province was to be beauty and its tone to be melancholy. He had also selected a dark bird of ill omen repeating at the end of each stanza the word *nevermore*. Next he selected a *topic*. "What," he asked himself, "is the most universally melancholy topic?" The obvious reply was *death*. "And when," he next asked himself, "is death most poetical?" And the reply was once again obvious: when it most closely allies itself to *beauty*. Therefore, Poe concluded, the most poetical topic in the world is the *death* of a *beautiful* woman, mourned by her bereaved lover.

STEP 5

Poe next had to combine the idea of a raven repeating one word with the bereaved lover lamenting the death of his beautiful lost one. He wanted the refrain to mean something different each time it was used. The question-answer technique suggested itself very quickly: *nevermore* would be the unvarying answer of the raven to the varying questions of the lover. The first question would be casual and unimportant, but each succeeding question would become climactically more serious. Poe decided to write first the climax

THE COMPOSITION OF "THE RAVEN"

stanza, that stanza in which the answer *nevermore* should involve the greatest sorrow and despair. This stanza is the one that is third from the end of the poem. He wrote the other stanzas so that they would lead up to this one.

STEP 6

The last matters of detail were perhaps the easiest since, like pieces of a puzzle nearly finished, they fell quite naturally into place. The lover and the raven had to be brought together. Should the encounter be indoors or outdoors? Poe decided to keep the lover in the room made sacred by the memories of his loved one. Poe made the night a stormy one for two reasons: first, the storm gave the raven a reason for seeking admission into the lover's room; second, the storm outside would contrast with the quietness of the room. He placed within the room a bust of Pallas so that the white marble would contrast with the dark plumage, and so that the scholarly, thoughtful nature of the lover could be established.

In such a way all the poem's details fell into place. With the details organized, and the climax stanza complete, Poe went on with the actual composition of the poem.

Other poems

The death of a beautiful woman mourned by the bereaved lover was a favorite subject for Poe. In what ways do the following two poems fit Poe's theories of poetry? Compare the poems to "The Raven." What are the similarities and the differences?

Annabel Lee

> It was many and many a year ago,
> In a kingdom by the sea,
> That a maiden there lived whom you may know

By the name of Annabel Lee:
And this maiden she lived with no other thought
Than to love and be loved by me.

She was a child and I was a child,
In this kingdom by the sea;
But we loved with a love that was more than love—
I and my Annabel Lee—
With a love that the winged seraphs of heaven
Coveted her and me.

And this was the reason that, long ago,
In this kingdom by the sea,
A wind blew out of a cloud, chilling
My beautiful Annabel Lee—
So that her highborn kinsmen came
And bore her away from me,
To shut her up in a sepulchre
In this kingdom by the sea.

The angels, not half so happy in Heaven,
Went envying her and me:—
Yes, that was the reason (as all men know,
In this kingdom by the sea)
That the wind came out of the cloud by night
Chilling and killing my Annabel Lee.

But our love it was stronger by far than the love
Of those who were older than we—
Of many far wiser than we—
And neither the angels in Heaven above,
Nor the demons down under the sea,
Can ever dissever my soul from the soul
Of the beautiful Annabel Lee:—

For the moon never beams, without bringing me dreams
Of the beautiful Annabel Lee;

And the stars never rise, but I feel the bright eyes
Of the beautiful Annabel Lee;
And so, all the night-tide, I lie down by the side
Of my darling, my darling, my life and my bride
In her sepulchre there by the sea—
In her tomb by the sounding sea.

To One in Paradise

Thou wast all that to me, love,
For which my soul did pine—
A green isle in the sea, love,
A fountain and a shrine,
All wreathed with fairy fruits and flowers,
And all the flowers were mine.
Ah, dream too bright to last!

Ah, starry Hope! that didst arise
But to be overcast!
A voice from out the Future cries,
"On! on!"—but o'er the Past
(Dim gulf!) my spirit hovering lies
Mute, motionless, aghast!

For, alas! alas! with me
The light of Life is o'er!
No more—no more—no more—
(Such language holds the solemn sea
To the sands upon the shore)
Shall bloom the thunder-blasted tree,
Or the stricken eagle soar!

And all my days are trances,
And all my nightly dreams
Are where thy dark eye glances,
And where thy footstep gleams—
In what ethereal dances,
By what ethereal streams.

EDGAR ALLAN POE

Poe as a word musician

Even the three poems above will show that Edgar Allan Poe was an extremely gifted word musician. His sound effects, rich with haunting rhythms, exciting rhymes and alliterations, swift and slow cadences, and bright onomatopoeias, are ingenious indeed. Poe could employ any music to fit any subject or theme. One of his most famous and most skillfully written poems is "The Bells." Notice how the sound effects suit the subject matter.

The Bells

I

Hear the sledges with the bells—
Silver bells!
What a world of merriment their melody foretells!
How they tinkle, tinkle, tinkle,
In the icy air of night!
While the stars that oversprinkle
All the heavens, seem to twinkle
With a crystalline delight;
Keeping time, time, time,
In a sort of Runic rhyme,
To the tintinnabulation that so musically wells
From the bells, bells, bells, bells,
Bells, bells, bells—
From the jingling and the tinkling of the bells.

II

Hear the mellow wedding bells—
Golden bells!
What a world of happiness their harmony foretells!
Through the balmy air of night
How they ring out their delight!—
From the molten-golden notes,
And all in tune,

THE BELLS: *Runic* = mysterious, magical

What a liquid ditty floats
To the turtle-dove that listens, while she gloats
On the moon!
Oh, from out the sounding cells
What a gush of euphony voluminously wells!
How it swells!
How it dwells
On the Future!—how it tells
Of the rapture that impels
To the swinging and the ringing
Of the bells, bells, bells—
Of the bells, bells, bells, bells,
Bells bells, bells—
To the rhyming and the chiming of the bells!

III

Hear the loud alarum bells—
Brazen bells!
What a tale of terror, now, their turbulency tells!
In the startled ear of night
How they scream out their affright!
Too much horrified to speak,
They can only shriek, shriek,
Out of tune,
In a clamorous appealing to the mercy of the fire,
In a mad expostulation with the deaf and frantic fire,
Leaping higher, higher, higher,
With a desperate desire,
And a resolute endeavor
Now—now to sit, or never,
By the side of the pale-faced moon.
Oh, the bells, bells, bells!
What a tale their terror tells
Of Despair!
How they clang, and clash, and roar!
What a horror they outpour
On the bosom of the palpitating air!

Yet the ear, it fully knows,
By the twanging
And the clanging,
How the danger ebbs and flows;
Yet the ear distinctly tells,
In the jangling
And wrangling,
How the danger sinks and swells,
By the sinking or the swelling in the anger of the bells—
Of the bells,—
Of the bells, bells, bells, bells,
Bells, bells, bells—
In the clamor and the clangor of the bells!

IV

Hear the tolling of the bells—
Iron bells!
What a world of solemn thought their monody compels!
In the silence of the night,
How we shiver with affright
At the melancholy menace of their tone!
For every sound that floats
From the rust within their throats
Is a groan.
And the people—ah, the people—
They that dwell up in the steeple,
All alone,
And who tolling, tolling, tolling,
In that muffled monotone,
Feel a glory in so rolling
On the human heart a stone—
They are neither man nor woman—
They are neither brute nor human—
They are ghouls:—
And their king it is who tolls:—
And he rolls, rolls, rolls
Rolls
A paean from the bells!

And his merry bosom swells
With the paean of the bells!
And he dances, and he yells;
Keeping time, time, time
In a sort of Runic rhyme,
To the paean of the bells—
Of the bells:—
Keeping time, time, time,
In a sort of Runic rhyme,
To the throbbing of the bells—
Of the bells, bells, bells—
To the sobbing of the bells;
Keeping time, time, time,
As he knells, knells, knells,
In a happy Runic rhyme,
To the rolling of the bells—
Of the bells, bells, bells:—
To the tolling of the bells—
Of the bells, bells, bells, bells,
Bells, bells, bells,—
To the moaning and the groaning of the bells.

 A poem which employs many of the musical qualities of "The Bells" and tells a story at the same time is the ballad "Ulalume." Notice the strong rhythm of the poem as well as its effective repetitions of rhymes and whole lines. In what ways does the poem resemble "The Raven"?

Ulalume—A Ballad

The skies they were ashen and sober;
The leaves they were crisped and sere—
The leaves they were withering and sere:
It was night, in the lonesome October
Of my most immemorial year:
It was hard by the dim lake of Auber

ULALUME: *Yaanek, Auber, Weir* = imaginary, poetic geography; *scoriac* = slag-like; *Astarte* = a moon goddess

In the misty mid region of Weir—
It was down by the dank tarn of Auber,
In the ghoul-haunted woodland of Weir.

Here once through an alley Titanic,
Of cypress, I roamed with my Soul—
Of cypress, with Psyche, my Soul.
These were days when my heart was volcanic
As the scoriac rivers that roll—
As the lavas that restlessly roll
Their sulfurous currents down Yaanek
In the ultimate climes of the Pole—
That groan as they roll down Mount Yaanek
In the realms of the Boreal Pole.

Our talk had been serious and sober,
But our thoughts they were palsied and sere—
Our memories were treacherous and sere;
For we knew not the month was October,
And we marked not the night of the year
(Ah, night of all nights of the year!)—
We noted not the dim lake of Auber
(Though once we had journeyed down here)—
We remembered not the dank tarn of Auber,
Nor the ghoul-haunted woodland of Weir.

And now, as the night was senescent
And star dials pointed to morn—
As the star-dials hinted of morn—
At the end of our path a liquescent
And nebulous lustre was born,
Out of which a miraculous crescent
Arose with a duplicate horn—
Astarte's bediamonded crescent
Distinct with its duplicate horn.

And I said: "She is warmer than Dian;
She rolls through an ether of sighs—

She revels in a region of sighs.
She has seen that the tears are not dry on
These cheeks, where the worm never dies,
And has come past the stars of the Lion,
To point us the path to the skies—
To the Lethean peace of the skies—
Come up, in despite of the Lion
To shine on us with her bright eyes—
Come up through the lair of the Lion,
With love in her luminous eyes."

But Psyche, uplifting her finger,
Said: "Sadly this star I mistrust—
Her pallor I strangely mistrust:
Ah, hasten!—ah, let us not linger.
Ah, fly! let us fly!—for we must."
In terror she spoke, letting sink her
Wings till they trailed in the dust—
In agony sobbed, letting sink her
Plumes till they trailed in the dust—
Till they sorrowfully trailed in the dust.

I replied: "This is nothing but dreaming:
Let us on by this tremulous light!
Let us bathe in this crystalline light!
Its Sibyllic spendor is beaming
With Hope and in Beauty to-night:—
See:—it flickers up the sky through the night!
Ah, we safely may trust to its gleaming,
And be sure it will lead us aright—
We surely may trust to a gleaming,
That cannot but guide us aright,
Since it flickers up to Heaven through the night."

Thus I pacified Psyche and kissed her,
And tempted her out of her gloom;
And conquered her scruples and gloom;

And we passed to the end of the vista,
But were stopped by the door of a tomb—
By the door of a legended tomb;
And I said: "What is written, sweet sister,
On the door of this legended tomb?"
She replied: "Ulalume—Ulalume!—
'Tis the vault of thy lost Ulalume!"

Then my heart it grew ashen and sober
As the leaves that were crisped and sere—
As the leaves that were withering and sere;
And I cried: "It was surely October
On *this* very night of last year
That I journeyed—I journeyed down here!—
That I brought a dread burden down here—
On this night of all nights of the year,
Ah, what demon hath tempted me here?
Well I know, now, this dim lake of Auber—
This misty mid region of Weir—
Well I know, now, this dank tarn of Auber,
This ghoul-haunted woodland of Weir."

Said we, then—the two, then: "Ah, can it
Have been that the woodlandish ghouls—
The pitiful, the merciful ghouls—
To bar up our way and to ban it
From the secret that lies in these wolds—
From the thing that lies hidden in these wolds—
Have drawn up the spectre of a planet
From the limbo of lunary souls—
This sinfully scintillant planet
From the Hell of the planetary souls?"

More poems

Legends about a city paved with gold are very old in the history of the discovery and exploration of the North American continent. Such legends became very popular again after the Gold Rush to California in 1849. The subject appealed to many writers; notice that Poe's El Dorado, however, is more than just a city of gold.

El Dorado

Gaily bedight,
A gallant knight,
In sunshine and in shadow,
Had journeyed long,
Singing a song,
In search of El Dorado.

But he grew old—
This knight so bold—
And o'er his heart a shadow
Fell as he found
No spot of ground
That looked like El Dorado.

And, as his strength
Failed him at length,
He met a pilgrim shadow—
"Shadow," said he,
"Where can it be—
This land of El Dorado?"

"Over the mountains
Of the Moon,
Down the Valley of the Shadow,
Ride, boldly ride,"
The shade replied,—
"If you seek for El Dorado!"

EL DORADO: *bedight* = dressed, arrayed

EDGAR ALLAN POE

Israfel, according to the religious followers of Islam, is a poet-angel, the very spirit of poetry in a divine figure. In his poem "Israfel," Poe uses the figure of the poet-angel to set forth his ideas about poetic inspiration and the poet's place in the world.

Israfel

In Heaven a spirit doth dwell
"Whose heart-strings are a lute;"
None sing so wildly well
As the angel Israfel,
And the giddy stars (so legend tells),
Ceasing their hymns, attend the spell
Of his voice, all mute.

Tottering above
In her highest noon,
The enamoured moon
Blushes with love,
While, to listen, the red levin
(With the rapid Pleiads, even,
Which were seven)
Pauses in Heaven.

And they say (the starry choir
And the other listening things)
That Israfeli's fire
Is owing to that lyre
By which he sits and sings—
The trembling living wire
Of those unusual strings.

But the skies that angel trod,
Where deep thoughts are a duty—
Where love's a grown-up God—
Where the Houri glances are

Imbued with all the beauty
Which we worship in a star.

Therefore, thou art not wrong,
Israfeli, who despisest
An unimpassioned song;
To thee the laurels belong,
Best bard, because the wisest!
Merrily live, and long!

The ecstasies above
With thy burning measures suit—
Thy grief, thy joy, thy hate, thy love,
With the fervor of thy lute—
Well may the stars be mute.

Yes, Heaven is thine; but this
Is a world of sweets and sours;
Our flowers are merely flowers,
And the shadow of thy perfect bliss
Is the sunshine of ours.

If I could dwell
Where Israfel
Hath dwelt, and he where I,
He might not sing so wildly well
A mortal melody,
While a bolder note than this might swell
From my lyre within the sky.

These last two poems were written for, and dedicated
to, women. The first, "To Helen," was written for Jane Stith
Stanard, a woman that Poe, as a young man, admired greatly.
The second is for Mrs. Maria Clemm, the mother of Poe's
wife. Both are classic poems of their kind.

To Helen

prototype of beautiful woman

Helen, thy beauty is to me
Like those Nicean barks of yore,
That gently, o'er a perfumed sea,
The weary, way-worn wanderer bore
To his own native shore.

On desperate seas long wont to roam,
Thy hyacinth hair, thy classic face,
Thy Naiad airs have brought me home
To the glory that was Greece,
And the grandeur that was Rome.

Lo! in yon brilliant window-niche
How statue-like I see thee stand,
The agate lamp within thy hand!
Ah, Psyche, from the regions which
Are Holy-Land!

To My Mother *in-law*

Because I feel that, in the Heavens above,
The angels, whispering to one another,
Can find, among their burning terms of love,
None so devotional as that of "Mother,"
Therefore by that dear name I long have called you—
You who are more than mother to me,
And fill my heart of hearts, where Death installed you
In setting my Virginia's spirit free.
My mother—my own mother, who died early,
Was but the mother of myself; but you
Are mother to the one I loved so dearly,
And thus are dearer than the mother I knew
By that infinity with which my wife
Was dearer to my soul than its soul-life.

Dearer to him than his mother

TO HELEN: *Nicean* = this musical word is probably from Latin poetry

67   MORE POEMS

Poe's stature

Forgotten for many years after his death, Edgar Allan Poe is today one of the most highly regarded American writers of the nineteenth century. He was first rediscovered by the French poet Baudelaire in 1855. Baudelaire, an exceptional poet himself, translated Poe's works into French, where they exerted a powerful influence on the Symbolist movement in French poetry. The Symbolist movement in turn went a long way in shaping and influencing the development of modern American poetry. In such a round-about way, Poe remains a powerful poetic figure more than a century after his death. His stories and poems, his theories of literature, his criticism, all have earned him undying fame.

FOUR

SIMILES, METAPHORS, AND SYMBOLS

HUMAN beings can hardly speak, write, or think for more than a few minutes without using comparisons. When we want to describe how fiercely someone played in a football game, we compare him to a tiger, a rock, or a demon. Consider only a few of the vast number of familiar comparisons: *crazy as a loon, proud as a peacock, stubborn as a mule, smart as a fox.* Sometimes the comparison may simply be one word: *mulish* or *foxy.*

The poetic names given to comparisons of unlike objects are *simile* and *metaphor.* The difference between a simile and a metaphor is very slight. The simile is a stated comparison; that is, it says that one object is like another object, as in *blind as a bat,* or *he played like a tiger.* Almost always similes use the words *like* and *as.* The metaphor, however, is an implied comparison. It says that one object *is* another object, as in *he was a tiger on the field,* or *she is a bat.* The difference between a metaphor and a simile is so slight that often in discussions of poetry the word *metaphor* is used to describe any kind of comparison.

But a definition is only the first step in understanding the importance and the use of metaphor. What does a metaphor do? Why is it so necessary? In what ways do poets, indeed all people, use metaphor in talking to other people? Like rhythm, rhyme, and other sound effects, metaphor is used very carefully by the poet to say exactly and vividly what he feels and sees and thinks.

Metaphor appeals to the senses

Metaphor can appeal very directly to the senses; it can, for instance, make us see a scene. Look at the following one-sentence description:

It is a beautiful lake set in lovely hills.

Does this description appeal to the senses? How clearly can the lake and the hills be seen by the imagination? Compare it with the following metaphorical description:

The lake was a mirror set in green velvet hills.

For most people, this second description illustrates the scene better because it presents a picture which the imagination can immediately visualize. The lake is compared to a *mirror* and the hills to *velvet:* both of these comparisons use objects that can be seen and felt. The first description does not use concrete describing words; *beautiful* and *lovely* are abstract words. Like *honesty, speed, strong,* or *happy,* they apply to ideas and concepts; but they are not the names of things that can be seen and touched. *Mirror, velvet, horse, hammer,* and *tree* are concrete words describing things that can be seen and touched. Abstract words, because they have no visual or tactile qualities, do not appeal to the imagination very readily. But the linking together of concrete words can jar the imagination. Because metaphors link together concrete words by comparing unlike objects, they have this effect. Metaphors awake a person's imagination so that he uses it to see and touch objects, to perceive colors and shapes, and even, if his imagination is acute enough, to taste and hear.

Read the descriptive phrases below. One description in each pair uses an abstract word and the other uses a concrete metaphor. Which descriptions seem to have more appeal to the senses? To what senses do they appeal?

a greedy eater	a bitter smell
a wolfish eater	an ammoniac smell
a strong tree	soft material
a marble-column tree	feathery material
a sharp edge	light-colored shirt
a razor edge	lemon-colored shirt

healthy cheeks
apple cheeks

Poets use metaphors because they appeal to the senses, and whatever appeals directly to the senses effectively captivates the imagination and grips the emotions.

Metaphor simplifies and illustrates ideas

In speaking with each other, people are continually relying on metaphors to simplify and illustrate ideas. This is no more true anywhere than in school. In the history class a teacher describing the conditions just before the outbreak of a war might compare them to a powder keg which would explode with the slightest jarring. Science books say that sound travels in *waves* and that electricity runs in a *current*. Biology teachers may say that the nerves carry messages from the fingertips to the brain. Now the nerves do not really carry messages, but the comparison of nerve impulses to messages simplifies and illustrates a complicated process.

A poet writing a poem or a student writing a composition often searches for the right word to use in a particular place. What is this search like? The following short poem describes it through the use of metaphor.

Word

STEPHEN SPENDER

> The word bites like a fish.
> Shall I throw it back free
> Arrowing to that sea
> Where thoughts lash tail and fin
> Or shall I pull it in
> To rhyme upon a dish?

Stephen Spender's short poem says that trying to get the right word is like fishing. Such a metaphor illustrates the idea quite well. What are some of the other comparisons made in this poem? Words and thoughts are compared to fish which "lash tail and fin." To what is the sea compared? The dish? Is there a consistency in the way the metaphor has been used? Metaphor is a valuable way to communicate; one idea often is best explained in terms of another.

Metaphor leads to deeper understanding

But metaphors do much more than appeal to the senses and illustrate ideas. By comparing two unlike things, a metaphor can show additional qualities of each. It can lead to new ideas and to new understanding. Each morning people awake and wind their watches for another day. But the poet, with his gift for metaphor, can compare his watch to the clockwork of the entire universe and ask, "Who winds the universal watch?" Such a comparison makes us understand time and the universe in a new way. Common objects and acts can suddenly take on new meaning through one quick, striking metaphor.

The train is such a common object. Notice how, through the use of metaphor, the poet presents a fresher, deeper understanding of a train. What is the metaphor that is used?

The Train

EMILY DICKINSON

> I like to see it lap the miles,
> And lick the valleys up,
> And stop to feed itself at tanks;
> And then, prodigious, step
>
> Around a pile of mountains,
> And, supercilious, peer
> In shanties by the sides of roads;
> And then a quarry pare
>
> To fit its sides, and crawl between,
> Complaining all the while
> In horrid, hooting stanza;
> Then chase itself down hill
>
> And neigh like Boanerges;
> Then, punctual as a star,
> Stop—docile and omnipotent—
> At its own stable door.

The verbs in the poem gradually make the comparison clear. In order of their use, these verbs are *lap, lick, feed, step, peer, pare, crawl, complaining, chase, neigh,* and *stop.* The first verb, *lap,* does suggest an animal of some sort. Since the train was often called the *iron horse,* the train—horse comparison suggests itself. The verb *neigh* in the last

THE TRAIN: *Boanerges* = a name given by Jesus to two of his disciples, meaning "sons of thunder"

stanza certainly makes the comparison clear, for only the horse neighs. The word *stable* concludes and completes the metaphor.

The comparison of train and horse made in this poem is very interesting. It leads to a newer understanding of both horse and train. The train and the horse are really very much alike: they are both dependent; they must be fed. Powerful though they are, they both stand at tanks and they are both docile at the stable door. Like a horse, the train seems to peer into windows, and it complains. Emily Dickinson's poem shows that the train, though powerful, is essentially as helpless as a horse. But this comparison doesn't make the train seem any less interesting; rather, the metaphor makes the train come alive in an unusual and novel way.

One well-known poet and teacher has said that a metaphor works like a *stereoscope,* an optical instrument that combines for the viewer the images of two two-dimensional pictures and achieves one three-dimensional picture. Just as the metaphor compares two unlike things to produce a third picture which is richer and more meaningful, so the stereoscope combines two somewhat unlike pictures of the same object to produce a third picture which is quite different from the two combined. If both pictures in the stereoscope were absolutely alike, the three-dimensional effect would be impossible. It is precisely because they are different from each other that they create the effect of something new.

The two pictures brought together by the stereoscope are made into one picture that has more solidity and depth. Like the stereoscope, the metaphor makes a richer, deeper picture. The Emily Dickinson poem is a picture which shows the strong and docile features of a train equally well; because the train is seen from two different points of view, it is seen more completely and more accurately.

The stereoscope effect of a metaphor may be seen again in the next poem. The following vocabulary will be helpful in your reading of the poem:

hypocritic	(line 1)	variant form of hypocritical
dervishes	(line 2)	members of a Muslim religious order known for its devotional exercises—bodily movements often leading to a trance
diadems	(line 4)	crowns
fagots	(line 4)	bundles of wood
pleached	(line 7)	interlaced
fillet	(line 11)	a ribbon or narrow strip of material used especially as a headband

Days

RALPH WALDO EMERSON

Daughters of Time, the hypocritic days
Muffled and dumb like barefoot dervishes,
And marching single in an endless file,
Bring diadems and fagots in their hands.
To each they offer gifts after his will,
Bread, kingdoms, stars, and sky that holds them all.
I, in my pleached garden, watched the pomp,
Forgot my morning wishes, hastily
Took a few herbs and apples, and the Day
Turned and departed silent. I, too late,
Under her solemn fillet saw the scorn.

The metaphor is clear enough: *Days* are compared to *Daughters of Time.* They offer beautiful gifts, ranging from crowns to bundles of wood, to each individual according to what he chooses. The "I" in the poem takes only a few herbs and apples, and the Day scornfully departs.

Why does this metaphor act like a stereoscope and give a deeper understanding of days? Everyone knows the dictionary definition of both *daughter* and *day*, yet when these two words are brought together by metaphor, we can understand each of them a little more clearly. The daughters are silent (muffled and dumb) so that they can pass without attracting notice. They cannot encourage or help individuals to take advantage of all that they offer. What the metaphor makes clear is that the Days are passive, but that individuals who are also passive and want little of life are missing great opportunities. The "I" of the poem chose a few modest things—herbs and apples—and the silent Day departed scornfully. The metaphor, by making a new picture of two different pictures, gives a deeper understanding of what days are.

To sum up, then, metaphor works in three ways to make the meaning of the poem more dramatic and more clear. Because it uses concrete words which appeal strongly to the senses, metaphor startles the imagination. In explanations of every kind in every subject, metaphor can also simplify and illustrate meaning. Lastly, like a stereoscope, the metaphor can give a richer, deeper view of a subject. It can provide a way of seeing things with greater understanding.

Exercise: Evaluating Metaphors

How can you distinguish between an effective metaphor and an ineffective one? What makes one metaphor better than another? There is no easy rule by which such questions can be answered. Some people argue that a metaphor should be consistent throughout a poem; others insist that a metaphor should not be too wild or farfetched; still others say that a metaphor has only to be colorful and exciting.

The use of metaphor in the poem "Trees" has been the subject of many heated discussions.

Trees

JOYCE KILMER

> I think that I shall never see
> A poem lovely as a tree.
>
> A tree whose hungry mouth is pressed
> Against the earth's sweet flowing breast;
>
> A tree that looks to God all day,
> And lifts her leafy arms to pray;
>
> A tree that may in summer wear
> A nest of robins in her hair;
>
> Upon whose bosom snow has lain;
> Who intimately lives with rain.
>
> Poems are made by fools like me,
> But only God can make a tree.

The points for and against this poem's use of metaphor can be summarized very briefly. The people who approve of it say that the metaphors show the various ways of looking at trees at various times. The people who think the use of metaphor is badly done say that the metaphors are mixed; the tree is seen pressing its mouth to the earth, lifting its arms to pray, wearing robins in its hair. The picture is very confusing.

Either in a composition or in a class discussion, try to decide whether metaphor is well or badly used in this poem. You might first consider the following questions:

1. Is consistency absolutely necessary in using metaphor?

2. What does a mixed metaphor do to the imagination which is visualizing the description?

3. How obvious should a metaphor be?

4. Does a sensational, or excessive, metaphor add or subtract? Why?

5. In what poems that you have read are metaphors very well used?

Symbol

Metaphors compare one object or action to another object or action. A symbol, on the other hand, *is one object coming to stand for, or represent, another.* Symbols are very common. In arithmetic, for example, the $\times$ is a symbol for multiplication and the $-$ is a symbol for subtraction. The Greek letter π is a symbol for 22/7. An unadorned ring is a marriage symbol; the stars on our flag are symbols for the fifty individual states; the cross is a symbol for Christianity. Many companies and groups have particular symbols by which they are recognized.

"Crossing the Bar" takes one object in nature, a sandbar under the ocean, and treats it in such a way that it becomes a symbol.

Crossing the Bar
ALFRED, LORD TENNYSON

Sunset and evening star,
And one clear call for me!
And may there be no moaning of the bar,
When I put out to sea,

But such a tide as moving seems asleep,
Too full for sound and foam,
When that which drew from out the boundless deep
Turns again home.

Twilight and evening bell,
And after that the dark!
And may there be no sadness of farewell
When I embark;

For though from out our bourne of Time and Place
The flood may bear me far,
I hope to see my Pilot face to face
When I have crossed the bar.

The sandbar in this poem symbolizes the separation between life and death. Crossing the bar means crossing from life into death.

Particular things often can become symbols for general ideas; that is, a wall may come to symbolize the idea of prejudice or imprisonment; a star may come to symbolize all that is distant or unattainable; a river can come to symbolize the flow of life. A poet often uses a particular object to represent another larger object or idea. Think about the symbol in the following poem.

Flower in the Crannied Wall
ALFRED, LORD TENNYSON

> Flower in the crannied wall,
> I pluck you out of the crannies,
> I hold you here, root and all, in my hand,
> Little flower—but if I could understand
> What you are, root and all, and all in all,
> I should know what God and man is.

The flower which the poet sees in the wall becomes more than a flower. For the poet it is a symbol of all the unknown and undiscovered meanings in the world and all the mystery in the life of God and man. Root and all, the flower is an unchartered world of itself. A particular object, a small flower, has become a symbol of a general idea, the mystery of life.

Denotation and connotation

The denotation of a word is its strict, exact dictionary definition; the connotation of a word is its wider, suggested meaning. The Fourth of July *denotes* a legal holiday celebrating the Declaration of Independence in 1776, but it may connote

DENOTATION AND CONNOTATION

hot weather, motor trips, parades, the odor of burnt fireworks, picnics, hot dogs and hamburgers, blue skies, and the colors red, white, and blue. November *denotes* the eleventh month of the year, having thirty days. But it may *connote* many things: cool nights, fallen leaves, bare, dark branches against a grey sky, thin ice on puddles of water, shorter days, snow flurries, Thanksgiving turkey, visits with relatives, and so on. The poem "Days" (p. 75) is an interesting study in denotation and connotation. Two lines in that poem read:

> **To each they offer gifts after his will,**
> **Bread, kingdoms, stars, and sky that holds them all.**

The denotation of these words is a simple matter, for the words themselves are quite common. The poet is really depending on the connotations of the words to convey his meaning. He does not mean simply *bread* or simply *kingdoms*. If he did, he would be saying that the days offer only four separate items. And do the days literally offer the *stars* and *sky?* Of course not, at least not in the denotative sense of those words. Each of the four words connotes many things:

Bread connotes material things, food, fuel, clothing, shelter, etc.

Kingdoms connotes authority, rank, responsibility, leadership, power, etc.

Stars connotes inspiration, beauty, truth, knowledge, love, constancy, etc.

Sky connotes vastness, eternity, faith, religion, God.

Remember that the "I" of the poem took only a *few herbs* and *apples*. Both by denotation and connotation, *herbs* and *apples* do not amount to very much. This is why the Day departed scornful.

Most words have both denotative and connotative meaning. *Dawn* suggests light, beginning, freshness, birth, etc., and *dusk* suggests darkness, ending, quietness, rest, death. The denotation of a word is unvarying. The connotation, however, often varies greatly. The poet uses his words carefully so that their connotations suit the sense of the poem and harmonize with the mood and feeling he is trying to create.

Exercise: Understanding Metaphors, Symbols, and Connotations

The poems in the next pages depend a great deal upon the use of metaphor, symbol, and connotation. Read the poems carefully and consider the questions after each.

A.

The Snake

EMILY DICKINSON

> A narrow fellow in the grass
> Occasionally rides;
> You may have met him—did you not,
> His notice sudden is.
>
> The grass divides as with a comb,
> A spotted shaft is seen;
> And then it closes at your feet
> And opens further on.
>
> He likes a boggy acre,
> A floor too cool for corn.
> Yet when a child, and barefoot,
> I more than once, at morn,
>
> Have passed, I thought, a whip-lash
> Unbraiding in the sun—
> When, stooping to secure it,
> It wrinkled and was gone.

Several of nature's people
I know, and they know me;
I feel for them a transport
Of cordiality;

But never met this fellow,
Attended or alone,
Without a tighter breathing,
And zero at the bone.

1. What comparison is made in the first stanza? What is the snake called in the second stanza?

2. What does the last stanza tell about the poet's feelings?

3. Do the metaphors of the first two stanzas indicate or foreshadow the poet's feeling about the snake, expressed in the last stanza?

4. Why does the poet call the snake a *whip-lash* in stanza four? What qualities does this metaphor suggest? What would be lost if she compared the snake to a *rope-coil?*

B.

The Fog

CARL SANDBURG

The fog comes
on little cat feet.

It sits looking
over harbor and city
on silent haunches
and then moves on.

1. The metaphor is made in the first two lines. What two things are compared? What words in the second group of lines continue the metaphor?

2. What are the similarities of the two things the metaphor brings together?

3. The poem describes a scene. To what senses does the metaphor appeal?

C.

The Eagle

ALFRED, LORD TENNYSON

> He clasps the crag with crooked hands;
> Close to the sun in lonely lands,
> Ring'd with the azure world, he stands.
>
> The wrinkled sea beneath him crawls;
> He watches from his mountain walls,
> And like a thunderbolt he falls.

1. Why do you think the poet uses the word *hands* in line one? Why not claws, which would be more accurate and more in tune with the *c* sounds?

2. How does this poem suggest that an eagle resembles man?

3. What are the connotations of *mountain walls?* Does the comparison of sea waves to wrinkles tell you anything about the eagle's position?

4. Discuss the simile of the last line. What qualities does it suggest that the eagle possesses?

5. For what aspects of nature might the eagle be a symbol?

D.

Lines from "The Love Song of J. Alfred Prufrock"

T. S. ELIOT

> The yellow fog that rubs its back upon the window-panes,
> The yellow smoke that rubs its muzzle on the window-panes
> Licked its tongue into the corners of the evening,
> Lingered upon the pools that stand in drains,
> Let fall upon its back the soot that falls from chimneys,
> Slipped by the terrace, made a sudden leap,
> And seeing that it was a soft October night,
> Curled once about the house, and fell asleep.

1. These lines make no open statement of comparison, yet the fog is being compared to some animal. What are the verb phrases that reveal this comparison? What is the animal?

2. Compare and contrast these lines with Carl Sandburg's "The Fog" on page 82. Which do you think is the more effective description? Why?

3. How does this description, like a stereoscope, give you a fresher, clearer idea of the way that a fog moves?

FIVE

ROBERT FROST
A New Englander of the World

EDGAR ALLAN POE died at the age of forty. At the same age, Robert Frost was an unknown writer on the verge of publishing his first book of poems. That book and subsequent books have placed Frost in the foremost rank of modern poets. Although he twice attempted and twice withdrew from college, Robert Frost lived to receive dozens of honorary degrees from great universities in Europe and America. For short periods of time, he taught at many American colleges; he won literary prizes on numerous occasions; he was a popular speaker in the lecture hall, on the radio, and on television; the Congress of the United States cited him for his poetry, a recognition rarely granted a man of letters; and in January, 1961, he was invited to compose and read a poem at the Inauguration of President Kennedy. No other poet of the twentieth century has been more honored and more loved.

He was born in 1874 of New England parents, in San Francisco, California. After the death of his father in 1885, he and his mother returned to New England, to Lawrence, Massachusetts, where his mother taught school. After his graduation from Lawrence High School as valedictorian and class poet, he attended first Dartmouth and then Harvard, but withdrew from each without taking a degree. In 1895, he married Elinor White, a classmate in high school, and thereafter worked at many jobs: in a cotton mill, in a shoe factory, on a farm, for a country newspaper, in several schools as a teacher. Meanwhile the poems he was writing were being rejected by the leading magazines of the country. From 1900 to 1909, he farmed near Derry, New Hampshire, and raised a family of four children. But in 1912, discouraged both with farming and with the reception of his poems, he sold his farm and moved with his family to England. It is ironic that America's most celebrated modern poet was first recognized in a country other than his own. With *A Boy's Will* in 1913 and *North of Boston* in 1914, Robert Frost became an established poet. When, in 1915, Frost returned to the United States and once again took up farming in New Hampshire, *North of Boston* had become a best seller in his native land.

Thereafter, writing poetry, teaching, and farming became his livelihood. *Mountain Interval* in 1916, *New Hampshire* in 1925, *West-Running Brook* in 1928, *Collected Poems* in 1930, and half a dozen other books, including *In the Clearing*, published in 1961 when Frost was eighty-six years old, were all hailed as poetry collections of a very high order. Four separate times his collections of poetry were awarded the Pulitzer Prize. Many colleges sought him as a teacher, and he taught at Middlebury, Michigan, Wesleyan, Amherst, Harvard, Yale, and Dartmouth. Yet he always kept his farm in northern New England.

Frost as a poet-teacher

A poem, Robert Frost once said, is an effort to find meaning and fulfillment. It "begins with a lump in the throat" and ends "in a clarification of life." He felt that the poem was a way of understanding; that, in his own words, it was "a stay against confusion." Each poem in its small way made sense out of the raw material of living; each poem organized the poet's thought and communicated it to the reader.

Many people mistakenly regard Robert Frost as a white-haired, cracker-barrel philosopher who, like a Santa Claus handing out presents, always gives out cheerful, warming advice to those who gather around him. Nothing could be farther from the truth. Although Frost's words show a persistent hope for mankind and a love for nature, and although his poetry is essentially optimistic, much of it shows an awareness of the isolation and sadness of life. Frost once described himself as a "pursuitist, not an escapist." In his pursuit of understanding, he discovered the tragic as well as the triumphant. And he teaches his readers about both the griefs and the joys of life.

"Out, Out—"

The buzz-saw snarled and rattled in the yard
And made dust and dropped stove-length sticks of wood,
Sweet-scented stuff when the breeze drew across it.
And from there those that lifted eyes could count
Five mountain ranges one behind the other
Under the sunset far into Vermont.
And the saw snarled and rattled, snarled and rattled,
As it ran light, or had to bear a load.
And nothing happened: day was all but done.
Call it a day, I wish they might have said
To please the boy by giving him the half hour
That a boy counts so much when saved from work.
His sister stood beside them in her apron
To tell them "Supper." At the word, the saw,
As if to prove that saws knew what supper meant,
Leaped out of the boy's hand, or seemed to leap—

He must have given the hand. However it was,
Neither refused the meeting. But the hand!
The boy's first outcry was a rueful laugh,
As he swung toward them holding up the hand
Half in appeal, but half as if to keep
The life from spilling. Then the boy saw all—
Since he was old enough to know, big boy
Doing a man's work, though a child at heart—
He saw all spoiled. "Don't let them cut my hand off—
The doctor, when he comes. Don't let them, sister!"
So. But the hand was gone already.
The doctor put him in the dark of ether.
He lay and puffed his lips out with his breath.
And then—the watcher at his pulse took fright.
No one believed. They listened at his heart.
Little—less—nothing!—and that ended it.
No more to build on there. And they, since they
Were not the one dead, turned to their affairs.

"Out, Out—" dramatizes the sudden, cruel, meaningless death of a young boy. The poem is a stark, shocking account. A "pursuitist" cannot help but see that such things do happen. But there are also moments of joy and high inspiration.

The Tuft of Flowers

I went to turn the grass once after one
Who mowed it in the dew before the sun.

The dew was gone that made his blade so keen
Before I came to view the levelled scene.

I looked for him behind an isle of trees;
I listened for his whetstone on the breeze.

But he had gone his way, the grass all mown,
And I must be, as he had been,—alone,

ROBERT FROST

"As all must be," I said within my heart,
"Whether they work together or apart."

But as I said it, swift there passed me by
On noiseless wing a bewildered butterfly,

Seeking with memories grown dim o'er night
Some resting flower of yesterday's delight.

And once I marked his flight go round and round,
As where some flower lay withering on the ground.

And then he flew as far as eye could see,
And then on tremulous wing came back to me.

I thought of questions that have no reply,
And would have turned to toss the grass to dry;

But he turned first, and led my eye to look
At a tall tuft of flowers beside a brook,

A leaping tongue of bloom the scythe had spared
Beside a reedy brook the scythe had bared.

I left my place to know them by their name,
Finding them butterfly weed when I came.

The mower in the dew had loved them thus,
By leaving them to flourish, not for us,

Nor yet to draw one thought of ours to him,
But from sheer morning gladness at the brim.

The butterfly and I had lit upon,
Nevertheless, a message from the dawn,

That made me hear the wakening birds around,
And hear his long scythe whispering to the ground,

And feel a spirit kindred to my own;
So that henceforth I worked no more alone;

But glad with him, I worked as with his aid,
And weary, sought at noon with him the shade;

And dreaming, as it were, held brotherly speech
With one whose thought I had not hoped to reach.

"Men work together," I told him from the heart,
"Whether they work together or apart."

Perhaps Frost's most consistent lesson has been to stress the importance of each person's individual self. Again and again he has stressed to his college students the importance of making up their own minds and of thinking for themselves. Frost's test of education was, "Does the way the teacher presents the course encourage the ability of the student to stand on his own two feet as a person?" Once the final examination that Frost gave a college poetry class consisted of one direction: "Write what will please me most." Some of the students wrote on poetry for the three hours; others said how much they had enjoyed the course; still others wrote very brief remarks about this book or that. One boy handed in an empty answer sheet; other than his own name, he had written nothing on the examination. His paper pleased Frost most, and he got the highest mark. Why do you think his response pleased Frost so much?

The following poem is about the difficult choices a person must make if he decides to trust his own individuality. Do you think the emotion expressed in the last line is a happy one or a sad one?

The Road Not Taken

Two roads diverged in a yellow wood,
And sorry I could not travel both
And be one traveler, long I stood
And looked down one as far as I could
To where it bent in the undergrowth;

Then took the other, as just as fair,
And having perhaps the better claim,
Because it was grassy and wanted wear;
Though as for that the passing there
Had worn them really about the same,

And both that morning equally lay
In leaves no step had trodden black.
Oh, I kept the first for another day!
Yet knowing how way leads on to way,
I doubted if I should ever come back.

I shall be telling this with a sigh
Somewhere ages and ages hence:
Two roads diverged in a wood, and I—
I took the one less traveled by,
And that has made all the difference.

talks about a man's big decision, doesn't take the one most people take

in end he is questioning

Nature in Frost's poetry

Frost's poetry has almost always concerned itself with the countryside of northern New England, and with its flinty, reticent people, its granite hills, its rocky farms, its streams and pastures and woods. The language of the poems is the language of ordinary speech: it is simple, direct, informal and chatty, like the talk of Yankee farmers.

But Frost is much more than a local poet; his ideas apply to all people in all places. In "Mending Wall" a stone

wall comes to stand for all barriers which separate people. In
"A Tuft of Flowers" a mower's thought leads to the con-
clusion that men always work together. In "A Road Not
Taken" a whole way of life is suggested. Objects in the New
England countryside come to have universal meaning.

In the next poem a tree at a bedroom window becomes
a mirror of the poet's own feelings.

Tree at My Window

Tree at my window, window tree,
My sash is lowered when night comes on;
But let there never be a curtain drawn
Between you and me.

Vague dream-head lifted out of the ground,
And thing next most diffuse to cloud,
Not all your light tongues talking aloud
Could be profound.

But tree, I have seen you taken and tossed,
And if you have seen me when I slept,
You have seen me when I was taken and swept
And all but lost.

That day she put our heads together,
Fate had her imagination about her,
Your head so much concerned with outer,
Mine with inner, weather.

The citizen of the world

In 1962 Robert Frost went to the Soviet Union as part of the
cultural exchanges the United States has been making with
that country. He was often asked to read "Mending Wall."
Many Russian youths asked Frost what he meant by the
wall. Some asked if he were referring to the wall that

separates East Berlin from West Berlin. Shrewdly, Robert Frost never indicated exactly what he had in mind. What does the wall represent to you?

Mending Wall   *ABOUT communication*

> Something there is that doesn't love a wall,
> That sends the frozen-ground-swell under it,
> And spills the upper boulders in the sun;
> And makes gaps even two can pass abreast.
> The work of hunters is another thing:
> I have come after them and made repair
> Where they have left not one stone on a stone,
> But they would have the rabbit out of hiding,
> To please the yelping dogs. The gaps I mean,
> No one has seen them made or heard them made,
> But at spring mending-time we find them there.
> I let my neighbor know beyond the hill;
> And on a day we meet to walk the line
> And set the wall between us once again.
> We keep the wall between us as we go.
> To each the boulders that have fallen to each.
> And some are loaves and some so nearly balls
> We have to use a spell to make them balance:
> "Stay where you are until our backs are turned!"
> We wear our fingers rough with handling them.
> Oh, just another kind of outdoor game,
> One on a side. It comes to little more:
> There where it is we do not need the wall:
> He is all pine and I am apple orchard.
> My apple trees will never get across
> And eat the cones under his pines, I tell him.
> He only says, "Good fences make good neighbors."
> Spring is the mischief in me, and I wonder
> If I could put a notion in his head:
> "Why do they make good neighbors? Isn't it
> Where there are cows? But here there are no cows.

YOU CAN HIDE BEHIND THE FENCE SO THEY AREN'T VULNERABLE

WONDERS WHY HE'S BUILDING A WALL

THE CITIZEN OF THE WORLD

Before I built a wall I'd ask to know
What I was walling in or walling out,
And to whom I was like to give offense.
Something there is that doesn't love a wall,
That wants it down." I could say "Elves" to him,
But it's not elves exactly, and I'd rather
He said it for himself. I see him there
Bringing a stone grasped firmly by the top
In each hand, like an old-stone savage armed.
He moves in darkness as it seems to me,
Not of woods only and the shade of trees.
He will not go behind his father's saying,
And he likes having thought of it so well
He says again, "Good fences make good neighbors."

(handwritten left margin: DOESN'T WANT TO TELL THE MAN THAT HE DOESN'T LIKE THE WALL)

(handwritten right margin: SAYS HE'S SAVAGE STONE-AGE MAN)

(handwritten right margin: REPEATS WHAT HE HEARD HIS FATHER SAID)

(handwritten below: NON-COMMUNICATION)

Robert Frost was the first and only poet ever asked to recite a poem at the Inauguration of an American President. In January, 1961, just before John F. Kennedy took the oath of office from the Chief Justice of the Supreme Court, Frost recited "The Gift Outright." Some have acclaimed it as the most patriotic poem ever written by an American. Can you see why?

The Gift Outright

The land was ours before we were the land's.
She was our land more than a hundred years
Before we were her people. She was ours
In Massachusetts, in Virginia,
But we were England's, still colonials,
Possessing what we were unpossessed by,
Possessed by what we now no more possessed.
Something we were withholding made us weak
Until we found it was ourselves
We were withholding from our land of living,
And forthwith found salvation in surrender.
Such as we were we gave ourselves outright

ROBERT FROST

(The deed of gift was many deeds of war) *who had to eight a lot*
To the land vaguely realizing westward,
But still unstoried, artless, unenhanced,
Such as she was, such as she would become.

The sonnet "A Soldier" was written in the 1920s, in the years immediately following World War I, yet its ideas are timeless. What metaphor does Frost use? What is his conclusion?

A Soldier

He is that fallen lance that lies as hurled,
That lies unlifted now, come dew, come rust,
But still lies pointed as it plowed the dust.
If we who sight along it round the world,
See nothing worthy to have been its mark,
It is because like men we look too near,
Forgetting that as fitted to the sphere,
Our missiles always make too short an arc.
They fall, they rip the grass, they intersect
The curve of earth, and striking, break their own;
They make us cringe for metal-point on stone.
But this we know, the obstacle that checked
And tripped the body, shot the spirit on
Further than target ever showed or shone.

mens goals always fall short

In the next poem, the poet Frost is alone in a snow storm. Notice that in this poem an ordinary event takes on a larger importance; it becomes more than a mere description. What do the snow-covered field and forest mean to Frost?

Desert Places

Snow falling and night falling fast oh fast
In a field I looked into going past,
And the ground almost covered smooth in snow,
But a few weeds and stubble showing last.

The woods around it have it—it is theirs.
All animals are smothered in their lairs.
I am too absent-spirited to count;
The loneliness includes me unawares.

And lonely as it is that loneliness
Will be more lonely ere it will be less—
A blanker whiteness of benighted snow
With no expression, nothing to express.

They cannot scare me with their empty spaces
Between stars—on stars where no human race is.
I have it in me much nearer home
To scare myself with my own desert places.

Conclusions

Robert Frost's poems prove many things. They prove that
the stuff of poetry is the stuff of people and places; they
prove that poetry is not always written in decorative, high-
flown language; they prove that poems can be good without being excessively difficult; they prove that poetry can be
read and enjoyed by millions even in the days of television
and movies. For poetry is communication—one man talking to another about human experience. And because his
words have been direct, his outlook keen, his conclusions
honest, and his spirit gallant, Robert Frost's talk has been
among the very best.

SIX

TONE

WORDS may be spoken in many different ways. They may be said quietly, loudly, modestly, boastfully, sincerely, or deceptively, depending on the speaker's tone of voice. Because *how* something is said is as important as *what* is said, the tone of voice a speaker uses will often determine the meaning of his words. The meaning will depend on the way the speaker stresses certain words, on the pitch of his voice, and on the feeling he puts into individual words and phrases.

Take as an example the simple sentence "Father gave the car to him," and notice that its meaning shifts each time it is said in a different way. Read the sentences below aloud, emphasizing the capitalized words.

1. FATHER gave the car to him. (There is no question about who gave it.)
2. Father GAVE the car to him. (It was not lent but actually given.)
3. Father gave the CAR to him. (He gave him nothing but the car.)
4. Father gave the car to HIM. (He gave it to him, not to his brother or sister.)

In each of these examples the words *Father gave the car to him* mean something slightly different. The speaker's emphasis, his *tone* of voice, makes one meaning emerge rather than another.

Poetry, like conversation, is communication; it is one person talking to another. The words of poetry are also said in a tone of voice, with a certain feeling and emphasis. The tone may be cheerful or it may be sorrowful, depending upon how the poet feels about what he is saying. *Tone* expresses the poet's attitude toward what he is saying.

What is the tone of the following poem, "War Is Kind," by Stephen Crane? Is the poet's voice sincere? Mocking? Is it bitter? Gentle?

War Is Kind

STEPHEN CRANE

> Do not weep maiden, for war is kind.
> Because your lover threw wild hands toward the sky
> And the affrighted steed ran on alone,
> Do not weep.
> War is kind.

>> Hoarse, blooming drums of the regiment,
>> Little souls who thirst for fight
>> These men were born to drill and die.
>> The unexplained glory flies above them,
>> Great is the battle-god, great, and his kingdom—
>> A field where a thousand corpses lie.

> Do not weep, babe, for war is kind.
> Because your father tumbled in the yellow trenches,
> Raged at his breast, gulped and died,
> Do not weep.
> War is kind.

Swift blazing flag of the regiment,
Eagle with crest of red and gold,
These men were born to drill and die.
Point for them the virtue of slaughter,
Make plain to them the excellence of killing
And a field where a thousand corpses lie.

Mother whose heart hung humble as a button
On the bright splendid shroud of your son,
Do not weep.
War is kind.

"War is Kind" is a very powerfully felt poem spoken in a bitterly angry tone of voice. The words *War is kind* do not really mean what they say; in fact, they mean the exact opposite. The words are ironic. Irony exists when the apparent meaning is different from, or even opposite to, the real meaning. Lines like *Point for them the virtue of slaughter* are very ironic. They do not mean what they seem to mean. The irony contributes to the anger of the poem, as you can see if you try reading it aloud. Should "War Is Kind" be read in a quiet, controlled anger, or in raging anger?

Tone in two poems

The tone of a poem should always be suitable to its subject. A religious poem would generally demand a solemn, thoughtful tone of voice, and a poem on death would require a grave tone. Thoughts on a box of Wheaties would be expressed with gaiety. A poem on war may be recited in a number of ways, and a poem on love could be bitter, skeptical, serious, funny, or reverent in tone.

The following two poems are very similar in subject; in both of them, the poet looks back upon past time with regret. Yet notice how different the poems are in tone.

A Lament

PERCY BYSSHE SHELLEY

O World! O Life! O Time!
On whose last steps I climb,
Trembling at that where I had
    stood before;
When will return the glory of
    your prime?
No more—Oh, never more!

Out of the day and night
A joy has taken flight:
Fresh spring, and summer, and
    winter hoar
Move my faint heart with grief,
    but with delight
No more—Oh never more!

Into My Heart

A. E. HOUSMAN

Into my heart an air that kills
From yon far country blows:
What are those blue remem-
    bered hills,
What spires, what farms are
    those?

That is the land of lost content,
I see it shining plain,
The happy highways where I
    went
And cannot come again.

Reading these two poems aloud will help to show the tone of each, but even without reading them aloud, certain facts about tone are clear. For one thing, the exclamation marks and the frequent use of *Oh* in Shelley's poem show how anguished, how strong his feelings are. *A Lament* is a barely controlled outburst of emotion; the first line, with its short exclamations, is especially emotional. The last line of each of the two stanzas is full of despair.

In Housman's short poem from *A Shropshire Lad*, there are no short, quick outbursts and no outspoken despair. Housman's lines, though they are full of regret, are stately, controlled statements. There is a calm acceptance of what must be. The tone is restrained and quiet.

Each poem succeeds in its own tone of voice, so that there is no question about one tone being better than another. Some students will prefer one poem to the other, but there is no clear right and wrong about tone. Which tone did you prefer? What are your reasons? Which poem do you think is more dramatic when it is read aloud?

Kinds of tone

It would be fruitless to attempt to name and categorize every possible tone of voice, just as it would be fruitless, indeed impossible, to define every emotion and every combination of emotions which human beings can feel. But by considering several of the more common tones of voice in a number of poems, you will get a good idea of how tone affects the meaning of a poem. You may want to read these poems aloud in order to hear the tone more clearly.

A HUMOROUS TONE

Many poems are said lightly, with tongue in cheek. Such poems may be as funny and amusing as any comic anecdote or comedian's joke. Can the following poem be read in a wholly serious tone of voice?

Penny Wise and Found Poolish

W. W. WATT

Win an Esther Williams Swimming Pool in Wheaties Lucky Drawings . . . 1st Prize Pool The Penthouse III . . . constructed with prime redwood, structural steel and enduring vinyl poolskin . . . No jingles to write . . . no boxtops to mail! Only one swimming pool will be awarded to members of a household.

—*Announcement on a box of Wheaties*

Miss Esther Williams
General Mills
Minneapolis, Minn.

Dear Esther:
Take pity on an old contester,

And do not dampen quite so clammily
Our hopes to be a two pool family.

We have two television sets
Both king- and queen-size cigarettes,
Two cars (American and foreign)
Two guides to bridge (Blackwood and Goren)
Two picture windows for the view,
Two hearts that always beat as two,
And now our dream of heaven is
Two Penthouse Pools marked "HERS" and "HIS."

Not writing jingles is a hard
Requirement for a seasoned bard,
So please forgive me if I send
A couple as a dividend:

"The pool for Wheaties champs to lave in
When they are full of riboflavin!"

"The poolskin pool of Neverwiltskin,
Smoother than common rumpelstiltskin!"

Believe me, Esther, if the rule
Allowing us a single pool
Is not unalterably final,
My passion will endure like vinyl.

I hope you will excuse my candor;
You are My Hero.
                          Love,
                          Leander

The tone of this poem is humorous and light; the poet
is not taking seriously the words he says. He is not really
going to be upset or brokenhearted because he can win only

one swimming pool for his family. The title, the words like *clammily, queen-size, Neverwiltskin,* and *rumpelstiltskin,* the signature at the end of the poem—all these are indications of a humorous tone of voice.

AN EXCITED, URGENT TONE

The tone of "Sea Fever" is excited and exuberant. The poet's memories of sea life, sharply recalled, convince him that he must go back to the restless, wandering life. There is an excited happiness in his words.

Sea Fever

JOHN MASEFIELD

I must go down to the seas again, to the lonely sea and the
    sky,
And all I ask is a tall ship and a star to steer her by,
And the wheel's kick and the wind's song and the white
    sail's shaking
And a gray mist on the sea's face and a gray dawn breaking.

I must go down to the seas again, for the call of the running
    tide,
Is a wild call and a clear call that may not be denied;
And all I ask is a windy day with the white clouds flying,
And the flung spray and the blown spume, and sea gulls cry-
    ing.

I must go down to the seas again to the vagrant gypsy life,
To the gull's way and the whale's way where the wind's
    like a whetted knife;
And all I ask is a merry yarn from a laughing fellow rover,
And a quiet sleep and a sweet dream when the long trick's
    over.

Notice the urgency of such phrases as *I must go down,* and *all I ask,* as well as the excitement of the *wind's song, sail's shaking*, and the *wild call*. This listing of all the things that he remembers, such as the *flung spray*, the *blown spume*, and the *sea gulls crying*, contributes toward the poem's excited, urgent tone.

A BITTER TONE

The next poem, like "War Is Kind," deals with the cruelty of warfare. What is the poet's tone of voice? Ragingly bitter or quietly so? Again try reading it aloud.

Does It Matter?

SIEGFRIED SASSOON

Does it matter?—losing your leg? ...
For people will always be kind;
And you need not show that you mind
When the others come in after hunting
To gobble their muffins and eggs.

Does it matter?—losing your sight? ...
There's such splendid work for the blind;
And people will always be kind,
As you sit on the terrace remembering
And turning your face to the light.

Do they matter?—those dreams from the pit?—
You can drink and forget and be glad;
And people won't say that you're mad;
For they know that you've fought for your country,
And no one will worry a bit!

The tone of this poem is ironic and bitter. It *seems* to say that it doesn't matter very much losing one's leg or eyesight, but of course it *really* says that it matters very much. One thing is said, but the opposite thing is meant. What words are especially bitter? How would you read the second line of the second stanza? The last line of the poem? You might compare your reading of the poem with a classmate's.

A JOYFUL TONE

The next poem is a very short part of a much longer work. The lines are spoken by a child who is a character in the longer story. Notice the child's youthful joy on a beautiful morning. The punctuation marks often help indicate the tone of voice; the exclamation mark at the end of the poem gives a clue to how much feeling is present.

Pippa's Song
ROBERT BROWNING

> The year's at the spring
> And day's at the morn;
> Morning's at seven;
> The hillside's dew-pearled;
> The lark's on the wing;
> The snail's on the thorn:
> God's in his heaven—
> All's right with the world!

The simple, short statements build quickly up to a joyful exclamation of faith in the last two lines. Pippa's words fairly sing out with their happiness.

A SERIOUS-HUMOROUS TONE

Poems may fuse humor and gaiety with high seriousness. One of the great tragedies of all literature is Shakespeare's *Hamlet*. Violence, death, and darkness pervade the play, but side by side with the serious and awful scenes are some very funny comic episodes. It is possible in a single poem to say something quite serious in a light or whimsical tone of voice, or to say something light in a somber way.

Almost everyone has had the experience of waiting to be waited on in some restaurant or lunch room. Such an experience and the emotions it may arouse make the stuff of the following brief poem.

Epitaph on a Waiter
DAVID MC CORD

By and by
God caught his eye.

What is the tone of this poem? Is it funny? Is it fierce and biting? Or is it a fusion of humor and scorn? Whatever your individual interpretation of the poem's tone may be, the hyperbole, or extravagant exaggeration, of waiting until *God caught his eye* is hardly realistic. Although there may be impatience and resentment in the words, the exaggeration is so great that the poem cannot be taken entirely seriously.

The following poem is another example of a humorous-serious poem. The descriptions seem odd and fanciful, but there is a serious undercurrent of meaning.

Disillusionment of Ten O'clock
WALLACE STEVENS

The houses are haunted
By white nightgowns.
None are green,
Or purple with green rings,
Or green with yellow rings,
Or yellow with blue rings.
None of them are strange,
With socks of lace
And beaded ceintures.
People are not going
To dream of baboons and periwinkles.
Only, here and there, an old sailor,

Drunk and asleep in his boots,
Catches tigers
In red weather.

Do you see what the poet is driving at? The houses are *haunted by white nightgowns;* all are uniformly colorless and standardized. There is no imagination, no life to them. *None of them are strange* and none of them have bright, striking colors and patterns. They are absolutely without any individual distinction.

With line 10 the poet turns from the nightgowns to the people who wear them. Their lives, too, are colorless and unimaginative. They are not going to dream of *baboons and periwinkles,* the wild, fierce, and beautiful things in life. Their dreams are like their nightgowns, pallid and bland.

In line 12 the poet tells us that only a drunken sailor, or people like him who lead adventurous lives, really have exciting, colorful dreams. This sailor *Catches tigers/In red weather,* red weather being a highly unusual way of describing torrid jungle heat.

The poet is saying something serious about the way people live; he is commenting on conformity and standardization. Yet there is humor and exaggeration in the way he makes his point. *Red weather* is a fanciful, farfetched expression; the descriptions of the nightgowns with the various colors are hard to take seriously. The poet makes a very serious statement about modern conformity, but his tone of voice is a mixture, or fusion, of humor and seriousness.

Shifts in tone

The tone of a poem need not stay consistent throughout all the lines. It may change, turn from lightness to melancholy or from grief to acceptance. It can begin in excited happiness and end in reverence. There is a change in the tone of voice in the next short poem.

My Heart Leaps Up

WILLIAM WORDSWORTH

My heart leaps up when I behold
A rainbow in the sky:
So was it when my life began;
So is it now I am a man:
So be it when I shall grow old,
    Or let me die!
The Child is father of the Man;
And I could wish my days to be
Bound each to each by natural piety.

[handwritten: wants to be good]

You can see that line 6, *Or let me die!* is said with a great deal of feeling. The first two lines of the poem are joyful; there is a happiness in the verb *leaps up*. There follow three short, almost breathless lines, each beginning with the word *so*, and leading dramatically up to the exclamation of line 6, which is the emotional peak of the poem.

The tone of the last three lines is quite different—the strong, joyful exclamation has given way to calm thought. The tone is even prayerful—a quiet, concluding statement of thought. Even in a short nine-line poem the tone may change as the ideas and emotions in the poem develop.

Dramatic monologues

The question of tone is particularly important in a special kind of a poem called the *dramatic monologue*. Dramatic monologues are like brief plays in which one character does all of the speaking. In the dramatic monologue there is a setting and there may or may not be other characters present. But only one character speaks.

TONE

The following brief poem is a dramatic monologue with a setting before some audience; the main character, a political orator, stands at a rostrum on which there is a glass of water.

"Next to of Course God"

E. E. CUMMINGS

"Next to of course god america i
love you land of the pilgrims' and so forth oh
say can you see by the dawn's early my
country 'tis of centuries come and go
and are no more what of it we should worry
in every language even deafanddumb
thy sons acclaim your glorious name by gorry
by jingo by gee be gosh by gum
why talk of beauty what could be more beautiful than these heroic happy dead
who rushed like lions to the roaring slaughter
they did not stop to think they died instead
then shall the voice of liberty be mute?"

He spoke. And drank rapidly a glass of water.

Does the lack of capitalization and punctuation cause you to read the poem fast or slowly? What does the speed of the speech contribute to the tone? What effect do all the clichés have on your opinion of the speaker's sincerity or insincerity?

The speaker in the next dramatic monologue is a duke who is describing a painting of his last duchess, now dead. He is talking directly to another person who has come to him to arrange a new marriage. Listen carefully to the speaker's tone of voice and observe what it reveals about his character.

DRAMATIC MONOLOGUES

My Last Duchess

ROBERT BROWNING

That's my last Duchess painted on the wall,
Looking as if she were alive. I call
That piece a wonder, now: Fra Pandolf's hands
Worked busily a day, and there she stands.
Will 't please you sit and look at her? I said
"Fra Pandolf" by design: for never read
Strangers like you that pictured countenance,
The depth and passion of its earnest glance,
But to myself they turned (since none puts by
The curtain I have drawn for you, but I)
And seemed as they would ask me, if they durst,
How such a glance came there; so, not the first
Are you to turn and ask thus. Sir, 'twas not
Her husband's presence only, called that spot
Of joy into the Duchess' cheek: perhaps
Fra Pandolf chanced to say "Her mantle laps
Over my lady's wrist too much," or "Paint
Must never hope to reproduce the faint
Half-flush that dies along her throat:" such stuff
Was courtesy, she thought, and cause enough
For calling up that spot of joy. She had
A heart—how shall I say?—too soon made glad,
Too easily impressed; she liked whate'er
She looked on, and her looks went everywhere.
Sir, 't was all one! My favor at her breast,
The dropping of the daylight in the West,
The bough of cherries some officious fool
Broke in the orchard for her, the white mule
She rode with round the terrace—all and each
Would draw from her alike the approving speech,
Or blush, at least. She thanked men,—good! but thanked
Somehow—I know not how—as if she ranked

MY LAST DUCHESS: *Fra Pandolf* = an imaginary painter; *Claus of
Innsbruck* = an imaginary sculptor

TONE

My gift of a nine-hundred-years-old name
With anybody's gift. Who'd stoop to blame
This sort of trifling? Even had you skill
In speech—(which I have not)—to make your will
Quite clear to such an one, and say, "Just this
Or that in you disgusts me; here you miss,
Or there exceed the mark"—and if she let
Herself be lessoned so, nor plainly set
Her wits to yours, forsooth, and made excuse,
—E'en then would be some stooping; and I choose
Never to stoop. Oh sir, she smiled, no doubt,
Whene'er I passed her; but who passed without
Much the same smile? This grew; I gave commands,
Then all smiles stopped together. There she stands
As if alive. Will 't please you rise? We'll meet
The company below, then. I repeat,
The Count your master's known munificence
Is ample warrant that no just pretense
Of mine for dowry will be disallowed;
Though his fair daughter's self, as I avowed
At starting, is my object. Nay, we'll go
Together down, sir. Notice Neptune, though,
Taming a sea-horse, thought a rarity,
Which Claus of Innsbruck cast in bronze for me!

Notice that the Duke is concerned about the dowry
he is to receive as a result of his next marriage. What was
the character of the last duchess? What was her great fault
according to the Duke? Try to define the Duke's tone of
voice.

Exercise: Reading for Tone

Read each of the following poems carefully and answer the questions
after each one. Although the poems are interesting for many reasons,
listen especially for the tone of voice in each.

A.

Carol with Variations

PHYLLIS MC GINLEY

The world has now 7,600,000 men under arms, excluding
navies, as against 5,900,000 in 1913,—news item in *The Sun*

Oh little town of Bethlehem, how still we see thee lie:
Your flocks are folded in to sleep, and sleep your little ones.
Behold, there is a star again that climbs the eastern sky,
And seven million living men are picking up their guns.

> Hark the happy cannons roar
> Glory to the Dictator
> Death and fear, and peace defiled,
> And a world unreconciled!

Once more the bells of Christendom ring out a proclamation
Of joy to all the universe, and mercy, and good will;
While brother shoots his brother down, and nation scowls at
            nation,
And seven million uniforms are decorate at drill.

> Hail to Dupont and to Krupp!
> Steel is strong and going up.
> Let the tidings glad be sent—
> 'Tis the Morn of Armament.

God rest you merry, gentlemen, whose will these armies are.
Go proudly in your colored shirts, let nothing you dismay.
(Oh, little town of Bethlehem, how fades your shining star?)
While seven million fighting men stand up on Christmas Day.

> Sing hosanna, sing Noel;
> Sing the gunner and the shell;
> Sing the candle, sing the lamp;

CAROL WITH VARIATIONS: *Krupp* = a German steel manufacturer

Sing the Concentration Camp.
Sing the Season born anew;
Sing of exile for the Jew.
Wreath the world with evergreen;
Praise the cunning submarine.
Sing the barbed and bitter wire,
Poison-gas and liquid fire,
Bullet, bomb, and hand-grenade,
And the heart of man, afraid.
Christ is come, the Light hath risen,
All our foes are safe in prison,
And the Christmastide begets
Seven million bayonets.

Hear the carol once again—
Peace on earth, good will to men.

1. Which lines deserve special emphasis? Why?

2. Describe the tone of the poem. What is the effect of using a Christmas carol background?

3. Find as many examples of *irony* as you can. Are the ironic phrases effective? Why?

4. Is the tone of the longer lines in any way different from the tone of the shorter ones? Show by selecting examples of each.

B.

Richard Cory

EDWIN ARLINGTON ROBINSON

Whenever Richard Cory went down town,
We people on the pavement looked at him:
He was a gentleman from sole to crown,
Clean favored and imperially slim.

And he was always quietly arrayed,
And he was always human when he talked;
But still he fluttered pulses when he said,
"Good morning," and he glittered when he walked.

DRAMATIC MONOLOGUES

And he was rich—yea, richer than a king—
And admirably schooled in every grace:
In fine, we thought, that he was everything
To make us wish that we were in his place.

So on we worked, and waited for the light,
And went without the meat, and cursed the bread:
And Richard Cory, one calm summer night,
Went home and put a bullet through his head.

1. Who do you think speaks the poem? What words show who it is?

2. What tone do the following expressions give the poem: *went down town, richer than a king, he was everything*? Are they informal and chatty or lofty and elegant?

3. Does the language of the poem suit the speaker of the poem? Why or why not?

4. In your own words describe the tone of voice in which this poem is spoken.

C.

Proud Maisie

SIR WALTER SCOTT

Proud Maisie is in the wood,
Walking so early;
Sweet Robin sits on the bush,
Singing so rarely.

"Tell me, thou bonny bird,
When shall I marry me?"
"When six braw gentlemen,
Kirkward shall carry ye."

"Who makes the bridal bed,
Birdie, say truly?"—
"The gray-headed sexton
That delves the grave duly."

PROUD MAISIE: *braw* = strong; *Kirkward* = churchward

"The glow-worm o'er grave and stone
Shall light thee steady;
The owl from the steeple sing,
'Welcome, proud lady.'"

1. This poem consists chiefly in questions and answers. What is Maisie asking about? What is the tone of her questions?

2. The robin is communicating some unhappy news to Maisie. What is the robin's tone? Is the irony of its answer in stanza 2 light or is it cruel?

3. Why is Maisie called proud? Where do you find hints of her pride?

D.

Home-Thoughts, from Abroad

ROBERT BROWNING

Oh, to be in England
Now that April's there,
And whoever wakes in England
Sees, some morning, unaware,
That the lowest boughs and the brush-wood sheaf
Round the elm-tree bole are in tiny leaf,
While the chaffinch sings on the orchard bough
In England—now!
And after April, when May follows,
And the whitethroat builds, and all the swallows!
Hark, where my blossomed pear-tree in the hedge
Leans to the field and scatters on the clover
Blossoms and dewdrops—at the bent spray's edge—
That's the wise thrush; he sings each song twice over,
Lest you should think he never could recapture
The first fine careless rapture!
And though the fields look rough with hoary dew,
And will be gay when noontide wakes anew
The buttercups, the little children's dower
—Far brighter than this gaudy melon-flower!

1. The poet, an Englishman, wrote "Home-Thoughts" while he was in Italy. Is he indoors or out? In a garden? On a street car? How can you tell?

2. What is the tone of the first eight lines of the poem? What is the tone of the last line?

3. How does the use of the dash help establish the tone of this poem? Where is it most effective?

4. What words and lines have the strongest feeling behind them? Give the reasons for your choice.

SEVEN

ALFRED EDWARD HOUSMAN
Poetry and the Afternoon Walk

ALFRED EDWARD HOUSMAN wrote relatively little poetry during his long life, but so high is its quality that his reputation as a poet is absolutely secure. By occupation A. E. Housman was a professor and a scholar. Even before his first poems appeared and even before his own family suspected he was writing poetry, Housman had gained international fame as an outstanding scholar of Greek and Latin literatures. Indeed many of his contemporaries regarded him as the greatest scholar of Latin in all Europe. Yet there is no question that today he is known to millions of English-speaking people first and foremost as a distinctive poet.

Housman was born in March, 1859, in Worcestershire, England; but while he was still an infant his family moved to Shropshire, which borders Wales. Shropshire was at that time still untouched by the industrial revolution, and Housman grew up in the beautiful rural setting of a lovely county, a county he was to celebrate in his poems. Even as a youth Housman showed himself to be a distinguished scholar. At the Bromsgrove School he stood at the top of his class and won numerous prizes. At Oxford he excelled in some subjects, deliberately neglected others, but grew fascinated by his own independent studies. After receiving his Oxford B.A. in 1881, Housman taught for a brief period before he accepted a position in the Patent Office in London. For ten years, from 1882 to 1892, he earned a modest salary for a six-hour day and used his free time to pursue his classical subjects and to write articles for learned journals. In 1892 he was appointed to a professorship of Latin at University College, London. After nineteen years at this post he was appointed Professor of Latin at Cambridge University. Here he continued to distinguish himself as scholar and teacher. Here he also found opportunity to indulge one of his favorite pursuits. All his life Housman had been an avid walker, and now each day he took an afternoon walk of two or three hours. Toward the end of his life, he was advised by doctors to avoid too much exercise. Housman, seventy-six years old, refused to follow their advice. He wrote to his brother: "I still go up my 44 steps two at a time, but that is in hopes of dropping dead at the top." Death came to him in 1936.

In 1885, during a visit to his native Shropshire, he first began to write poetry. Generally quiet, reserved, and dedicated to long hours of solitary study, Housman told no one of his poems so that when in 1896 *A Shropshire Lad* was published members of his own family were surprised. This little book of ballads was quickly accepted as a classic. It was followed in 1922 by *Last Poems,* another small collection, and in 1936 by *More Poems,* published posthumously.

Housman's method of writing poems

In 1933 Housman was honored by being asked to deliver the Leslie Stephen Lecture at the University of Cambridge, a lecture always reserved for distinguished men. Housman's lecture, afterwards published as a book with the title *The Name and Nature of Poetry*, described the method by which he came to write his poems. After his usual morning's work and the lunch which followed, Housman would set out for a two to three hours' walk in the surrounding countryside. He writes:

> As I went along, thinking of nothing in particular, only looking at things around me and following the progress of the seasons, there would flow into my mind, with sudden and unaccountable emotion, sometimes a line or two of verse, sometimes a whole stanza at once, accompanied, not preceded by a vague notion of the poem they were destined to be part of.

When he reached home he wrote down the lines he had in his head. Often, of course, there were gaps to be filled and much rewriting to be done. Sometimes the next day's walk would complete the poem; sometimes the poem would remain unfinished for long periods of time. The following is the last poem from *A Shropshire Lad*.

63

I hoed and trenched and weeded,
And took the flowers to fair:
I brought them home unheeded;
The hue was not the wear.

So up and down I sow them
For lads like me to find,
When I shall lie below them,
A dead man out of mind.

Some seeds the birds devour,
And some the season mars,
But here and there will flower
The solitary stars,

And fields will yearly bear them
As light-leaved spring comes on,
And luckless lads will wear them
When I am dead and gone.

About this poem Housman said:

> Two of the stanzas, I do not say which, came
> into my head, just as they are printed. . . . A third
> stanza came with a little coaxing after tea. One
> more was needed, but it did not come: I had to
> turn to and compose it. . . . I wrote it thirteen
> times, and it was more than a twelve-month be-
> fore I got it right.

Which of the stanzas do you think came first? Which
is the one which took a year to finish? Why? Character-
istically, Housman himself never gave the answers.

A Shropshire lad

Of Housman's three volumes of poetry, *A Shropshire Lad* is
clearly the most significant; *Last Poems* and *More Poems*
are really continuations of the first book. *A Shropshire Lad*
consists of sixty-three short ballad poems. All of them are
simple and direct in language and all of them are uniform
in rhythm. The poems, most of them charged with strong
emotion, are reflections of a Shropshire farm lad and they
deal with various aspects of the life he knew: young love, the

fame of a young athlete, a fight between brothers, the death of friends. Many of them are tinged with sadness and pessimism; others are light and joyous. Housman worked carefully to revise and polish his lines until he had exactly what he wanted in both style and content. Notice his skillful choosing of words.

To an Athlete Dying Young

The time you won your town the race
We chaired you through the marketplace;
Man and boy stood cheering by,
And home we brought you shoulder-high.

Today, the road all runners come,
Shoulder-high we bring you home,
And set you at your threshold down,
Townsman of a stiller town.

Smart lad, to slip betimes away
From fields where glory does not stay,
And early though the laurel grows
It withers quicker than the rose.

Eyes the shady night has shut
Cannot see the record cut,
And silence sounds no worse than cheers
After earth has stopped the ears.

Now you will not swell the rout
Of lads that wore their honors out,
Runners whom renown outran
And the name died before the man.

So set, before its echoes fade,
The fleet foot on the sill of shade,
And hold to the low lintel up
The still-defended challenge-cup.

And round that early-laureled head
Will flock to gaze the strengthless dead,
And find unwithered on its curls
The garland briefer than a girl's.

8

"Farewell to barn and stack and tree,
Farewell to Severn shore.
Terence, look your last at me,
For I come home no more.

"The sun burns on the half-mown hill,
By now the blood is dried;
And Maurice amongst the hay lies still
And my knife is in his side.

"My mother thinks us long away;
'Tis time the field were mown.
She had two sons at rising day,
Tonight she'll be alone.

"And here's a bloody hand to shake,
And, oh, man, here's goodbye;
We'll sweat no more on scythe and rake,
My bloody hands and I.

"I wish you strength to bring you pride,
And a love to keep you clean,
And I wish you luck, come Lammastide,
At racing on the green.

122   ALFRED EDWARD HOUSMAN

"Long for me the rick will wait,
And long will wait the fold,
And long will stand the empty plate,
And dinner will be cold."

Reveille

Wake: the silver dusk returning
Up the beach of darkness brims,
And the ship of sunrise burning
Strands upon the eastern rims.

Wake: the vaulted shadow shatters,
Trampled to the floor it spanned,
And the tent of night in tatters
Straws the sky-pavilioned land.

Up, lad, up: 'tis late for lying.
Hear the drums of morning play;
Hark, the empty highways crying,
"Who'll beyond the hills away?"

Towns and countries woo together,
Forelands beacon, belfries call;
Never lad that trod on leather
Lived to feast his heart with all.

Up, lad: thews that lie and cumber
Sunlit pallets never thrive;
Morns abed and daylight slumber
Were not meant for man alive.

Clay lies still, but blood's a rover;
Breath's a ware that will not keep.
Up, lad: when the journey's over
There'll be time enough to sleep.

7

When smoke stood up from Ludlow,
And mist blew off from Teme,
And blithe afield to plowing
Against the morning beam
I strode beside my team,

The blackbird in the coppice
Looked out to see me stride,
And hearkened as I whistled
The trampling team beside,
And fluted and replied:

"Lie down, lie down, young yeoman;
What use to rise and rise?
Rise man a thousand mornings
Yet down at last he lies,
And then the man is wise."

I heard the tune he sang me,
And spied his yellow bill;
I picked a stone and aimed it
And threw it with a will.
Then the bird was still.

Then my soul within me
Took up the blackbird's strain,
And still beside the horses
Along the dewy lane
It sang the song again:

"Lie down, lie down, young yeoman;
The sun moves always west;
The road one treads to labor
Will lead one home to rest,
And that will be the best."

ALFRED EDWARD HOUSMAN

Dead guy comes back to life

"Is my team plowing,
That I was used to drive
And hear the harness jingle
When I was man alive?"

Aye, the horses trample,
The harness jingles now;
No change though you lie under
The land you used to plough.

"Is football playing
Along the river shore,
With lads to chase the leather,
Now I stand up no more?"

Aye, the ball is flying,
The lads play heart and soul;
The goal stands up, the keeper
Stands up to keep the goal.

"Is my girl happy,
That I thought hard to leave,
And has she tired of weeping
As she lies down at eve?"

Aye, she lies down lightly,
She lies not down to weep;
Your girl is well contented.
Be still, my lad, and sleep.

"Is my friend hearty,
Now I am thin and pine,
And has he found to sleep in
A better bed than mine?"

Yes, lad, I lie easy,
I lie as lads would choose;
I cheer a dead man's sweetheart—
Never ask me whose.

49

Think no more, lad; laugh, be jolly:
Why should men make haste to die?
Empty heads and tongues a-talking
Make the rough road easy walking,
And the feather pate of folly
Bears the falling sky.

Oh, 'tis jesting, dancing, drinking
Spins the heavy world around.
If young hearts were not so clever,
Oh, they would be young forever:
Think no more; 'tis only thinking
Lays lads underground.

13

When I was one-and-twenty
I heard a wise man say,
"Give crowns and pounds and guineas,
But not your heart away;
Give pearls away and rubies,
But keep your fancy free."
But I was one-and-twenty,
No use to talk to me.

When I was one-and-twenty
I heard him say again,
"The heart out of the bosom
Was never given in vain;
'Tis paid with sighs a plenty

And sold for endless rue."
And I am two-and-twenty,
And oh, 'tis true, 'tis true.

Housman's lighter side

Many readers have wondered about Housman's pessimism. So many of his poems seem to say that all things of beauty must soon come to an end. Death and violence seem to be the natural ends in the world of his poetry.

The death of Housman's mother when he was only twelve was a cruel blow to a thoughtful, sensitive boy. Housman's sister recalls that once, as a youth of thirteen, he assigned his brothers and sisters the task of writing a poem; the subject he chose was Death. She writes: "A tender attachment had existed between mother and son; and this loss to him seems to have aroused in him an early resentment against nature's relentless ways of destruction." Death, she goes on to say, became an obsession with him even in boyhood.

Be that as it may, A. E. Housman should not be regarded as a dour, gloomy, life-hating old man. He was an active, friendly teacher for about forty years. Although he never married, he remained devoted to his brothers and sisters and their families. He wrote them often, visited them each year, and shared their sorrows and joys. He had a lifelong love of the outdoors. And he seems to have had a keen sense of humor.

He enjoyed writing light and humorous verse on various animals. One of his better-known light poems is the following.

The Elephant

A tail behind, a trunk in front,
Completes the usual elephant.

An elephant with trunk behind,
Is much more difficult to find;
And if throughout the world you hunt
To find one with the tail in front,
I fear the search will take you long,
The force of habit is so strong.

The next short poem was written for his very young nephew. It was accompanied in its first version by a sketch of a large bear and an empty baby carriage.

A bear untamable and wild
Has just devoured an infant child.
The infant child is not aware
It has been eaten by the bear.

A summing up

Like the Latin poetry that he loved and studied so well, Housman's poems are bare and stark; they have no word decorations, no elaborately developed metaphors or figures of speech. His poems are concise and keenly to the point— no word is wasted—and his rhythms are flawless. Like so many of the Latin poets, Housman sings of the brevity of love and spring and of life itself. There is a deep melancholy in much of his poetry.

Many readers have insisted that A. E. Housman is a minor poet, because he produced so little work. But the question of whether he is a major or a minor poet need not be an important one. What is important is that his poems are still read and still enjoyed by readers all over the world. *A Shropshire Lad* is a slim book, but it is already a classic one in English literature. Its strange beauty and power have given A. E. Housman a permanent place among the fine poets of the English language.

ALFRED EDWARD HOUSMAN

EIGHT

THE WHOLE POEM:
STATEMENT AND MEANING

EVERY word has a meaning and any sensible arrangement of words will necessarily convey a meaning. Because poetry is communication, because it is one person talking to another, the poem must inevitably make a statement. Rhythm, rhyme, and other sound effects are very important to poetry because they help to bring out and emphasize the meaning. Tone, or the writer's attitude toward what he is saying, is important because meaning may be communicated seriously or humorously, with coolness or with anger, mildly or powerfully. Metaphor also makes meaning clear; it simplifies an idea at the same time that it leads to greater understanding. All these are a part of poetry; but in the end, the reader must always understand and deal with the statement of the poem.

It is important to realize, however, that statement or meaning does not by itself make poetry, just as rhythm by itself or alliteration by itself or metaphor by itself will not make poetry. The meaning of a poem should not and cannot be reduced to a slogan or a brief "message." An audience watching a movie does not think solely in terms of what the movie means; it does not go "message hunting" throughout the showing of the film. Instead the audience enjoys the photography, the suspense, the humor, the acting, and the conflicts simultaneously. In short, it enjoys the whole movie. So with poetry. The statement that walls are bad does not make a poem, but Robert Frost's "Mending Wall" (p. 93) is a poem because it dramatizes the idea so well. Taken together, used in harmony, fused together into a meaningful whole, rhythm, rhyme, sound effects, tone, metaphor, symbol, and connotation dramatize meaning. The whole poem must mean, but it must mean imaginatively. It must stimulate the emotions and thoughts of the reader.

A poem may be about any subject. It can deal with any aspect of life: love, death, time, change, happiness, grief, courage, social conditions, faith, loyalty, kindness, or cruelty. A poet may, for instance, talk about the joy of love, the melancholy of love, the brevity of love, the beauty of love, or the holiness of love. The reader does not have to agree with the poet's attitude in order to read and enjoy the poem. If a movie or a song or a play or a painting is well done, if it is a unified, meaningful presentation of life, if it is imaginative, it will be a rich, rewarding experience for the audience. In a similar way, the poem which excites emotions and stirs thoughts will gain the admiration of readers who may not agree with all the ideas that are expressed. But a good poem will tend to convince and captivate the reader.

The discussions of the three poems in the next pages will help you to experience the poem as a whole, to see it as a fusion of the various aspects of language that you have been studying. Each of them is discussed very briefly. The first two are poems written in rather recent times while the third, a sonnet by Shakespeare, is more than 350 years old. All three of them are short poems.

Although each poem makes a statement, remember that a poem is more than a mere "message." Try to understand how the elements of poetic language—rhythm, rhyme, sound, tone, metaphor, symbol, and connotation—are unified into the whole meaning of the poem.

Poem I

The Golf Links

SARAH CLEGHORN

> The golf links lie so near the mill
> That almost every day
> The laboring children can look out
> And see the men at play.

"The Golf Links" makes a statement against child labor. Instead of making a flat, dull statement that child labor is a social wrong, it dramatizes its meaning by using contrasts. Notice that Sarah Cleghorn sets two scenes in this brief poem—the golf links and the mill. She also presents two sets of characters—the men and the children. The places and the people are contrasted with each other: one place is for recreation and the other for work; one group is at play while the other is at work. Ordinarily the children might be expected to be outdoors playing in the fresh air while the men were at work. But not in this imaginative short poem. The poet conveys her meaning by reversing the ordinary roles of the men and the children. The reversal is a striking and surprising way to convey her meaning—far better than a lifeless generality about child labor.

Notice how both the rhythm and alliteration help to make the statement a forceful one. The poem is perfectly iambic throughout, with one exception. In the third line there are two consecutive unstressed syllables in the word *láboring*. This situation makes the next stressed syllable a little more forceful than it would otherwise be, so that the first part of *children* gets extra emphasis. This emphasis by rhythm stresses just who it is that is laboring: *children* and not men; it also enforces the surprise of learning that the men are not working.

The alliteration of the letter *l* throughout the poem is very effective in dramatizing the meaning. Notice that the *l*inks *l*ie near the mi*ll* but that the *l*aboring chi*l*dren do nothing but *l*ook out of the mi*ll*. The letter *l* links together all the important words and ideas and underlines the monotony and repetition of the children's labor.

The poem is ironic, but the irony can be expressed in several different tones of voice. It is ironic in tone because the poem shows that the *real* truth is different from the *expected* truth: the men and not the children are doing the playing. But the poem, especially in the last two lines, may be read in a hot, angry tone of voice, or it may be read in a light, satiric tone of voice. Either tone emphasizes the meaning of the poem. A lifeless, expressionless tone would subtract from the statement.

This particular poem uses no metaphors. But contrast, rhythm, alliteration, and tone, means by which a poet can dramatize an idea, are all fused into a unified whole.

Poem II

Nothing Gold Can Stay

ROBERT FROST

> Nature's first green is gold,
> Her hardest hue to hold.
> Her early leaf's a flower;
> But only so an hour.
> Then leaf subsides to leaf.
> So Eden sank to grief,
> So dawn goes down to day.
> Nothing gold can stay.

One of the beauties of this brief poem lies in the way the meaning is conveyed. Its statement is this: the freshest, the most beautiful moments in nature, in the day, and in all life are the beginnings, which are short-lived and transitory. The idea is a very old one and a very common one, but in "Nothing Gold Can Stay" Robert Frost gives it an original, imaginative dramatization.

The tone of the poem is direct and straightforward: there is no irony, no humor, no bitterness. Unlike "The Golf Links" there is no protest or sharpness in the words. Frost is serious and objective about what he is saying.

The word *gold* is an interesting place to begin our discussion. This word has important denotative and connotative meanings in this poem. The word *denotes* a valuable metal, yellow in color; it *connotes* beauty and wealth. In the poem both the denotations and the connotations of the word are important to the meaning. For instance, in the last line, *gold* means both the valuable metal and early beauty.

The word *Eden* also has important connotations. It means, of course, the garden where Adam and Eve first dwelt. But its connotations go far beyond the place meaning. Eden connotes innocence, freshness, perfect harmony, immortality, goodness—the conditions of the life Adam and Eve led until the Fall. Then, after the Fall, grief came into the world. No *Eden,* no *gold* can preserve for long its early beauty.

Notice the rhythm of the poem. With few exceptions it is an iambic pattern. The most important exception comes in the last line. The first syllable in each line is unstressed, but the first syllable of *Nóthing* in the last line receives a stress, and a heavy one because it is unexpected. This rhythmic stress adds weight to the meaning of the line. Notice that the last line is the only one that has five syllables. Such rhythmic variety makes the last line stand out.

The many alliterations, assonances, and rhymes of the poem link together the significant words and ideas. The first line alliterates the letter *g;* the *g* sound is brought in again in line 6 with the word *grief* and in line 7 with *goes.* The poem says that the green and gold of early nature go down to grief. The important idea-words are linked together by the *g* sound. The second line alliterates the *h,* and the last word of line 4, *hour,* begins with a silent *h* and also rhymes with the word *flower.* The *flower-hour* rhyme is almost a two-word summary of the poem's meaning that early beauty does not last. The assonance of *Eden, leaf,* and *grief* is also part of the statement, since the leaf and Eden, like the flower, come to grief. Three important verbs of the last four lines, *subsides, sank,* and *goes,* all abound in the *s* sound and all of them emphasize the idea of falling or decaying. Each pair of rhyme words, *gold-hold, flower-hour, leaf-grief, day-stay,* tells the story of passing things.

These sound combinations illustrate how important sound is to the meaning of a poem. Meaning and sound are very compactly, very intensely fused to each other. The very compactness of the poem emphasizes its statement about the brevity of things.

Poem III

Sonnet 73

WILLIAM SHAKESPEARE

That time of year thou may'st in me behold
When yellow leaves, or none, or few, do hang
Upon those boughs which shake against the cold—
Bare ruin'd choirs where late the sweet birds sang.

In me thou see'st the twilight of such day
As after sunset fadeth in the west,

Which by and by black night doth take away,
Death's second self, that seals up all in rest.

In me thou see'st the glowing of such fire
That on the ashes of his youth doth lie,
As the death-bed whereon it must expire,
Consumed with that which it was nourished by.

This thou perceiv'st, which makes thy love more strong
To love that well which thou must leave ere long.

Neither "The Golf Links" nor "Nothing Gold Can Stay"
uses metaphor in making its statement, but Shakespeare's
sonnet is highly metaphoric. The sonnet is one person talking to another; the speaker of the poem is talking to someone he loves. He says that he is on the threshold of death and
that her love is more strong because she loves that which
must soon die. But the speaker's statement avoids dull, lifeless, abstract words. Through metaphor it makes its meaning concrete and immediate.

Remember that metaphor has a number of functions
in communication. First, it appeals directly to the senses by
using concrete words; second, it simplifies and illustrates
complicated ideas; and third, by bringing together two unlike objects, it can often lead to a deeper understanding of
ideas.

Each of the three quatrains, or four-line stanzas, uses a
metaphor to convey and illustrate the speaker's meaning. In
the first quatrain, he compares his age to that time of year
when few or no yellow leaves cling to the boughs. He describes these leafless boughs as *Bare ruin'd choirs* because
there is no more music and singing in them. The few leaves
that remain shake in the cold. The speaker compares the
autumn of the year and the autumn of his life, a com-

parison which makes one realize that a life is very much like a year with its four seasons.

In the second quatrain he compares his advanced age to the twilight; the sun, like a man's life, fades into the west where night, called in another metaphor *death's second self,* seals it up. Here the declining life is compared to the declining day, and the coming of night is like the coming of death.

In the third quatrain life is compared to a fire. The speaker says that the fires of his youth have burned out. There is left only the glow of old age, still warm upon the ashes of his youth. The ashes of his youth are compared to a death-bed where the last glow of his life will die out. The metaphor makes one understand clearly how brief life is.

Each of the three quatrains compares the speaker's life with something else—with the seasons, with a single day, and with a fire. Notice that the three things are progressively briefer. The three metaphors complement each other. Each of them shows in its way what approaching death is like. Warmth, light, energy, all ebb away in these metaphors.

Even a hasty reading of the poem will reveal the tone. Its subject, the connotations of the words it uses, its feeling —all three are somber and melancholy. There is no irony, no anger, no bitterness, no joy, no humor. The words are said in a thoughtful, quiet way. The speaker's words are profoundly sad.

Like the metaphors and the tone, the rhythm of the sonnet enforces the statement of the poem. This, like all sonnets, is generally iambic pentameter; but there are a few interruptions of this pattern. The first three lines of the poem are strictly iambic, but the fourth line receives heavy consecutive stresses.

Báre rúin'd chŏirs whĕre lăte thĕ sweét bírds sáng

The line is said with strong, grief-stricken emotion. It is full of regret. The spondaic syllables bring out the emotion of the words.

The last line of the second stanza also receives rhythmic emphasis because the lines open with heavy spondaic beats instead of the usual iambic:

Déath's sécond sélf, thǎt séals ǔp áll ǐn rést.

The important word of the eleventh line, *death-bed*, also has the stress of a spondaic rhythm. These three examples show how closely the meaning and the rhythm of the poem work together.

All the elements in this sonnet—tone, rhythm, metaphor, and so forth—are welded into the whole poem's meaning. The meaning is made clear by a series of metaphors whose tone is somber, and the connotations of all the words suggest grief and dying. The rhythm is heavy and broken where the emotion is strong. All the elements work as one to make the entire sonnet a dramatic, exciting statement.

Conclusions

Whether it be in baseball, in modern art, or in some foreign language, there is no enjoyment without understanding and appreciation. The first part of this book has tried to show you, through the lives of four poets, and through discussions of sound, metaphor, tone, and meaning, something about the composition of poems. Ahead, in the anthology section of the book, you will find a large selection of poems of many varieties: narrative poems, humorous poems, free verse, character poems, poems on timeless themes, sonnets, and poems of the present day.

The earliest poem in the book was written several hundred years ago by a poet of the past; the latest was written just a short time ago. Many of the poems have been enjoyed by readers for a great many years; others are new —the favorites of the future. But they are all good poems, and they represent hours of enjoyment and enlightenment for all who would read. There is laughter and wonder in poetry; there is story and surprise; there is the new and the eternal. Because poets have always been among our greatest teachers, poems have always been a fundamental part of growing up and of learning. Enjoying poems is like enjoying a wise speaker or storyteller. All students are capable of enjoying poems because no student is without imagination or without feeling when confronted with the world's beauties, terrors, and truths. Each human being has felt as a poet has felt; each human being is a potential poet.

Exercise: Distinguishing Good Poetry from Bad

When is a poem good? When is it bad? These are important questions which many young students of poetry ask. Generally speaking, the good poem may be distinguished from the bad poem in four ways.

In Good Poetry	In Bad Poetry
1. The elements of language (rhythm, tone, metaphor, etc.) are unified and in harmony with each other.	1. The elements of language are disorganized.
2. Sound and sense are fused.	2. Sound and sense are unrelated.
3. The language is dramatic, exciting, and full of suggestions.	3. The language is dull, full of clichés and flat phrases.
4. The emotion is genuine.	4. The emotion is excessive, trivial, or false.

The best way to distinguish good poetry from bad is to study some examples of each. Bearing in mind the four guideposts outlined above, read and study each of the two pairs of poems below, and then answer the questions after each pair. One of each pair is a bad poem.

I.　A. *The Symphony*

"O Trade! O Trade! would thou wert dead!
The Time needs heart—'tis tired of head:
We're all for love," the violins said.
"Of what avail the rigorous tale
Of bill for coin and box for bale?
Grant thee, O Trade! thine uttermost hope:
Level red gold with blue sky-slope,
And base it deep as devils grope:
When all's done, what hast thou won
Of the only sweet that's under the sun?"

B. *The Instruments*

The trumpet's loud clangor
Excites us to arms
With shrill notes of anger
And mortal alarms.

The double, double, double beat
Of the thundering drum
Cries, "Hark! the foes come!
Charge! Charge! 'tis too late to retreat!"

The soft complaining flute
In dying notes discovers
The woes of hopeless lovers,
Whose dirge is whispered by the warbling lute.

1. Both of these poems try to imitate in words the sound of musical instruments. What sound effects does each poet use?

2. In which poem do you think sound and sense are better fused? Choose examples to back up your opinion.

3. Find examples of imaginative language and dull language in the poems. Which has more of the former?

4. Evaluate the emotions expressed in each poem.

II.   A. *Composed Upon Westminster Bridge*

Earth has not anything to show more fair:
Dull would he be of soul who could pass by
A sight so touching in its majesty:
This city now doth, like a garment, wear
The beauty of the morning; silent, bare,
Ships, towers, domes, theaters, and temples lie
Open unto the fields, and to the sky;
All bright and glittering in the smokeless air.
Never did sun more beautifully steep
In his first splendor, valley, rock, or hill;
Ne'er saw I, never felt, a calm so deep!
The river glideth at his own sweet will:
Dear God! the very houses seem asleep;
And all that mighty heart is lying still.

B. *On a Beautiful Landscape*

Beautiful landscape! I could look on thee
For hours, unmindful of the storm and strife,
And mingled murmurs of tumultuous life.
Here, all is still as fair; the stream, the tree,
The mellow sunshine on the bank: no tear
No thought of Time's swift wing, or gentle night,
That comes to steal away the long sweet light—
No sighs of sad humanity are here.
Here is no tint of mortal change; the day,—
Beneath whose light the dog and peasant-boy
Gambol, with look, and almost bark, of joy,—
Still seems, though centuries have past to stay.
Then gaze again, that shadowed scenes may teach
Lessons of peace and love, beyond all speech.

1. Both of these sonnets describe a scene. Which presents the more vivid description, made up of sharp, individual pictures?

2. Compare the language of the two sonnets. Which poem contains flat, generalized phrases and predictable adjectives? Are there any

words in either that seem out of tune with the emotions? What are they?

3. Which sonnet reads more smoothly? Find examples of both the careful use of meter and the awkward use of it. In which sonnet does the rhythm help the meaning? How does it do so?

4. Compare the endings of the two sonnets. Which is more dramatic? Why?

5. Compare the emotions expressed in each sonnet. In which one do you think they are more genuinely felt? Explain your answer.

III.　　A. *The Robin*

When snows are gone and skies are clear,
When breezes stir and leaves flutter, dear,
The robin comes and sings with cheer
Of life reborn, so dry thy tear.

From spring to summer, the robin hops;
His cheerful song he never stops.
The grasses reach, the red rose pops,
Life goes on, dear; it never stops.

　　B. *The Throstle*

"Summer is coming, summer is coming.
I know it, I know it, I know it.
Light again, leaf again, life again, love again,"
Yes, my wild little poet.

Sing the new year in under the blue.
Last year you sang it as gladly.
"New, new, new, new!" Is it then *so* new
That you should carol so madly?

"Love again, song again, nest again, young again,"
Never a prophet so crazy!
And hardly a daisy as yet little friend,
See, there is hardly a daisy.

"Here again, here, here, here, happy year!"
O warble unchidden, unbidden!
Summer is coming, is coming, my dear,
And all the winters are hidden.

1. Compare the language of one poem with that of the other. In which poem is it flat, dull, or inappropriate? Quote examples to back up your opinion.

2. Why do you think the poet uses so much alliteration and repetition in the second poem? Does he succeed in his purpose?

3. What is the relation between sound and sense in the first poem?

4. Both poems use a bird to show that life is continuous and unending. Who is the speaker in the first poem? To whom does he speak? Who is the principal speaker in the second poem? To whom does he speak? Which form of dialogue, one without replies or one with them, dramatizes the idea more effectively? Why?

NINE

WILLIAM BUTLER YEATS
The Poet and His Nation

MANY things about William Butler Yeats as a man may distract a reader from his very great poetry. There is Yeats the believer in magic, supernatural spirits, and ghosts, the man who took elves and fairies quite seriously. There is Yeats who communed with the dead and who believed that personality was determined by the phases of the moon. There is Yeats the dreamy, romantic lover of the beautiful outdoors. There is Yeats the founder of the famous Abbey Theatre in Dublin, which nurtured the Irish renaissance in playwriting. There is Yeats the devoted lover of Maud Gonne for more than two decades. There is Yeats the leader of a lifelong crusade in the cause of a native Irish literature. And there is Yeats the Senator of the Irish Free State. But most important of all, there is Yeats the poet. There is no question about it: At the time of his death in 1939, William Butler Yeats had been recognized by most of his peers as the great poet of the century writing in the English language.

Yeats was born of a Protestant family near Dublin in 1865 and spent most of his early youth at Sligo in northwestern Ireland. When he was ten his family moved to London where Yeats attended school for five years. This move was the first of a number between London and Ireland. At school Yeats seems to have been a poor student, a backward, dreamy child who was fond of going off on long walks by himself. Spelling was one of his poorest subjects and all his life he remained a poor speller. Although he read a great deal, he cared little for systematic learning.

His father, John Butler Yeats, was a very well-known painter who recognized and tried to develop his son's poetic talents. But he was bitterly disappointed when his son chose, at the age of nineteen, to matriculate at an academy of art rather than at Trinity College, Dublin. The son's love of literature proved stronger than his interest in art, however, and in 1886, after three years of art school, William Butler Yeats resolved to become a professional writer. For many months, as a young free-lance journalist, Yeats wrote on various subjects; but his special interest was Irish folklore. His father continued to encourage poetry instead of the drudgery of newspaper work. Once Yeats turned to poetry, success came with remarkable swiftness.

In 1888, at the age of twenty-two, he published his first book, *Fairy and Folk Tales,* a compilation of Irish stories. The next year he published his first book of original poems, *The Wandering of Oisin,* and found himself a recognized and respected poet. The career that was to lead to the highest international honors was well under way. Soon he was on friendly terms with many of the leading writers of the time: George Bernard Shaw, Oscar Wilde, George Russell, William Morris, John Synge, Ezra Pound, and a great many others. He founded and led the Rhymers' Club, a group of young poets. He founded and inspired the Irish Literary Society in London and edited a volume of Irish verse. He became a nationalist working for Irish independence from Britain, and he continued to write poetry. For Yeats the 1890s were a busy and productive decade. In 1902, with the financial help of his patroness, Lady Gregory, he founded the Irish National Theatre Society in Dublin and began writing plays as well as poems. By 1908, when the first collected edition of his poems was published, Yeats had an established reputation as an Irish nationalist leader and a writer of plays and poetry.

In 1889 Yeats met and fell instantly in love with Maud Gonne, a beautiful, eloquent, and domineering worker for Irish independence. Dragging Yeats at her heels from meeting to meeting, she soon learned that he was a fine speaker who had an ability to win people over to his side. Inspired by Maud Gonne's enthusiasm, Yeats took up the cause of Irish nationalism. Although Yeats courted her for thirteen years and loved her for many years more, they were never married, for she was devoted to politics and to propaganda and he was devoted to art. She married an army officer, a Major MacBride, in 1903. This ended the great romance, but not the love, of William Butler Yeats' life.

Yeats had always been interested in magic and mysticism. While it may seem difficult to believe about a great poet, Yeats really believed in spirits and in ghosts. He believed also that the living could communicate with the dead. In 1917, after decades of devotion to Maud Gonne, he married a medium, George Hyde-Lees, and began to record her messages from the "unseen world." Even on their honeymoon, Mrs. Yeats, through what she called "automatic handwriting," was recording messages from the world of the dead. Although she was a spiritualist and a medium, Mrs. Yeats also had shrewd, practical common sense. She was an excellent wife to the poet and she bore him a daughter and a son; their marriage was lasting and happy. The interests of the "unseen world" did not keep them from the responsibilities and joys of the everyday world. "Willie," Mrs. Yeats is reported to have said to her husband, "you are a great poet, but you are no saint."

Early poetry of Yeats

The early poems of Yeats are very romantic; in them one feels a great love for nature and a strong sense of music. Even as a youth growing up in the Sligo countryside, Yeats had loved to walk and dream in the lovely landscapes. In his *Autobiography* he tells of his excitement when, as a boy of ten, his father read aloud to him all of Henry David Thoreau's *Walden.* His early poems show his sensitivity to the beauties of the outdoors and his awareness of the ordinary folk who lived on the farms around the small country villages. Perhaps they are not the greatest poems of Yeats, but they are among the most popular and the most musical.

The Falling of the Leaves

Autumn is over the long leaves that love us,
And over the mice in the barley sheaves;
Yellow the leaves of the rowan above us,
And yellow the wet wild-strawberry leaves.

The hour of the waning of love has beset us,
And weary and worn are our sad souls now;
Let us part, ere the season of passion forget us,
With a kiss and a tear on thy drooping brow.

The Lake Isle of Innisfree

I will arise and go now, and go to Innisfree,
And a small cabin build there, of clay and wattles made:
Nine bean-rows will I have there, a hive for the honeybee,
And live alone in the bee-loud glade.

And I shall have some peace there, for peace comes dropping
    slow,
Dropping from the veils of the morning to where the cricket
    sings;

THE LAKE ISLE OF INNISFREE: *wattles* = interwoven twigs

There midnight's all a glimmer, and noon a purple glow,
And evening full of the linnet's wings.

I will arise and go now, for always night and day
I hear the lake water lapping with low sounds by the shore;
While I stand on the roadway, or on the pavements grey,
I hear it in the deep heart's core.

The Ballad of Father Gilligan

The old priest Peter Gilligan
Was weary night and day;
For half his flock were in their beds,
Or under green sods lay.

Once, while he nodded on a chair,
At the moth-hour of eve,
Another poor man sent for him,
And he began to grieve.

"I have no rest, nor joy, nor peace,
For people die and die";
And after cried he, "God forgive!
My body spake, not I!"

He knelt, and leaning on the chair
He prayed and fell asleep;
And the moth-hour went from the fields,
And stars began to peep.

They slowly into millions grew,
And leaves shook in the wind;
And God covered the world with shade,
And whispered to mankind.

Upon the time of sparrow-chirp
When the moths came once more,

BALLAD OF FATHER GILLIGAN: *mavrone* = alas

The old priest Peter Gilligan
Stood upright on the floor.

"Mavrone, mavrone! the man has died
While I slept on the chair";
He roused the horse out of its sleep,
And rode with little care.

He rode now as he never rode,
By rocky lane and fen;
The sick man's wife opened the door:
"Father! you come again!"

"And is the poor man dead?" he cried.
"He died an hour ago."
The old priest Peter Gilligan
In grief swayed to and fro.

"When you were gone, he turned and died
As merry as a bird."
The old priest Peter Gilligan
He knelt him at that word.

"He Who hath made the night of stars
For souls who tire and bleed,
Sent one of His great angels down
To help me in my need.

"He Who is wrapped in purple robes,
With planets in His care,
Had pity on the least of things
Asleep upon a chair."

When You Are Old

When you are old and grey and full of sleep,
And nodding by the fire, take down this book,

And slowly read, and dream of the soft look
Your eyes had once, and of their shadows deep;

How many loved your moments of glad grace,
And loved your beauty with love false or true,
But one man loved the pilgrim soul in you,
And loved the sorrows of your changing face;

And bending down beside the glowing bars,
Murmur, a little sadly, how Love fled
And paced upon the mountains overhead
And hid his face amid a crowd of stars.

The Lamentation of the Old Pensioner

Although I shelter from the rain
Under a broken tree
My chair was nearest to the fire
In every company
That talked of love or politics,
Ere Time transfigured me.

Though lads are making pikes again
For some conspiracy,
And crazy rascals rage their fill
At human tyranny,
My contemplations are of Time
That has transfigured me.

There's not a woman turns her face
Upon a broken tree,
And yet the beauties that I loved
Are in my memory;
I spit into the face of Time
That has transfigured me.

The Fiddler of Dooney

When I play on my fiddle in Dooney,
Folk dance like a wave of the sea;
My cousin is priest in Kilvarnet,
My brother in Mocharabuiee.

I passed my brother and cousin:
They read in their books of prayer;
I read in my book of songs
I bought at the Sligo fair.

When we come at the end of time
To Peter sitting in state,
He will smile on the three old spirits,
But call me first through the gate;

For the good are always the merry,
Save by an evil chance,
And the merry love the fiddle,
And the merry love to dance:

And when the folk there spy me,
They will all come up to me,
With "Here is the fiddler of Dooney!"
And dance like a wave of the sea.

Into the Twilight

Out-worn heart, in a time out-worn,
Come clear of the nets of wrong and right;
Laugh, heart, again in the grey twilight,
Sigh, heart, again in the dew of the morn.

Your mother Eire is always young,
Dew ever shining and twilight grey;
Though hope fall from you and love decay,
Burning in fire of a slanderous tongue.

Come, heart, where hill is heaped upon hill:
For there the mystical brotherhood
Of sun and moon and hollow and wood
And river and stream work out their will;

And God stands winding His lonely horn,
And time and the world are ever in flight;
And love is less kind than the grey twilight,
And hope is less dear than the dew of the morn.

The Ragged Wood

O hurry where by water among the trees
The delicate-stepping stag and his lady sigh,
When they have but looked upon their images—
Would none had ever loved but you and I!

Or have you heard that sliding silver-shoed
Pale silver-proud queen-woman of the sky,
When the sun looked out of his golden hood?—
O that none ever loved but you and I!

O hurry to the ragged wood, for there
I will drive all those lovers out and cry—
O my share of the world, O yellow hair!
No one has ever loved but you and I.

Later poetry of Yeats

Mystic, dreamer, lover of nature though he was, Yeats was
never far from the affairs of state for very long. The Irish
theatre, the Nationalist movement, the governing of the Irish
Free State, World War I, these were all serious concerns of
his. His early poems were dreamy, romantic conceptions of
rural life, but his later poems are deeply involved with the
issues of the world around him. Part of Yeats' genius lies in
his ability to do many things at once. From the busy years

when he was a senator in the government of the Irish Free State, he went on to write many of his greatest poems.

Writing poems was not an easy process for Yeats. Even at the height of his career he felt that he had finished a full day's labor when he had composed six lines of poetry. As a very young poet he often spent an entire week on six lines; as an old man he found writing a stanza an exhausting experience. Before beginning to work on the lines of the poem, Yeats wrote down a prose outline of what he had in mind. He then took his prose outline and began to put the ideas into verse. Such a process invariably involved many drafts, for Yeats persisted in trying dozens of possible variations. This trial and error method might go on for hours, though only a line or two would result.

Beginning in 1897 and continuing for twenty years, Yeats spent his summers writing at Coole Park, the summer home of Lady Gregory, his patroness and friend. There, under her general supervision, he lived, ate, and wrote his poems and plays. In 1919, with the publication of *The Wild Swans at Coole*, Yeats began on his late and greatest poetry. In 1923 he was awarded the Nobel Prize for Literature, the highest literary award in the world. His poems during the last two decades of his life are among the finest, the most dramatic poems written in the English language.

The Wild Swans at Coole

> The trees are in their autumn beauty,
> The woodland paths are dry,
> Under the October twilight the water
> Mirrors a still sky;
> Upon the brimming water among the stones
> Are nine-and-fifty swans.
>
> The nineteenth autumn has come upon me
> Since I first made my count;

I saw, before I had well finished,
All suddenly mount
And scatter wheeling in great broken rings
Upon their clamorous wings.

I have looked upon those brilliant creatures,
And now my heart is sore.
All's changed since I, hearing at twilight,
The first time on this shore,
The bell-beat of their wings above my head,
Trod with a lighter tread.

Unwearied still, lover by lover,
They paddle in the cold
Companionable streams or climb the air;
Their hearts have not grown old;
Passion or conquest, wander where they will,
Attend upon them still.

But now they drift on the still water,
Mysterious, beautiful;
Among what rushes will they build,
By what lake's edge or pool
Delight men's eyes when I awake some day
To find they have flown away?

An Irish Airman Foresees His Death

I know that I shall meet my fate
Somewhere among the clouds above;
Those that I fight I do not hate,
Those that I guard I do not love;
My country is Kiltartan Cross,
My countrymen Kiltartan's poor,
No likely end could bring them loss
Or leave them happier than before.
Nor law, nor duty bade me fight,

Nor public men, nor cheering crowds,
A lonely impulse of delight
Drove to this tumult in the clouds;
I balanced all, brought all to mind,
The years to come seemed waste of breath,
A waste of breath the years behind
In balance with this life, this death.

A Deep-Sworn Vow

Others because you did not keep
That deep-sworn vow have been friends of mine;
Yet always when I look death in the face,
When I clamber to the heights of sleep,
Or when I grow excited with wine,
Suddenly I meet your face.

The Leaders of the Crowd

They must to keep their certainty accuse
All that are different of a base intent;
Pull down established honor; hawk for news
Whatever their loose fantasy invent
And murmur it with bated breath, as though
The abounding gutter had been Helicon
Or calumny a song. How can they know
Truth flourishes where the student's lamp has shone,
And there alone, that have no solitude?
So the crowd come they care not what may come.
They have loud music, hope everyday renewed
And heartier loves; that lamp is from the tomb.

The Wheel

Through winter-time we call on spring,
And through the spring on summer call,
And when abounding hedges ring
Declare that winter's best of all;

WILLIAM BUTLER YEATS

And after that there's nothing good
Because the spring-time has not come—
Nor know that what disturbs our blood
Is but its longing for the tomb.

On Easter day, 1916, a group of extreme Irish nation-
alists staged a fanatic rebellion against the British rule over
Ireland. The revolt was quickly crushed and many of the
finest leaders in the Nationalist movement were killed. One
of these, Major MacBride, was the husband of Maud Gonne.
Deeply moved by this uprising, about which he had known
nothing, Yeats wrote "Easter, 1916." The following is the
last stanza of that poem.

Too long a sacrifice
Can make a stone of the heart.
O when may it suffice?
That is Heaven's part, our part
To murmur name upon name,
As a mother names her child
When sleep at last has come
On limbs that had run wild.
What is it but night fall?
No, no, not night but death;
Was it needless death after all?
For England may keep faith
For all that is done and said.
We know their dream; enough
To know they dreamed and are dead;
And what if excess of love
Bewildered them till they died?
I write it out in verse—
MacDonagh and MacBride
And Connolly and Pearse
Now and in time to be,
Wherever green is worn,

Are changed, changed utterly:
A terrible beauty is born.

September 25, 1916

Politics

"In our time the destiny of man presents its meaning in political terms."—Thomas Mann

How can I, that girl standing there,
My attention fix
On Roman or on Russian
Or on Spanish politics?
Yet here's a travelled man that knows
What he talks about,
And there's a politician
That has read and thought,
And maybe what they say is true
Of war and war's alarms,
But O that I were young again
And held her in my arms!

A Prayer for My Daughter

Once more the storm is howling, and half hid
Under this cradle-hood and coverlid
My child sleeps on. There is no obstacle
But Gregory's wood and one bare hill
Whereby the haystack- and roof-levelling wind,
Bred on the Atlantic, can be stayed;
And for an hour I have walked and prayed
Because of the great gloom that is in my mind.

I have walked and prayed for this young child an hour
And heard the sea-wind scream upon the tower,
And under the arches of the bridge, and scream
In the elms above the flooded stream;

A PRAYER FOR MY DAUGHTER: *Queen* = Venus, goddess of love;
bandy-legged smith = Vulcan, her husband

Imagining in excited reverie
That the future years had come,
Dancing to a frenzied drum,
Out of the murderous innocence of the sea.

May she be granted beauty and yet not
Beauty to make a stranger's eye distraught,
Or hers before a looking-glass, for such,
Being made beautiful overmuch,
Consider beauty a sufficient end,
Lose natural kindness and maybe
The heart-revealing intimacy
That chooses right, and never find a friend.

Helen being chosen found life flat and dull
And later had much trouble from a fool,
While that great Queen, that rose out of the spray,
Being fatherless could have her way
Yet chose a bandy-legged smith for man.
It's certain that fine women eat
A crazy salad with their meat
Whereby the Horn of Plenty is undone.

In courtesy I'd have her chiefly learned;
Hearts are not had as a gift but hearts are earned
By those that are not entirely beautiful;
Yet many, that have played the fool
For beauty's very self, has charm made wise,
And many a poor man that has roved,
Loved and thought himself beloved,
From a glad kindness cannot take his eyes.

May she become a flourishing hidden tree
That all her thoughts may like the linnet be,
And have no business but dispensing round
Their magnanimities of sound,
Nor but in merriment begin a chase,

Nor but in merriment a quarrel.
O may she live like some green laurel
Rooted in one dear perpetual place.

My mind, because the minds that I have loved,
The sort of beauty that I have approved,
Prosper but little, has dried up of late,
Yet knows that to be choked with hate
May well be of all evil chances chief.
If there's no hatred in a mind
Assault and battery of the wind
Can never tear the linnet from the leaf.

An intellectual hatred is the worst,
So let her think opinions are accursed.
Have I not seen the loveliest woman born
Out of the mouth of Plenty's horn,
Because of her opinionated mind
Barter that horn and every good
By quiet natures understood
For an old bellows full of angry wind?

Considering that, all hatred driven hence,
The soul recovers radical innocence
And learns at last that it is self-delighting,
Self-appeasing, self-affrighting,
And that its own sweet will is Heaven's will;
She can, though every face should scowl
And every windy quarter howl
Or every bellows burst, be happy still.

And may her bridegroom bring her to a house
Where all's accustomed, ceremonious;
For arrogance and hatred are the wares
Peddled in the thoroughfares.
How but in custom and in ceremony

Are innocence and beauty born?
Ceremony's a name for the rich horn,
And custom for the spreading laurel tree.

June 1919

Difficult poetry of Yeats

Yeats is often one of the most difficult poets to read. For one thing, his vocabulary, his sentence structure, and his allusions to the past sometimes are beyond the experience of high school students. For another thing, Yeats had his own private set of symbols which he described in a short prose work called *A Vision*. Gyres, geometric shapes, phases of the moon, cycles of history—all these are part of his elaborate symbol making. A student need not know the content of *A Vision* in order to read and understand most of Yeats' poems, but many poems are made more clear by it.

One such poem is "The Second Coming." In *A Vision* Yeats maintains that history repeats itself in patterns, that every twenty centuries one way of life gives way to another. In "The Second Coming" Yeats sees the end of the Judeo-Christian era and the birth of some new, rather brutish way of life. Notice the ugly symbol Yeats uses to picture this new way of life.

The Second Coming
Turning and turning in the widening gyre
The falcon cannot hear the falconer;
Things fall apart; the centre cannot hold;
Mere anarchy is loosed upon the world,
The blood-dimmed tide is loosed, and everywhere
The ceremony of innocence is drowned;
The best lack all conviction, while the worst
Are full of passionate intensity.

THE SECOND COMING: *Spiritus Mundi* = literally, spirit of the world; here, the source of ideas

Surely some revelation is at hand;
Surely the Second Coming is at hand.
The Second Coming! Hardly are those words out
When a vast image out of *Spiritus Mundi*
Troubles my sight: somewhere in the sands of the desert
A shape with a lion body and the head of a man,
A gaze blank and pitiless as the sun,
Is moving its slow thighs, while all about it
Reel shadows of the indignant desert birds.
The darkness drops again; but now I know
That twenty centuries of stony sleep
Were vexed to nightmare by a rocking cradle,
And what rough beast, its hour come round at last,
Slouches toward Bethlehem to be born?

The first stanza describes the breakup of the modern world. What symbols does Yeats use to show that things are falling apart?

In the second stanza Yeats envisions a rough beast slouching toward Bethlehem to be born. What does the rough beast connote to you? Why Bethlehem? To what does the "rocking cradle" refer?

"The Second Coming" is a difficult poem, and it can be variously interpreted. Another difficult poem, often hailed as one of the finest that Yeats wrote, is "Sailing to Byzantium." Hundreds of pages have been written about this poem's meaning. Read it carefully at least twice. Do you see that Yeats wants to leave the world of mortal flesh and enter the eternity of art?

Sailing to Byzantium

I

That is no country for old men. The young
In one another's arms, birds in the trees

—Those dying generations—at their song,
The salmon-falls, the mackerel-crowded seas,
Fish, flesh, fowl, commend all summer long
Whatever is begotten, born, and dies.
Caught in that sensual music all neglect
Monuments of unaging intellect.

II

An aged man is but a paltry thing,
A tattered coat upon a stick, unless
Soul clap its hands and sing, and louder sing
For every tatter in its mortal dress,
Nor is there singing school but studying
Monuments of its own magnificence;
And therefore I have sailed the seas and come
To the holy city of Byzantium.

III

O sages standing in God's holy fire
As in the gold mosaic of a wall,
Come from the holy fire, perne in a gyre,
And be the singing-masters of my soul.
Consume my heart away; sick with desire
And fastened to a dying animal
It knows not what it is; and gather me
Into the artifice of eternity.

IV

Once out of nature I shall never take
My bodily form from any natural thing,
But such a form as Grecian goldsmiths make
Of hammered gold and gold enamelling
To keep a drowsy Emperor awake;
Or set upon a golden bough to sing
To lords and ladies of Byzantium
Of what is past, or passing, or to come.

Conclusion

Many of Yeats' distinguished contemporaries—poets, teachers, and critics—were skeptical about his poetry. People like T. S. Eliot, for instance, at one time felt that Yeats' "supernatural world" had no relation to the modern world. Others felt that a man who believed in ghosts and fairies could hardly say anything of importance to a citizen of the twentieth century. The poet Robert Graves, the hero Lawrence of Arabia, the critic Middleton Murry, all doubted the significance of Yeats at one time or another.

But at his death in 1939, William Butler Yeats was almost universally respected as a great poet. In his poem "In Memory of W. B. Yeats," the poet W. H. Auden said about him: "You were silly like us; your gift survived it all." The stature of a poet is determined not by his religion, his friends, his oddities, or his personal interests; in the last analysis *a poet is measured by his poetry.* And the poetry of William Butler Yeats will be read as long as literature survives.

Part Two

AN

ANTHOLOGY

OF POEMS

BALLADS AND NARRATIVE POETRY

A folk ballad is a song that tells a story. At one time or another all folk ballads were sung; today many of them are still sung, but the music of a great many others has been lost. Sung or not, they have always had a strong appeal to readers and listeners. The stories ballads tell are plain in language and full of action. Ballads use a great deal of dialogue, much repetition, but few explanatory details of background. They tell basic stories that will appeal to all peoples and ages: of courage, of strength, of love, of struggle, of death, of heroes, and of outlaws.

The origin of folk ballads is not entirely clear. There is no record of the original authors, those anonymous poets who composed and sang their stories. But why should the authors of ballads written in fairly recent times be as unknown as the authors of the ballads written in 16th- and 17th-century Britain? One theory, held by relatively few people, is that no single poet wrote the ballad, that ballads were composed by groups meeting and singing together in peasant cottages, in mining camps, on the railroad beds. Another theory is that they were written by individual authors but taken over by successive groups and generations of people who changed the words and forgot the original writer. No explanation seems complete.

What is more important for our purposes is the existence, not the origin, of these ballads. There are no other poems quite like them. Swift, dramatic, full of incident, often abrupt, ballads continue to delight readers of all ages.

Casey Jones

ANONYMOUS

Come all ye rounders if you want to hear
The story of a brave engineer;
Casey Jones was the hogger's name,
On a big eight-wheeler, boys, he won his fame.
Caller called Casey at half-past four,
He kissed his wife at the station door,
Mounted to the cabin with orders in hand,
And took his farewell trip to the promised land.

> Casey Jones, he mounted to the cabin,
> Casey Jones, with orders in his hand!
> Casey Jones, he mounted to the cabin,
> Took his farewell trip into the promised land.

Put in your water and shovel in your coal,
Put your head out the window, watch the drivers roll,
I'll run her till she leaves the rail,
'Cause we're eight hours late with the Western Mail!
He looked at his watch and his watch was slow,
Looked at the water and the water was low,
Turned to his fireboy and said,
"We'll get to 'Frisco, but we'll all be dead!"

(Refrain)

Casey pulled up Reno Hill,
Tooted for the crossing with an awful shrill,
Snakes all knew by the engine's moans
That the hogger at the throttle was Casey Jones.
He pulled up short two miles from the place,
Number Four stared him right in the face,
Turned to his fireboy, said "You'd better jump,
'Cause there's two locomotives going to bump!"

(Refrain)

Casey said, just before he died,
"There's two more roads I'd like to ride."
Fireboy said, "What can they be?"
"The Rio Grande and the Old S.P."
Mrs. Jones sat on her bed a-sighing,
Got a pink that Casey was dying,
Said, "Go to bed, children; hush your crying,
'Cause you'll get another papa on the Salt Lake Line."

Casey Jones! Got another papa!
Casey Jones, on the Salt Lake Line!
Casey Jones! Got another papa!
Got another papa on the Salt Lake Line!

Jesse James

ANONYMOUS

It was on a Wednesday night, the moon was shining bright,
They robbed the Danville train.
And the people they did say, for many miles away,
'Twas the outlaws Frank and Jesse James.

Jesse had a wife to mourn him all her life,
The children they are brave.
'Twas a dirty little coward shot Mister Howard,
And laid Jesse James in his grave.

Jesse was a man was a friend to the poor,
He never left a friend in pain.
And with his brother he robbed the Chicago bank
And then held up the Glendale train.

It was Robert Ford, the dirty little coward,
I wonder how he does feel,
For he ate of Jesse's bread and he slept in Jesse's bed,
Then he laid Jesse James in his grave.

It was his brother Frank that robbed the Gallatin bank,
And carried the money from the town.
It was in this very place that they had a little race,
For they shot Captain Sheets to the ground.

They went to the crossing not very far from there,
And there they did the same;
And the agent on his knees he delivered up the keys
To the outlaws Frank and Jesse James.

It was on a Saturday night, Jesse was at home
Talking to his family brave,
When the thief and the coward, little Robert Ford,
Laid Jesse James in his grave.

How people held their breath when they heard of Jesse's death,
And wondered how he ever came to die.
'Twas one of the gang, dirty Robert Ford,
That shot Jesse James on the sly.

Jesse went to rest with his hand on his breast;
He died with a smile on his face.
He was born one day in the county of Clay,
And came from a solitary race.

Johnie Armstrong

ANONYMOUS

There dwelt a man in faire Westmerland,
Johnie Armstrong men did him call,
He had neither lands nor rents coming in,
Yet he kept eight score men in his hall.

He had horse and harness for them all,
Goodly steeds were all milke-white;
O the golden bands an about their necks,
And their weapons, they were all alike.

JOHNIE ARMSTRONG: *taine* = taken

Newes then was brought unto the king
That there was sick a won as hee,
That lived like a bold outlaw,
And robbed all the north country.

The king he writt a letter then,
A letter which was large and long;
He signed it with his owne hand;
And he promised to doe him no wrong.

When this letter came Johnie untill,
His heart it was blythe as birds on a tree:
"Never was I sent for before any king,
My father, my grandfather, nor none but mee.

"And if we goe the king before,
I would we went most orderly;
Every man of you shall have his scarlet cloak,
Laced with silver laces three.

"Every won of you shall have his scarlet cloak,
Laced with silver lace so white;
O the golden bands an about your necks,
Black hatts, white feathers, all alyke."

By the morrow morning at ten of the clock,
Towards Edenburough gon was hee,
And with him all his eight score men;
Good Lord, it was a goodly sight for to see!

When Johnie came before the king,
He fell down on his knee;
"O pardon, my soveraine leige," he said,
"O pardon my eight score men and mee!"

"Thou shalt have no pardon, thou traitor strong,
For thy eight score men nor thee;

For tomarrow morning by ten of the clock,
Both thou and them shall hang on the gallow-tree."

But Johnie looke'd over his left shoulder,
Good Lord, what a grievous look looked hee!
Saying, "Asking grace of a graceless face—
Why there is none for you nor me."

But Johnie had a bright sword by his side,
And it was made of the mettle so free,
That had not the king stept his foot aside,
He had smitten his head from his faire body.

Saying, "Fight on, my merry men all,
And see that none of you be taine;
For rather then men shall say we were hange'd
Let them report how we were slaine."

Then, God wott, faire Eddenburrough rose,
And so besett poore Johnie rounde,
That fourscore and ten of Johnie's best men
Lay gasping all upon the ground.

Then like a mad man Johnie laide about,
And like a mad man then fought he,
Untill a false Scot came Johnie behinde,
And runn him through the faire body.

Saying, "Fight on, my merry men all,
And see that none of you be taine;
For I will stand by and bleed but awhile,
And then I will come and fight again."

Newes then was brought to young Johnie Armstrong,
As he stood by his nurse's knee,
Who vowed if ere he live'd for to be a man,
On the treacherous Scots revenged hee'd be.

The Douglas Tragedy

ANONYMOUS

"Rise up, rise up, now, Lord Douglas," she says,
"And put on your armour so bright;
Let it never be said that a daughter of thine
Was married to a lord under night.

"Rise up, rise up, my seven bold sons,
And put on your armour so bright,
And take better care of your youngest sister,
For your eldest's away the last night."

He's mounted her on a milk-white steed,
And himself on a dapple grey,
With a buglet horn hung down by his side,
And lightly they rode away.

Lord William lookit oer his left shoulder,
To see what he could see,
And there he spy'd her seven brethren bold,
Come riding over the lee.

"Light down, light down, Lady Margret," he said,
"And hold my steed in your hand,
Until that against your seven brethren bold,
And your father, I mak a stand."

She held his steed in her milk-white hand,
And never shed one tear,
Until that she saw her seven brethren fa,
And her father hard fighting, who lovd her so dear.

"O hold your hand, Lord William!" she said,
"For your strokes they are wondrous sair;

THE DOUGLAS TRAGEDY: *many a ane* = many a one; *dighted* = wiped;
gang = go; *quire* = choir; *braid* = broad; *plat* = intertwined

BALLADS AND NARRATIVE POETRY

True lovers I can get many a ane,
But a father I can never get mair."

O she's taken out her handkerchief,
It was o the holland so fine,
And aye she dighted her father's bloody wounds,
That were redder than the wine.

"O chuse, o chuse, Lady Margret," he said,
"O whether will ye gang or bide?"
"I'll gang, I'll gang, Lord William," she said,
"For ye have left me no other guide."

He's lifted her on a milk-white steed,
And himself on a dapple grey,
With a buglet horn hung down by his side
And slowly they baith rade away.

O they rade on, and on they rade,
And a' by the light of the moon,
Until they came to yon wan water,
And there they lighted down.

They lighted down to take a drink
Of the spring that ran sae clear,
And down the stream ran his gude heart's blood,
And sair she gan to fear.

"Hold up, hold up, Lord William," she says,
"For I fear that you are slain;"
"'Tis naething but the shadow of my scarlet cloak,
That shines in the water sae plain."

O they rade on, and on they rade,
And a' by the light of the moon,
Until they came to his mother's ha door,
And there they lighted down.

"Get up, get up, lady mother," he says,
"Get up and let me in!
Get up, get up, lady mother," he says,
"For this night my fair lady I've win.

"O mak my bed, lady mother," he says,
"O mak it braid and deep,
And lay Lady Margret close at my back,
And the sounder I will sleep."

Lord William was dead lang ere midnight,
Lady Margret lang ere day,
And all true lovers that go thegither,
May they have mair luck than they!

Lord William was buried in St. Mary's kirk,
Lady Margret in Mary's quire;
Out o the lady's grave grew a bonny red rose,
And out o the knight's a briar.

And they twa met, and they twa plat,
And fain they wad be near;
And a' the warld might ken right weel
They were twa lovers dear.

But bye and rade the Black Douglas,
And wow but he was rough!
For he pulld up the bonny briar,
And flang 't in St. Mary's Loch.

Bonnie George Campbell

ANONYMOUS

High upon Highlands,
And low upon Tay,
Bonnie George Campbell
Rode out on a day;
Saddled and bridled,

And gallant to see:
Home came his good horse,
But home came not he.

Out ran his old mother,
Wild with despair;
Out ran his bonnie bride,
Tearing her hair.
He rode saddled and bridled,
With boots to the knee:
Home came his good horse,
But never came he.

"My meadow lies green,
And my corn is unshorn,
My barn is unbuilt,
And my babe is unborn."
He rode saddled and bridled,
Careless and free:
Safe home came the saddle,
But never came he.

Edward, Edward

ANONYMOUS

"Why does your sword so drip with blood,
        Edward, Edward?
Why does your sword so drip with blood,
  And why so sad are ye, O?"
"O I have killed my hawk so good,
        Mother, mother,
O I have killed my hawk so good
  And I had no more but he, O."

"Your hawk's blood was never so red,
        Edward, Edward,
Your hawk's blood was never so red,

My dear son, I tell thee, O."
"O I have killed my red-roan steed,
          Mother, mother,
O I have killed my red-roan steed,
    That was so fair and free, O."

"Your steed was old and your stable's filled,
          Edward, Edward,
Your steed was old and your stable's filled,
    Now say what may it be, O."
"It was my father that I killed,
          Mother, mother,
It was my father that I killed,
    Alas, and woe is me, O."

"What penance will ye do for that,
          Edward, Edward?
What penance will ye do for that,
    My dear son, now tell me, O?"
"I'll set my feet in yonder boat,
          Mother, mother,
I'll set my feet in yonder boat,
    And I'll fare across the Sea, O."

"What will ye do with your towers and hall,
          Edward, Edward?
What will ye do with your towers and hall,
    That are so fair to see, O?"
"I'll let them stand till down they fall,
          Mother, mother,
I'll let them stand till down they fall,
    For here nevermore may I be, O."

"What will ye leave to your babes and your wife,
          Edward, Edward?
What will ye leave to your babes and your wife,
    When ye go over the sea, O?"

175   BALLADS AND NARRATIVE POETRY

"The world's room—let them beg through life,
      Mother, mother,
The world's room—let them beg through life,
  For them nevermore will I see, O."

"And what will ye leave to your own mother dear,
      Edward, Edward?
And what will ye leave to your own mother dear,
  My dear son, now tell me, O?"
"The curse of Hell from me shall ye bear,
      Mother, mother,
The curse of Hell from me shall ye bear:
  Such counsel ye gave to me, O!"

John Henry

ANONYMOUS

John Henry was a lil baby,
Sittin' on his mama's knee,
Said: "De Big Bend Tunnel on de C.&O. road
Gonna cause de death of me,
Lawd, lawd, gonna cause de death of me."

Cap'n says to John Henry,
"Gonna bring me a steam drill 'round,
Gonna take dat steam drill out on de job,
Gonna whop dat steel on down,
Lawd, lawd, gonna whop dat steel on down."

John Henry tol' his cap'n,
Lightnin' was in his eye:
"Cap'n, bet yo' las' red cent on me,
Fo' I'll beat it to de bottom or I'll die,
Lawd, lawd, I'll beat it to the bottom or I'll die."

Sun shine hot an' burnin',
Wer'n't no breeze a-tall,

JOHN HENRY: *intrels* = entrails, innards

Sweat ran down like water down a hill,
Dat day John Henry let his hammer fall,
Lawd, lawd, dat day John Henry let his hammer fall.

John Henry went to de tunnel,
An' they put him in de lead to drive,
De rock so tall an' John Henry so small,
Dat he lied down his hammer an' he cried,
Lawd, lawd, dat he lied down his hammer an' he cried.

John Henry started on de right hand,
De steam drill started on de lef'—
"Before I'd let dis steam drill beat me down,
I'd hammer my fool self to death,
Lawd, lawd, I'd hammer my fool self to death."

Drill man tol' John Henry,
"Fella', darn yo' soul,
You might beat dis steam and drill of mine,
When de rocks in dis mountain turn to gol'."

John Henry said to his shaker,
"Fella', why don' you sing?
I'm throwin' twelve poun's from my hips on down,
Jes' listen to de col' steel ring,
Lawd, lawd, jes' listen to de col' steel ring."

Oh, the captain said to John Henry,
"I b'lieve this mountain's sinkin' in."
John Henry said to his captain, oh my!
"Ain' nothin' but my hammer suckin' win',
Lawd, lawd, ain' nothin' but my hammer suckin' win'."

John Henry tol' his captain,
"Look yonder what I see—
Yo' drill's done broke an' yo' hole's done choke,

An' you cain' drive steel like me,
Lawd, lawd, an' you cain' drive steel like me."

John Henry told his shaker,
"Shaker, you better pray,
For, if I miss dis six-foot steel,
Tomarrow'll be yo' buryin' day,
Lawd, lawd, tomarrow'll be yo' buryin' day."

De man dat invented de steam drill,
Thought he was mighty fine.
John Henry drove his fifteen feet,
An' de steam drill only made nine,
Lawd, lawd, an' de steam drill only made nine.

De hammer dat John Henry swung,
It weighed over nine pound;
He broke a rib in his lef'-han' side,
An' his intrels fell on de groun',
Lawd, lawd, an' his intrels fell on de groun'.

All de womens in de Wes',
When dey heared of John Henry's death,
Stood in de rain, flagged de eas'-boun' train,
Goin' where John Henry fell dead,
Lawd, lawd, goin' where John Henry fell dead.

John Henry's lil mother,
She was all dressed in red,
She jumped in bed, covered up her head,
Said she didn' know her son was dead,
Lawd, lawd, didn' know her son was dead.

Dey took John Henry to de graveyard,
An' dey buried him in de san',
An' every locomotive come roarin' by,
Says "Dere lays a steel-drivin' man,
Lawd, lawd, dere lays a steel-drivin' man."

The Three Ravens

ANONYMOUS

There were three ravens sat on a tree,
Downe a downe, hay downe, hay downe
There were three ravens sat on a tree,
With a downe
There were three ravens sat on a tree,
They were as black as they might be.
With a down derrie, derrie, derrie,
    downe, downe.

The one of them said to his mate,
"Where shall we our breakfast take?"

"Downe in yonder greene field,
There lies a knight slain under his shield.

"His hounds they lie downe at his feete,
So well they can their master keepe.

"His haukes they flie so eagerly,
There's no fowle dare him come nie."

Downe there comes a fallow doe,
As great with yong as she might goe.

She lifts up his bloudy hed,
And kist his wounds that were so red.

She got him up upon her backe,
And carried him to earthen lake.

She buried him before the prime,
She was dead herselfe ere even-song time.

God send every gentleman,
Such haukes, such hounds, and such a leman.

THE THREE RAVENS: *lake* = pit; *leman* = loved one, wife

The Bailiff's Daughter of Islington

ANONYMOUS

There was a youth, and a well-beloved youth,
And he was an esquire's son,
He loved the bailiff's daughter dear,
That lived in Islington.

But she was coy, and she would not believe
That he did love her so,
No, nor at any time she would
Any countenance to him show.

But when his friends did understand
His fond and foolish mind,
They sent him up to fair London,
An apprentice for to bind.

And when he had been seven long years,
And his love he had not seen;
"Many a tear have I shed for her sake
When little she thought of me."

All the maids of Islington
Went forth to sport and play;
All but the bailiff's daughter dear;
She secretly stole away.

She put off her gown of grey,
And put on her puggish attire;
She's up to fair London gone,
Her true-love to require.

As she went along the road,
The weather being hot and dry,
There was she aware of her true-love,
At length came riding by.

She stept to him, as red as any rose,
And took him by the bridle-ring:
"I pray you, kind sir, give me one penny,
To ease my weary limb."—

"I prithee, sweetheart, canst thou tell me
Where that thou wast born?"—
"At Islington, kind sir," said she,
"Where I have had many a scorn."—

"I prithee, sweetheart, canst thou tell me
Whether thou dost know
The bailiff's daughter of Islington?"—
"She's dead, sir, long ago."—

"Then will I sell my goodly steed,
My saddle and my bow;
I will into some far countrey,
Where no man doth me know."—

"Oh stay, Oh stay, thou goodly youth!
She's alive, she is not dead;
Here she standeth by thy side,
And is ready to be thy bride."—

"Oh farewell grief, and welcome joy,
Ten thousand times and o'er!
For now I have seen my own true-love,
That thought I should have seen no more."

BALLADS AND NARRATIVE POETRY

The Demon Lover

ANONYMOUS

"O where have you been, my long, long love,
This long seven years and mair?"
"I'm come to seek my former vows
Ye granted me before."

"O hold your tongue of your former vows,
For they will breed sad strife;
O hold your tongue of your former vows,
For I am become a wife."

He turned him right and round about,
And the tear blinded his ee:
"I wad never hae trodden on Irish ground,
If it had not been for thee.

"I might hae had a king's daughter,
Far, far beyond the sea;
I might have had a king's daughter,
Had it not been for love o thee."

"If ye might have had a king's daughter,
Yer self ye had to blame;
Ye might have taken the king's daughter,
For ye knew that I was nane.

"If I was to leave my husband dear,
And my two babes also,
O what have you to take me to,
If with you I should go?"

"I hae seven ships upon the sea—
The eighth brought me to land—
With four-and-twenty bold mariners,
And music on every hand."

She has taken up her two little babes,
Kissed them baith cheek and chin:

THE DEMON LOVER: *ain* = own; *drumlie* = gloomy

"O fair ye weel, my ain two babes,
For I'll never see you again."

She set her foot upon the ship,
No mariners could she behold;
But the sails were o the taffetie,
And the masts o the beaten gold.

She had not sailed a league, a league,
A league but barely three,
When dismal grew his countenance,
And drumlie grew his ee.

They had not sailed a league, a league,
A league but barely three,
Until she espied his cloven foot,
And she wept right bitterlie.

"O hold your tongue of your weeping," says he,
"Of your weeping now let me be;
I will shew you how the lillies grow
On the banks of Italy."

"O what hills are yon, yon pleasant hills,
That the sun shines sweetly on?"
"O yon are the hills of heaven," he said,
"Where you will never win."

"O whaten a mountain is yon," she said,
"All so dreary wi frost and snow?"
"O yon is the mountain of hell," he cried,
"Where you and I will go."

He strack the tap-mast wi his hand,
The fore-mast wi his knee,
And he brake that gallant ship in twain,
And sank her in the sea.

Literary ballads are a development of the folk ballad. The important differences between the two ballad forms are these: folk ballads were written to be sung, while literary ballads were not; folk ballads have a questionable origin, but literary ballads are the works of known poets; folk ballads may have several versions, some cruder than others, but a literary ballad is a single, polished poem.

In other words, certain poets, attracted by the style of the folk ballad, attempted to write story poems using many of the same characteristics. Like folk ballads, literary ballads tell a swift, action-filled story in plain language. Literary ballads concentrate on a single character or event, they use repetition, and they often tell their stories through dialogue, just as folk ballads do. Literary ballads, like folk ballads, tell elemental stories of love, death, courage, violence, and heroism.

Lochinvar

SIR WALTER SCOTT

O, young Lochinvar is come out of the west,
Through all the wide border his steed was the best;
And save his good broadsword he weapons had none,
He rode all unarmed, and he rode all alone.
So faithful in love, and so dauntless in war,
There never was knight like the young Lochinvar.

He staid not for brake, and he stopped not for stone,
He swam the Eske river where ford there was none;
But ere he alighted at Netherby gate,
The bride had consented, the gallant came late;
For a laggard in love, and a dastard in war,
Was to wed the fair Ellen of brave Lochinvar.

LOCHINVAR: *galliard* = lively dance; *scaur* = steep bank

So boldly he entered the Netherby Hall,
Among bride's-men, and kinsmen, and brothers, and all:
Then spoke the bride's father, his hand on his sword,
(For the poor craven bridegroom said never a word,)
"O come ye in peace here, or come ye in war,
Or to dance at our bridal, young Lord Lochinvar?"

"I long wooed your daughter, my suit you denied;—
Love swells like the Solway, but ebbs like its tide—
And now am I come, with this lost love of mine,
To lead but one measure, drink one cup of wine.
There are maidens in Scotland more lovely by far,
That would gladly be bride to the young Lochinvar."

The bride kissed the goblet: the knight took it up,
He quaffed off the wine, and he threw down the cup.
She looked down to blush, and she looked up to sigh,
With a smile on her lips, and a tear in her eye.
He took her soft hand, ere her mother could bar,—
"Now tread we a measure!" said young Lochinvar.

So stately his form, and so lovely her face,
That never a hall such a galliard did grace;
While her mother did fret, and her father did fume,
And the bridegroom stood dangling his bonnet and plume;
And the bride-maidens whispered, " 'Twere better by far,
To have matched our fair cousin with young Lochinvar."

One touch to her hand, and one word in her ear,
When they reached the hall-door, and the charger stood near;
So light to the croupe the fair lady he swung,
So light to the saddle before her he sprung!—
"She is won! we are gone, over bank, bush, and scaur;
They'll have fleet steeds that follow," quoth young Lochinvar.

There was mounting 'mong Graemes of the Netherby clan:
Forsters, Fenwicks, and Musgraves, they rode and they ran:
There was racing and chasing, on Cannobie Lee,
But the lost bride of Netherby ne'er did they see.
So daring in love, and so dauntless in war,
Have ye e'er heard of a gallant like young Lochinvar?

Jock O' Hazeldean
SIR WALTER SCOTT

"Why weep ye by the tide, ladie?
Why weep ye by the tide?
I'll wed ye to my youngest son,
And ye sall be his bride.
And ye sall be his bride, ladie,
Sae comely to be seen"—
But aye she loot the tears down fa'
For Jock o' Hazeldean.

"Now let this willfu' grief be done,
And dry that cheek so pale;
Young Frank is chief of Errington,
And lord of Langley dale;
His step is first in peaceful ha'
His sword in battle keen"—
But aye she loot the tears down fa'
For Jock o' Hazeldean.

"A chain of gold ye sall not lack,
Nor braid to bind your hair;
Nor mettled hound, nor managed hawk,
Nor palfrey fresh and fair;
And you, the foremost o' them a',
Shall ride our forest queen"—
But aye she loot the tears down fa'
For Jock o' Hazeldean.

JOCK O' HAZELDEAN: *loot* = let; *ha'* = hall

The kirk was decked at morningtide,
The tapers glimmered fair;
The priest and bridegroom wait the bride,
And dame and knight are there.
They sought her baith by bower and ha'—
The ladie was not seen!
She's o'er the Border, and awa'
Wi' Jock o' Hazeldean.

La Belle Dame sans Merci
JOHN KEATS

O what can ail thee, knight at arms,
Alone and palely loitering?
The sedge has withered from the lake,
And no birds sing!

O what can ail thee, knight at arms,
So haggard and so woe-begone?
The squirrel's granary is full,
And the harvest's done.

I see a lily on thy brow,
With anguish moist and fever dew;
And on thy cheeks a fading rose
Fast withereth too.

I met a lady in the meads,
Full beautiful, a faery's child;
Her hair was long, her foot was light,
And her eyes were wild.

I made a garland for her head,
And bracelets, too, and fragrant zone;

LA BELLE DAME SANS MERCI: *sedge* = coarse marsh grass; *meads* =
meadows; *grot* = grotto

She looked at me as she did love,
And made sweet moan.

I set her on my pacing steed,
And nothing else saw all day long;
For sidelong would she bend, and sing
A faery's song.

She found me roots of relish sweet,
And honey wild, and manna dew;
And sure in language strange she said,
"I love thee true."

She took me to her elfin grot,
And there she wept and sighed full sore;
And there I shut her wild, wild eyes
With kisses four.

And there she lulled me asleep,
And there I dreamed, ah woe betide!
The latest dream I ever dreamt,
On the cold hillside.

I saw pale kings, and princes too,
Pale warriors, death-pale were they all,
Who cried, "La Belle Dame sans Merci
Thee hath in thrall!"

I saw their starved lips in the gloam
With horrid warning gaped wide—
And I awoke and found me there,
On the cold hill's side.

And this is why I sojurn here,
Alone and palely loitering;
Though the sedge is withered from the lake,
And no birds sing.

The Skeleton in Armor

HENRY WADSWORTH LONGFELLOW

"Speak! speak! thou fearful guest!
Who, with thy hollow breast
Still in rude armor drest,
    Comest to daunt me!
Wrapt not in Eastern balms,
But with thy fleshless palms
Stretched, as if asking alms,
    Why dost thou haunt me?"

Then, from those cavernous eyes
Pale flashes seemed to rise,
As when the Northern skies
    Gleam in December;
And, like the water's flow
Under December's snow,
Came a dull voice of woe
    From the heart's chamber.

"I was a Viking old!
My deeds, though manifold,
No Skald in song has told,
    No Saga taught thee!
Take heed, that in thy verse
Thou dost the tale rehearse,
Else dread a dead man's curse;
    For this I sought thee.

"Far in the Northern Land,
By the wild Baltic's strand,
I, with my childish hand,
    Tamed the gerfalcon;

THE SKELETON IN ARMOR: *Skald* = poet or story teller; *gerfalcon* = a falcon common to the north; *Skaw* = a northern point in Denmark; *Skoal* = a Scandinavian salutation, customary when drinking to health

And, with my skates fast-bound,
Skimmed the half-frozen Sound,
That the poor whimpering hound
   Trembled to walk on.

"Oft to his frozen lair
Tracked I the grisly bear,
While from my path the hare
   Fled like a shadow;
Oft through the forest dark
Followed the were-wolf's bark,
Until the soaring lark
   Sang from the meadow.

"But when I older grew,
Joining a corsair's crew,
O'er the dark sea I flew
   With the marauders.
Wild was the life we led;
Many the souls that sped,
Many the hearts that bled,
   By our stern orders.

"Many a wassail-bout
Wore the long Winter out;
Often our midnight shout
   Set the cocks crowing,
As we the Berserk's tale
Measured in cups of ale,
Draining the oaken pail,
   Filled to o'erflowing.

"Once as I told in glee
Tales of the stormy sea,
Soft eyes did gaze on me,
   Burning yet tender;

And as the white stars shine
On the dark Norway pine,
On that dark heart of mine
   Fell their soft splendor.

"I wooed the blue-eyed maid,
Yielding, yet half afraid,
And in the forest's shade
   Our vows were plighted.
Under its loosened vest
Fluttered her little breast,
Like birds within their nest
   By the hawk frighted.

"Bright in her father's hall
Shields gleamed upon the wall,
Loud sang the minstrels all,
   Chanting his glory;
When of old Hildebrand
I asked his daughter's hand,
Mute did the ministrels stand
   To hear my story.

"While the brown ale he quaffed,
Loud then the champion laughed,
And as the wind-gusts waft
   The sea-foam brightly,
So the loud laugh of scorn,
Out of those lips unshorn,
From the deep drinking-born
   Blew the foam lightly.

"She was a Prince's child,
I but a Viking wild,
And though she blushed and smiled,
   I was discarded!

Should not the dove so white
Follow the sea-mew's flight,
Why did they leave that night
 Her nest unguarded?

"Scarce had I put to sea,
Bearing the maid with me,
Fairest of all was she
 Among the Norsemen!
When on the white sea-strand,
Waving his armed hand,
Saw we old Hildebrand,
 With twenty horsemen.

"Then launched they to the blast,
Bent like a reed each mast,
Yet we were gaining fast,
 When the wind failed us;
And with a sudden flaw
Came round the gusty Skaw,
So that our foe we saw
 Laugh as he hailed us.

"And as to catch the gale
Round veered the flapping sail,
'Death!' was the helmsman's hail,
 'Death without quarter!'
Mid-ships with iron keel
Struck we her ribs of steel;
Down her black hulk did reel
 Through the black water!

"As with his wings aslant,
Sails the fierce cormorant,
Seeking some rocky haunt,
 With his prey laden,—

So toward the open main,
Beating to sea again,
Through the wild hurricane,
    Bore I the maiden.

"Three weeks we westward bore,
And when the storm was o'er,
Cloud-like we saw the shore
    Stretching to leeward;
There for my lady's bower
Built I the lofty tower,
Which, to this very hour,
    Stands looking seaward.

"There lived we many years;
Time dried the maiden's tears;
She had forgot her fears,
    She was a mother;
Death closed her mild blue eyes,
Under that tower she lies;
Ne'er shall the sun arise
    On such another!

"Still grew my bosom then,
Still as a stagnant fen!
Hateful to me were men,
    The sunlight hateful!
In the vast forest here,
Clad in my warlike gear,
Fell I upon my spear,
    Oh, death was grateful!

"Thus, seamed with many scars,
Bursting these prison bars,
Up to its native stars
    My soul ascended!

There from the flowing bowl
Deep drinks the warrior's soul,
Skoal! to the Northland! skoal!"
Thus the tale ended.

The Elf-King

JOHANN WOLFGANG VON GOETHE

Who gallops so late through wind and wild?
It is a father with his child.
Closely he shields the boy in his arm;
He holds him fast; he folds him warm.

"My son, why hide you your face in fear?"
"See you not the Elf-King, Father dear—
The King of the Elves with his crown and train?"
"My son, 'tis only the mist and the rain."

"Thou lovely child, come go with me!
The gayest games I'll play with thee;
The brightest blooms in our garden spring;
My mother will deck you in gold like a king."

"My father, my father, can you not hear
What the Elf-King whispers bending near?"
"Hush, my child, in my arms entwined!
'Tis the withered leaves in the sighing wind."

"Beautiful boy, come go with me,
My daughters fair shall wait on thee.
They nightly dance in a fairy ring;
They'll rock thee and dance for thee and sing."

"My father, my father, see you not where
The Elf-King's daughter beckons there?"

"My son, my son, naught can I see
But the glimmer gray of the willow tree."

"I love you beautiful boy, and so
I'll force you to come if you say me no."

"He clutches me, Father!" cries out the son,
"A hurt to me the Elf-King's done."

The father shudders; he gallops amain;
He clasps the child as it moans in pain.
He reaches the courtyard in anguished dread.
Within his arms, the boy—was dead.

"How They Brought the Good News from Ghent to Aix"

ROBERT BROWNING

I sprang to the stirrup, and Joris, and he;
I gallop'd, Dirck gallop'd, we gallop'd all three;
"Good speed!" cried the watch, as the gate-bolts undrew;
"Speed!" echo'd the wall to us galloping through;
Behind shut the postern, the lights sank to rest,
And into the midnight we gallop'd abreast.

Not a word to each other; we kept the great pace
Neck by neck, stride by stride, never changing our place;
I turn'd in my saddle and made its girths tight,
Then shorten'd each stirrup, and set the pique right,
Rebuckled the cheek-strap, chain'd slacker the bit,
Nor gallop'd less steadily Roland a whit.

'Twas moonset at starting; but while we drew near
Lokeren, the cocks crew and twilight dawn'd clear;
At Boom, a great yellow star came out to see;
At Duffeld, 't was morning as plain as could be;

And from Mecheln church-steeple we heard the half-chime,
So, Joris broke silence with, "Yet there is time!"

At Aershot, up leap'd of a sudden the sun,
And against him the cattle stood black every one,
To stare thro' the mist at us galloping past,
And I saw my stout galloper Roland at last,
With resolute shoulders, each butting away
The haze, as some bluff river headland its spray:

And his low head and crest, just one sharp ear bent back
For my voice, and the other prick'd out on his track;
And one eye's black intelligence,—ever that glance
O'er its white edge at me, his own master, askance!
And the thick heavy spume-flakes which aye and anon
His fierce lips shook upwards in galloping on.

By Hasselt, Dirck groan'd; and cried Joris, "Stay spur!
Your Roos gallop'd bravely, the fault's not in her,
We'll remember at Aix"—for one heard the quick wheeze
Of her chest, saw the stretch'd neck and staggering knees,
And sunk tail, and horrible heave of the flank,
As down on her haunches she shudder'd and sank.

So, we were left galloping, Joris and I,
Past Looz and past Tongres, no cloud in the sky;
The broad sun above laugh'd a pitiless laugh,
'Neath our feet broke the brittle bright stubble like chaff;
Till over by Dalhem a dome-spire sprang white,
And "Gallop," gasp'd Joris, "for Aix is in sight!"

"How they'll greet us!"—and all in a moment his roan
Roll'd neck and croup over, lay dead as a stone;
And there was my Roland to bear the whole weight
Of the news which alone could save Aix from her fate,
With his nostrils like pits full of blood to the brim,
And with circles of red for his eye-sockets' rim.

Then I cast loose my buffcoat, each holster let fall,
Shook off both my jack-boots, let go belt and all,
Stood up in the stirrups, lean'd, patted his ear,
Call'd my Roland his pet name, my horse without peer;
Clapp'd my hands, laugh'd and sang, any noise, bad or good,
Till at length into Aix Roland gallop'd and stood.

And all I remember is—friends flocking around
As I sat with his head 'twixt my knees on the ground;
And no voice but was praising this Roland of mine,
As I pour'd down his throat our last measure of wine,
Which (the burgesses voted by common consent)
Was no more than his due who brought good news from Ghent.

An Incident of the French Camp
ROBERT BROWNING

You know, we French stormed Ratisbon:
A mile or so away,
On a little mound, Napoleon
Stood on our storming-day;
With neck out-thrust, you fancy how,
Legs wide, arms locked behind,
As if to balance the prone brow
Oppressive with its mind.

Just as perhaps he mused, "My plans
That soar, to earth may fall,
Let once my army-leader Lannes
Waver at yonder wall,—"
Out 'twixt the battery-smokes there flew
A rider, bound on bound
Full galloping; nor bridle drew
Until he reached the mound.

Then off there flung in smiling joy,
And held himself erect

By just his horse's mane, a boy:
You hardly could suspect—
(So tight he kept his lips compressed,
Scarce any blood came through)
You looked twice e'er you saw his breast
Was all but shot in two.

"Well," cried he, "Emperor, by God's grace
We've got you Ratisbon!
The Marshall's in the market-place,
And you'll be there anon
To see your flag-bird flap his vans
Where I, to heart's desire,
Perched him!" The chief's eye flashed; his plans
Soared up again like fire.

The chief's eye flashed; but presently
Softened itself, as sheathes
A film the mother eagle's eye
When her bruised eaglet breathes;
"You're wounded!" "Nay," his soldier's pride
Touched to the quick, he said:
"I'm killed, Sire!" And his chief beside,
Smiling, the boy fell dead.

The Battle of Blenheim
ROBERT SOUTHEY

It was a summer evening,
Old Kaspar's work was done,
And he before his cottage door
Was sitting in the sun;
And by him sported on the green
His little grandchild Wilhelmine.

She saw her brother Peterkin
Roll something large and round

Which he beside the rivulet
In playing there had found;
He came to ask what he had found
That was so large and smooth and round.

Old Kaspar took it from the boy
Who stood expectant by;
And then the old man shook his head,
And with a natural sigh
" 'Tis some poor fellow's skull," said he,
"Who fell in the great victory.

"I find them in the garden,
For there's many here about;
And often when I go to plow
The ploughshare turns them out.
For many thousand men," said he,
"Were slain in that great victory."

"Now tell us what 'twas all about,"
Young Peterkin he cries;
And little Wilhelmine looks up
With wonder-waiting eyes;
"Now tell us all about the war,
And what they fought each other for."

"It was the English," Kaspar cried,
"Who put the French to rout;
But what they fought each other for
I could not well make out.
But everybody said," quoth he,
"That 'twas a famous victory.

"My father lived at Blenheim then,
Yon little stream hard by;
They burnt his dwelling to the ground,
And he was forced to fly:

BALLADS AND NARRATIVE POETRY

So with his wife and child he fled,
Nor had he where to rest his head.

"With fire and sword the country round
Was wasted far and wide,
And many a childing mother then
And new-born baby died:
But things like that, you know, must be
At every famous victory.

"They say it was a shocking sight
After the field was won;
For many thousand bodies here
Lay rotting in the sun:
But things like that, you know, must be
After a famous victory.

"Great praise the Duke of Marlbro' won
And our good Prince Eugene;"
"Why, 'twas a very wicked thing!"
Said little Wilhelmine;
"Nay . . . nay . . . my little girl," quoth he,
"It was a famous victory."

"And everybody praised the Duke
Who this great fight did win."
"But what good came of it at last?"
Quoth little Peterkin:—
"Why, that I cannot tell," said he,
"But 'twas a famous victory!"

The Skater of Ghost Lake
WILLIAM ROSE BENÉT

Ghost Lake's a dark lake, a deep lake and cold:
Ice black as ebony, frostily scrolled;
Far in its shadows a faint sound whirrs;
Steep stand the sentineled deep, dark firs.

A brisk sound, a swift sound, a ring-tinkle-ring;
Flit-flit,—a shadow, with a stoop and a swing,
Flies from a shadow through the crackling cold.
Ghost Lake's a deep lake, a dark lake and old!

Leaning and leaning with a stride and a stride,
Hands locked behind him, scarf blowing wide,
Jeremy Randall skates, skates late,
Star for a candle, moon for a mate.

Black is the clear glass now that he glides,
Crisp is the whisper of long lean strides,
Swift is his swaying—but pricked ears hark.
None comes to Ghost Lake late after dark!

Cecily only—yes, it is she!
Stealing to Ghost Lake, tree after tree,
Kneeling in snow by the still lake side,
Rising with feet winged, gleaming, to glide.

Dust of the ice swirls. Here is his hand.
Brilliant his eyes burn. Now, as was planned,
Arm across arm twined, laced to his side,
Out on the dark lake lightly they glide.

Dance of the dim moon, a rhythmical reel,
A swaying, a swift tune—skurr of the steel;
Moon for a candle, maid for a mate,
Jeremy Randall skates, skates late.

Black as if lacquered the wide lake lies;
Breath as a frost-fume, eyes seek eyes;
Souls are a sword-edge tasting the cold.
Ghost Lake's a deep lake, a dark lake and old!

Far in the shadows hear faintly begin
Like a string pluck-plucked of a violin,

Muffled in mist on the lake's far bound,
Swifter and swifter, a low singing sound!

Far in the shadows and faint on the verge
Of blue cloudy moonlight, see it emerge,
Flit-flit,—a phantom, with a stoop and a swing . . .
Ah, it's a night bird, burdened of wing!

Pressed close to Jeremy, laced to his side,
Cecily Culver, dizzy you glide.
Jeremy Randall sweepingly veers
Out on the dark ice far from the piers.

"Jeremy!" "Sweetheart?" "What do you fear?"
"Nothing, my darling,—nothing is here!"
"Jeremy?" "Sweetheart?" "What do you flee?"
"Something—I know not; something I see!"

Swayed to a swift stride, brisker of pace,
Leaning and leaning, they race and they race;
Ever that whirring, that crisp sound thin
Like a string pluck-plucked of a violin;

Ever that swifter and low singing sound
Sweeping behind them, winding them round;
Gasp of their breath now that chill flakes fret;
Ice black as ebony—blacker—like jet!

Ice shooting fangs forth—sudden—like spears;
Crackling of lightning—a roar in their ears!
Shadowy, a phantom swerves off from its prey . . .
No, it's a night bird flit-flits away!

Low-winging moth-owl, home to your sleep!
Ghost Lake's a still lake, a cold lake and deep.
Faint in its shadows a far sound whirrs.
Black stand the ranks of its sentinel firs.

Skipper Ireson's Ride

JOHN GREENLEAF WHITTIER

Of all the rides since the birth of time,
Told in story or sung in rhyme,—
On Apuleius's Golden Ass,
Or one-eyed Calender's horse of brass,
Witch astride of a human back,
Islam's prophet on Al-Borak,—
The strangest ride that ever was sped
Was Ireson's out from Marblehead!
　Old Floyd Ireson, for his hard heart,
　Tarred and feathered and carried in a cart
　By the women of Marblehead!

Body of turkey, head of owl,
Wings a-droop like a rained-on fowl,
Feathered and ruffled in every part,
Skipper Ireson stood in the cart.
Scores of women, old and young,
Strong of muscle, and glib of tongue,
Pushed and pulled up the rocky lane,
Shouting and singing the shrill refrain:
　"Here's Flud Oirson, fur his horrd horrt
　Torr'd an' futherr'd an' corr'd in a corrt
　By the women o' Morble'ead!"

Wrinkled scolds with hands on hips,
Girls in bloom of cheek and lips,
Wild-eyed, free-limbed, such as chase
Bacchus round some antique vase,
Brief of skirt, with ankles bare,
Loose of kerchief and loose of hair,
With conch-shells blowing and fish-horns' twang,
Over and over the Maenads sang:

SKIPPER IRESON'S RIDE: *Apuleius's Golden Ass = The Golden Ass,* a
book by Apuleius, 2nd century A.D.; about a man transformed into a
mule

"Here's Flud Oirson, fur his horrd horrt,
Torr'd an' futherr'd an' corr'd in a corrt
By the women o' Morble'ead!"

Small pity for him!—He sailed away
From a leaking ship in Chaleur Bay,—
Sailed away from a sinking wreck,
With his own town's-people on her deck!
"Lay by! Lay by!" they called to him.
Back he answered, "Sink or swim!
Brag of your catch of fish again!"
And off he sailed through the fog and rain.
   Old Floyd Ireson, for his hard heart,
   Tarred and feathered and carried in a cart
   By the women of Marblehead!

Fathoms deep in dark Chaleur
That wreck shall lie forevermore.
Mother and sister, wife and maid,
Looked from the rocks of Marblehead
Over the moaning and rainy sea,—
Looked for the coming that might not be!
What did the winds and the sea birds say
Of the cruel captain who sailed away?—
   Old Floyd Ireson, for his hard heart,
   Tarred and feathered and carried in a cart
   By the women of Marblehead.

Through the street, on either side,
Up flew windows, doors swung wide;
Sharp-tongued spinsters, old wives gray,
Treble lent the fish-horn's bray.
Sea-worn grandsires, cripple-bound,
Hulks of old sailors run aground,
Shook head, and fist, and hat, and cane,
And cracked with curses the hoarse refrain:
   "Here's Flud Oirson, fur his horrd horrt,

Torr'd an' futherr'd an' corr'd in a corrt
By the women o' Morble'ead!"

Sweetly along the Salem road
Bloom of orchard and lilac showed.
Little the wicked skipper knew
Of the fields so green and the sky so blue.
Riding there in his sorry trim,
Like an Indian idol glum and grim,
Scarcely he seemed the sound to hear
Of voices shouting far and near:
    "Here's Flud Oirson, fur his horrd horrt,
    Torr'd an' futherr'd an' corr'd in a corrt
    By the women o' Morble'ead!"

"Hear me, neighbors!" at last he cried,—
"What to me is this noisy ride?
What is the shame that clothes the skin
To the nameless horror that lives within?
Waking or sleeping, I see a wreck,
And hear a cry from a reeling deck!
Hate me and curse me,—I only dread
The hand of God and the face of the dead!"
    Said Old Floyd Ireson, for his hard heart,
    Tarred and feathered and carried in a cart
    By the women of Marblehead!

Then the wife of the skipper lost at sea
Said, "God has touched him! why should we?"
Said an old wife mourning her only son,
"Cut the rogue's tether and let him run!"
So with soft relentings and crude excuse,
Half scorn, half pity, they cut him loose,
And gave him a cloak to hide him in,
    Poor Floyd Ireson, for his hard heart,
    Tarred and feathered and carried in a cart
    By the women of Marblehead!

Jim Bludso, of the Prairie Belle

JOHN HAY

Wall, no! I can't tell whar he lives,
Because he don't live, you see;
Leastways, he's got out of the habit
Of livin' like you and me.
Whar have you been for the last three year
That you haven't heard folks tell
How Jimmy Bludso passed in his checks
The night of the Prairie Bell?

He weren't no saint,—them engineers
Is all pretty much alike,—
One wife in Natchez-under-the-Hill
And another one here, in Pike;
A keerless man in his talk, was Jim
And an awkward hand in a row,
But he never flunked, and he never lied,—
I reckon he never knowed how.

And this was all the religion he had,—
To treat his engine well;
Never be passed on the river;
To mind the pilot's bell;
And if the Prairie Belle took fire,—
A thousand times he swore,
He'd hold her nozzle agin the bank
Till the last soul got ashore.

All boats has their day on the Mississip,
And her day come at last,—
The Movastar was a better boat,
But the Belle she wouldn't be passed.
And so she come tearin' along that night—
The oldest craft on the line—
With a Negro squat on her safety valve,
And her furnace crammed, rosin and pine.

JIM BLUDSO, OF THE PRAIRIE BELLE: *galoot* = slang for a disreputable looking man

The fire bust out as she clared the bar,
And burnt a hole in the night,
And quick as a flash she turned, and made
For that willer-bank on the right.
There was runnin' and cursin', but Jim yelled out,
Over all the infernal roar,
"I'll hold her nozzle agin the bank
Till the last galoot's ashore."

Through the hot, black breath of the burnin' boat
Jim Bludso's voice was heard,
And they all had trust in his cussedness,
And knowed he would keep his word.
And, sure's you're born, they all got off
Afore the smokestacks fell,—
And Bludso's ghost went up alone
In the smoke of the Prairie Belle.

He weren't no saint,—but at jedgment
I'd run my chance with Jim,
'Longside of some pious gentlemen
That wouldn't shook hands with him.
He seen his duty, a dead-sure thing,—
And went for it thar and then;
And Christ ain't a going to be too hard
On a man that died for men.

The Ballad of East and West

RUDYARD KIPLING

Oh, East is East, and West is West, and never the twain shall
    meet,
Till Earth and Sky stand presently at God's great Judgment Seat;
But there is neither East nor West, Border, nor Breed, nor Birth,
When two strong men stand face to face, though they come from
    the ends of the earth.

THE BALLAD OF EAST AND WEST: *Guides* = trusted native troops who
served with the British; *kite* = a small hawk with long narrow wings;
ling = heather

Kamal is out with twenty men to raise the Border side,
And he has lifted the Colonel's mare that is the Colonel's pride.
He has lifted her out of the stable-door between the dawn and
    the day,
And turned the calkins upon her feet, and ridden her far away.
Then up and spoke the colonel's son that led a troop of the
    Guides:
"Is there never a man of all my men can say where Kamal hides?"
Then up and spoke the Mohammed Khan, the son of Ressaldar:
"If you know the track of the morning mist, ye know where his
    pickets are.
At dusk he harries the Abazai—at dawn he is into Bonair,
But he must go by Fort Bukloh to his own place to fare.
So if ye gallop to Fort Bukloh as fast as a bird can fly,
By the favor of God ye may cut him off ere he win to the tongue
    of Jagai.
But if he be past the Tongue of Jagai, right swiftly turn ye then,
For the length and the breadth of that grisly plain is sown with
    Kamal's men.
There is rock to the left, and rock to the right, and low lean thorn
    between,
And ye may hear a breech-bolt snick where never a man is seen."
The Colonel's son has taken horse, and a raw rough dun was
    he,
With a mouth of a bell and a heart of Hell and the head of a
    gallows-tree.
The Colonel's son to the Fort has won, they bid him stay to eat—
Who rides at the tail of a Border thief, he sits not long at his meat.
He's up and away from Fort Bukloh as fast as he can fly,
Till he was aware of his father's mare in the gut of the Tongue of
    Jagai,
Till he was aware of his father's mare with Kamal upon her back,
And when he could spy the white of her eye, he made the pistol
    crack,
He has fired once, he has fired twice, but the whistling ball went
    wide.

"Ye shoot like a soldier," Kamal said. "Show now if ye can ride!"
It's up and over the Tongue of Jagai, as blown dust-devils go,
The dun he fled like a stag of ten, but the mare like a barren doe.
The dun he leaned against the bit and slugged his head above,
But the red mare played with the snaffle bars, as a maiden plays
  with a glove.
There was rock to the left and rock to the right, and the low lean
  thorn between,
And thrice he heard a breech-bolt snick tho' never a man was
  seen.
They have ridden the low moon out of the sky, their hoofs drum
  up the dawn,
The dun he went like a wounded bull, but the mare like a new-
  roused fawn.
The dun he fell at the watercourse—in a woeful heap fell he,
And Kamal has turned the red mare back, and pulled the rider
  free.
He has knocked the pistol out of his hand—small room was there
  to strive,
" 'Twas only by favor of mine," quoth he, "ye rode so long alive:
There was not a rock for twenty mile, there was not a clump of
  tree,
But covered a man of my own men with a rifle cocked on his
  knee.
If I had raised my bridle hand, as I have held it low,
If I had bowed my head on my breast, as I have held it high,
The kite that whistles above us now were gorged till she could not
  fly."
Lightly answered the Colonel's son: "Do good to bird and beast,
But count who come for the broken meats before thou makest a
  feast.
If there should follow a thousand swords to carry my bones away,
Belike the price of a jackal's meal were more than a thief could
  pay.
They will feed their horse on the standing crop, their men on the
  garnered grain,

The thatch of the byres will serve their fires when all the cattle
 are slain.
But if thou thinkest the price be fair,—thy brethren wait to sup,
The hound is kin to the jackal-spawn,—howl, dog, and call them
 up!
And if thou thinkest the price be high, in steer and gear and stack,
Give me my father's mare again, and I'll fight my own way back!"
Kamal has gripped him by the hand and set him upon his feet.
"No talk shall be of dogs," said he, "when wold and gray wolf
 meet.
May I eat dirt if thou hast hurt of me in deed or breath;
What dam of lances brought thee forth to jest at the dawn with
 Death?"
Lightly answered the Colonel's son: "I hold by the blood of my
 clan:
Take up the mare for my father's gift—by God, she has carried a
 man!"
The red mare ran to the Colonel's son, and nuzzled against his
 breast;
"We be two strong men," said Kamal then, "but she loveth the
 younger best.
So she shall go with a lifter's dower, my turquoise-studded rein,
My 'broidered saddle and saddlecloth, and silver stirrups twain."
The Colonel's son a pistol drew, and held it muzzle end,
"Ye have taken the one from a foe," said he. "Will ye take the
 mate from a friend?"
"A gift for a gift," said Kamal straight; "a limb for the risk of a
 limb.
Thy father has sent his son to me, I'll send my son to him!"
With that he whistled his only son, that dropped from a mountain
 crest—
He trod the ling like a buck in spring, and he looked like a lance
 in rest.
"Now here is thy master," Kamal said, "who leads a troop of the
 Guides,
And thou must ride at his left side as shield on shoulder rides.

          AN ANTHOLOGY OF POEMS

Till Death or I cut loose the tie, at camp and board and bed,
Thy life is his—thy fate it is to guard him with thy head.
So, thou must eat the White Queen's meat, and all her foes are thine,
And thou must harry thy father's hold for the peace of the Border-line.
And thou must make a trooper tough and hack thy way to power—
Belike they will raise thee to Ressaldar when I am hanged in Peshawur!"

They have looked each other between the eyes, and there have found no fault.
They have taken the Oath of the Brother-in-Blood on leavened bread and salt;
They have taken the Oath of the Brother-in-Blood on fire and fresh-cut sod,
On the hilt and the haft of the Khyber knife, and the Wondrous Names of God.
The Colonel's son he rides the mare and Kamal's boy the dun,
And two have come back to Fort Bukloh where there went forth but one.
And when they drew to the Quarter-Guard, full twenty swords flew clear—
There was not a man but carried his feud with the blood of a mountaineer.
"Ha' done! ha' done!" said the Colonel's son. "Put up the steel at your sides!
Last night ye struck at a Border thief—tonight 'tis a man of the Guides!"

Oh, East is East, and West is West, and never the twain shall meet,
Till Earth and Sky stand presently at God's great Judgment Seat;
But there is neither East or West, Border, nor Bred, nor Birth,
When two strong men stand face to face, though they come from the ends of the earth!

Danny Deever

RUDYARD KIPLING

"What are the bugles blowin' for?" said Files-on-Parade.
"To turn you out, to turn you out," the Color Sergeant said.
"What makes you look so white, so white?" said Files-on-Parade.
"I'm dreadin' what I've got to watch," the Color Sergeant said.
　For they're hangin' Danny Deever, you can 'ear the dead march
　　play,
　The regiment's in 'ollow square—they're hangin' him today;
　They've taken of his buttons off an' cut his stripes away,
　An' they're hangin' Danny Deever in the mornin'.

"What makes the rear-rank breathe so 'ard?" said Files-on-Parade.
"It's bitter cold, it's bitter cold," the Color Sergeant said.
"What makes that front-rank man fall down?" says Files-on-
　Parade.
"A touch o' sun, a touch o' sun," the Color Sergeant said.
　They are hangin' Danny Deever, they are marchin' of 'im
　　round,
　They 'ave 'alted Danny Deever by 'is coffin on the ground;
　An' 'e'll swing in 'arf a minute for a sneakin', shootin' hound—
　O they're hangin' Danny Deever in the mornin'!

" 'Is cot was right-'and cot to mine," said Files-on-Parade.
" 'E's sleepin' out an' far tonight," the Color Sergeant said.
"I've drunk 'is beer a score o' times," said Files-on-Parade.
" 'E's drinkin' bitter beer alone," the Color Sergeant said.
　They are hangin' Danny Deever, you must mark 'im to 'is place,
　For 'e shot a comrade sleepin'—you must look 'im in the face;
　Nine 'undred of 'is county an' the regiment's disgrace,
　While they're hangin' Danny Deever in the mornin'.

"What's that so black agin the sun?" said Files-on-Parade.
"It's Danny fightin' 'ard for life," the Color Sergeant said.
"What's that that whimpers over'ead?" said Files-on-Parade.
"It's Danny's soul that's passin' now," the Color Sergeant said.

　　　　　　　　　　　　AN ANTHOLOGY OF POEMS

For they're done with Danny Deever, you can 'ear the quick-
    step play,
The regiment's in column, an' they're marchin' us away;
Ho! the young recruits are shakin', an' they'll want their beer
    today,
After hangin' Danny Deever in the mornin'.

The Highwayman

ALFRED NOYES

Part One

The wind was a torrent of darkness among the gusty trees,
The moon was a ghostly galleon tossed upon cloudy seas,
The road was a ribbon of moonlight over the purple moor,
And the highwayman came riding—
    Riding—riding—
The highwayman came riding, up to the old inn-door.

He'd a French cocked-hat on his forehead, a bunch of lace at his
    chin,
A coat of the claret velvet, and breeches of brown doe-skin;
They fitted with never a wrinkle: his boots were up to the thigh!
And he rode with a jewelled twinkle,
    His pistol butts a-twinkle,
His rapier hilt a-twinkle, under the jewelled sky.

Over the cobbles he clattered and clashed in the dark inn-yard,
And he tapped with his whip on the shutters, but all was locked
    and barred;
He whistled a tune to the window, and who should be waiting
    there
But the landlord's black-eyed daughter,
    Bess, the landlord's daughter,
Plaiting a dark red love-knot into her long black hair.

And dark in the dark old inn-yard a stable-wicket creaked
Where Tim the ostler listened; his face was white and peaked;
His eyes were hollows of madness, his hair like mouldy hay,
But he loved the landlord's daughter,
   The landlord's red-lipped daughter.
Dumb as a dog he listened, and he heard the robber say—

"One kiss, my bonny sweetheart, I'm after a prize to-night,
But I shall be back with the yellow gold before the morning light;
Yet, if they press me sharply, and harry me through the day,
Then look for me by moonlight,
   Watch for me by moonlight,
I'll come to thee by moonlight, though hell should bar the way."

He rose upright in the stirrups; he scarce could reach her hand,
But she loosed her hair i' the casement! His face burnt like a
      brand
As the black cascade of perfume came tumbling over his breast;
And he kissed its waves in the moonlight,
   (Oh, sweet black waves in the moonlight!)
Then he tugged at his rein in the moonlight, and galloped away
   to the West.

Part Two

He did not come in the dawning; he did not come at noon;
And out o' the tawny sunset, before the rise o' the moon,
When the road was a gipsy's ribbon, looping the purple moor,
A red-coat troop came marching—
   Marching—marching—
King George's men came marching, up to the old inn-door.

They said no word to the landlord, they drank his ale instead,
But they gagged his daughter and bound her to the foot of her
      narrow bed;
Two of them knelt at her casement, with muskets at their side!

There was death at every window;
    And hell at one dark window;
For Bess could see, through her casement, the road that he would
    ride.

They had tied her up to attention, with many a sniggering jest;
They had bound a musket beside her, with the barrel beneath her
    breast!
"Now keep good watch!" and they kissed her. She heard the dead
    man say—
Look for me by moonlight;
    Watch for me by moonlight;
I'll come to thee by moonlight, though hell should bar the way!

She twisted her hands behind her; but all the knots held good!
She writhed her hands till her fingers were wet with sweat or
    blood!
They stretched and strained in the darkness, and the hours
    crawled by like years,
Till, now, on the stroke of midnight,
    Cold, on the stroke of midnight,
The tip of one finger touched it! The trigger at least was hers!

The tip of one finger touched it; she strove no more for the rest!
Up, she stood up to attention, with the barrel beneath her breast,
She would not risk their hearing; she would not strive again;
For the road lay bare in the moonlight;
    Blank and bare in the moonlight;
And the blood of her veins in the moonlight throbbed to her love's
    refrain.

Tlot-tlot; tlot-tlot! Had they heard it? The horse-hoofs ringing
    clear;
Tlot-tlot, tlot-tlot, in the distance? Were they deaf that they did
    not hear?
Down the ribbon of moonlight, over the brow of the hill,

The highwayman came riding,
   Riding, riding!
The red-coats looked to their priming! She stood up straight and
      still!

Tlot-tlot, in the frosty silence! Tlot-tlot, in the echoing night!
Nearer he came and nearer! Her face was like a light!
Her eyes grew wide for a moment; she drew one last deep breath,
Then her fingers moved in the moonlight,
   Her musket shattered the moonlight,
Shattered her breast in the moonlight and warned him—with her
      death.

He turned; he spurred to the Westward; he did not know who
      stood
Bowed with her head o'er the musket, drenched with her own
      red blood!
Not till the dawn he heard it, his face grew grey to hear
How Bess, the landlord's daughter,
   The landlord's black-eyed daughter,
Had watched for her love in the moonlight, and died in the dark-
      ness there.

Back, he spurred like a madman, shrieking a curse to the sky,
With the white road smoking behind him and rapier brandished
      high!
Blood-red were his spurs i' the golden noon; wine-red was his
      velvet coat,
When they shot him down on the highway,
   Down like a dog on the highway,
And he lay in his blood on the highway, with the bunch of lace
      at his throat.

And still of a winter's night, they say, when the wind is in the
      trees,
When the moon is a ghostly galleon tossed upon cloudy seas,

When the road is a ribbon of moonlight over the purple moor,
A highwayman comes riding—
    Riding—riding—
A highwayman comes riding, up to the old inn-door.

Over the cobbles he clatters and clangs in the dark inn-yard;
He taps with his whip on the shutters, but all is locked and
        barred;
He whistles a tune to the window, and who should be waiting
        there
But the landlord's black-eyed daughter,
    Bess, the landlord's daughter,
Plaiting a dark red love-knot into her long black hair.

The Listeners

WALTER DE LA MARE

"Is there anybody there?" said the Traveller,
Knocking on the moonlit door;
And his horse in the silence champed the grasses
Of the forest's ferny floor.
And a bird flew up out of the turret,
Above the Traveller's head:
And he smote upon the door again a second time;
"Is anybody there?" he said.
But no one descended to the Traveller;
No head from the leaf-fringed sill
Leaned over and looked into his grey eyes,
Where he stood perplexed and still.
But only a host of phantom listeners
That stood in the lone house then
Stood listening in the quiet of the moonlight
To that voice from the world of men:
Stood thronging the faint moonbeams on the dark stair,

217   BALLADS AND NARRATIVE POETRY

That goes down to the empty hall,
Hearkening in an air stirred and shaken
By the lonely Traveller's call.
And he felt in his heart their strangeness,
Their stillness answering his cry
While his horse moved, cropping the dark turf,
'Neath the starred and leafy sky;
For he suddenly smote on the door, even
Louder, and lifted his head:—
"Tell them I came and no one answered,
That I kept my word," he said.
Never the least stir made the listeners,
Though every word he spake
Fell echoing through the shadowiness of the still house
From the one man left awake:
Ay, they heard his foot on the stirrup,
And the sound of iron on stone,
And how the silence surged softly backward,
When the plunging hoofs were gone.

Ballad: O What Is That Sound?

W. H. AUDEN

O what is that sound which so thrills the ear
Down in the valley drumming, drumming?
Only the scarlet soldiers, dear,
            The soldiers coming.

O what is that light I see flashing so clear
Over the distance brightly, brightly?
Only the sun on their weapons, dear,
            As they step lightly.

O what are they doing with all that gear;
What are they doing this morning, this morning?
Only their usual maneuvers, dear,
            Or perhaps a warning.

O why have they left the road down there;
Why are they suddenly wheeling, wheeling?
Perhaps a change in the orders, dear;
       Why are you kneeling?

O haven't they stopped for the doctor's care;
Haven't they reined their horses, their horses?
Why, they are none of them wounded, dear,
       None of these forces.

O is it the parson they want with white hair;
Is it the parson, is it, is it?
No, they are passing his gateway, dear,
       Without a visit.

O it must be the farmer who lives so near;
It must be the farmer so cunning, so cunning?
They have passed the farm already, dear,
       . And now they are running.

O where are you going? Stay with me here!
Were the vows you swore me deceiving, deceiving?
No, I promised to love you, dear,
       But I must be leaving.

O it's broken the lock and splintered the door,
O it's the gate where they're turning, turning;
Their feet are heavy on the floor
       And their eyes are burning.

LIGHT AND HUMOROUS VERSE

Imagine a world without humor! Imagine a world with no enter-
tainment, no enjoyment, no quick laughter to provide relief and
distraction from the serious concerns of everyday life. Without
humor, life would be intolerable. In moments of discouragement
or grief, in the darkest tragedies, in times of crisis, humor relieves
tensions and lightens burdens. It restores a true sense of propor-
tion. It is no wonder that every nation has loved its finest humor-
ists.

But humor does much more than provide relief and distraction.
Mark Twain called humor mankind's greatest moral instrument;
he said that humor was the best means to reveal the hypocrisy,
the weaknesses, and the foolishness that fill the world. Humor is,
as one poet put it, "An ally of uncompromising honesty." Many of
the following poems will give you uncomplicated amusement,
but many others are comments on our civilization. Behind the
humor there will often be a serious idea.

Elegy on the Death of a Mad Dog
OLIVER GOLDSMITH

> Good people all, of every sort,
> Give ear unto my song;
> And if you find it wondrous short,
> It cannot hold you long.

> In Islington there was a man
> Of whom the world might say
> That still a godly race he ran,
> Whene'er he went to pray.

A kind and gentle heart he had,
To comfort friend and foes;
The naked every day he clad,
When he put on his clothes.

And in that town a dog was found,
As many dogs there be,
Both mongrel, puppy, whelp, and hound
And cur of low degree.

This dog and man at first were friends;
But when a pique began,
The dog to gain his private ends,
Went mad and bit the man.

Around from all the neighboring streets
The wondering people ran,
And swore the dog had lost his wits,
To bite so good a man.

The wound it seemed both sore and sad
To every Christian eye;
And while they swore the dog was mad,
They swore the man would die.

But soon a wonder came to light,
That showed the rogues they lied;
The man recovered of the bite;
The dog it was that died.

A Fable

RALPH WALDO EMERSON

The mountain and the squirrel
Had a quarrel;
And the former called the latter "Little Prig."
Bun replied,

"You are doubtless very big;
But all sorts of things and weather
Must be taken in together
To make up a year
And a sphere.
And I think it's no disgrace
To occupy my place.
If I'm not so large as you,
You are not half so small as I,
And not half so spry.
I'll not deny you make
A very pretty squirrel track;
Talents differ: all is well and wisely put;
If I cannot carry forests on my back,
Neither can you crack a nut."

"Ah, Are You Digging on My Grave?"

THOMAS HARDY

"Ah, are you digging on my grave,
My loved one?—planting rue?"
—"No: yesterday he went to wed
One of the highest wealth has bred.
'It cannot hurt her now,' he said,
'That I should not be true.' "

"Then who is digging on my grave?
My nearest dearest kin?"
—"Ah, no: they sit and think, 'What use!
What good will planting flowers produce?
No tendance of her mound can loose
Her spirits from Death's gin.' "

"But someone digs upon my grave?
My enemy?—prodding sly?"
—"Nay: when she heard you had passed the Gate

That shuts on all flesh soon or late,
She thought you no more worth her hate,
And cares not where you lie."

"Then who is digging on my grave?
Say—since I have not guessed!"
—"O it is I, my mistress dear,
Your little dog, who still lives near,
And much I hope my movements here
Have not disturbed your rest?"

"Ah, yes! *You* dig upon my grave . . .
Why flashed it not on me
That one true heart was left behind!
What feeling do we ever find
To equal among human kind
A dog's fidelity!"

"Mistress, I dug upon your grave
To bury a bone, in case
I should be hungry near this spot
When passing on my daily trot.
I am sorry, but I quite forgot
It was your resting place."

The Sloth

THEODORE ROETHKE

In moving-slow he has no peer.
You ask him something in his ear;
He thinks about it for a Year;

And then, before he says a Word
There, upside down (unlike a bird)
He will assume that you have heard—

LIGHT AND HUMOROUS VERSE

A most EX-as-per-at-ing Lug.
But should you call his manner Smug,
He'll sigh and give his branch a Hug;

Then off again to Sleep he goes,
Still swaying gently by his Toes,
And you just know he knows he knows.

To a Louse
(*On Seeing One on a Lady's Bonnet at Church*)
ROBERT BURNS

Ha! wh'are ye gaun, ye crowlin' ferlie!
Your impudence protects you sairly;
I canna say but ye strunt rarely,
Owre gauze and lace;
Though faith! I fear ye dine but sparely
On sic a place.

Ye ugly, creepin', blastit wonner,
Detested, shunned by saunt an' sinner!
How dare ye set your fit upon her,
Sae fine a lady?
Gae somewhere else, and seek your dinner
On some poor body.

Swith, in some beggar's haffet squattle;
There ye may creep, and sprawl, and sprattle
Wi'ther kindred jumping cattle,
In shoals and nations;
Where horn nor bane ne'er dare unsettle
Your thick plantations.

TO A LOUSE: *crowlin' ferlie* = crawling wonder; *sairly* = greatly; *strunt* = strut; *blastit wonner* = blasted wonder; *fit* = foot; *Swith ... squattle* = Depart! Sprawl in some beggar's temple; *sprattle* = struggle; *horn nor bane* = comb nor poison; *onie grozet* = any gooseberry; *rozet* = rosin; *Wad ... droddum* = Put an end to you; *wyliecoat* = flannel vest; *Lunardi* = a bonnet named for an aeronaut of the day

Now haud ye there, ye're out o' sight,
Below the fatt'rels, snug an' tight;
Na, faith ye yet! ye'll no be right
Till ye've got on it,
The very topmost tow'ring height
O' Miss's bonnet.

My sooth! right bauld ye set your nose out,
As plump and gray as onie grozet;
O for some rank mercurial rozet,
Or fell red smeddum!
I'd gie you sic a hearty dose o't,
Wad dress your drodum!

I wad na been surprised to spy
You on an auld wife's flannen toy;
Or aiblins some bit duddie boy,
On's wyliecoat;
But Miss's fine Lunardi! fie,
How daur ye do 't?

O Jenny, dinna toss your head,
An' set your beauties a' abread!
Ye little ken what cursed speed
The blastie's makin'!
Thae winks and finger ends, I dread,
Are notice takin'!

O wad some Pow'r the giftie gie us
To see oursels as ithers see us!
It wad frae mony a blunder free us!
And foolish notion:
What airs in dress an' gait wad lea'e us,
And e'en devotion!

The Firefly

OGDEN NASH

The firefly's flame
Is something for which science has no name.
I can think of nothing eerier
Than flying around with an unidentified glow on a person's
posteerier.

The Sea-Gull

OGDEN NASH

Hark to the whimper of the sea-gull;
He weeps because he's not an ea-gull.
Suppose you were, you silly sea-gull,
Could you explain it to your she-gull?

Hem and Haw

BLISS CARMAN

Hem and Haw were the sons of sin,
Created to shally and shirk;
Hem lay 'round and Haw looked on
While God did all the work.

Hem was a fogy, and Haw was a prig,
For both had the dull, dull mind;
And whenever they found a thing to do,
They yammered and went it blind.

Hem was the father of bigots and bores;
As the sands of the sea were they.
And Haw was the father of all the tribe
Who criticize today.

But God was an artist from the first,
And knew what he was about;
While over his shoulder sneered these two,
And advised him to rub it out.

They prophesied ruin ere man was made;
"Such folly must surely fail!"
And when he was done, "Do you think, my Lord,
He's better without a tail?"

And still in the honest working world,
With posture and hint and smirk,
These sons of the devil are standing by
While man does all the work.

They balk endeavor and baffle reform,
In the sacred name of law;
And over the quavering voice of Hem
Is the droning voice of Haw.

The World State

G. K. CHESTERTON

Oh, how I love Humanity,
    With love so pure and pringlish,
And how I hate the horrid French,
    Who never will be English!

The International Idea,
    The largest and the clearest,
Is welding all the nations now,
    Except the one that's nearest.

This compromise has long been known,
    This scheme of partial pardons,
In ethical societies
    And small suburban gardens—

The villas and the chapels where
I learned with little labor
The way to love my fellow man
And hate my next-door neighbor.

Inventory

DOROTHY PARKER

Four be the things I am wiser to know:
Idleness, sorrow, a friend, and a foe.

Four be the things I'd been better without:
Love, curiosity, freckles, and doubt.

Three be the things I shall never attain:
Envy, content, and sufficient champagne.

Three be the things I shall have till I die:
Laughter and hope and a sock in the eye.

Jabberwocky

LEWIS CARROLL

'Twas brillig, and the slithy toves
Did gyre and gimble in the wabe:
All mimsy were the borogroves,
And the mome raths outgrabe.

"Beware the Jabbervock, my son!
The jaws that bite, the claws that catch!
Beware the Jubjub bird, and shun
The frumious Bandersnatch!"

He took his vorpal sword in hand;
Long time the manxome foe he sought—
So rested he by the Tumtum tree,
And stood awhile in thought.

And, as in uffish thought he stood,
The Jabberwock, with eyes of flame,
Came whiffling through the tulgey wood,
And burbled as it came!

One, two! One, two! And through and through
The vorpal blade went snicker-snack!
He left it dead, and with its head
He went galumphing back.

"And hast thou slain the Jabberwock?
Come to my arms, my beamish boy!
O frabjous day! Callooh, Callay!"
He chortled in his joy.

'Twas brillig, and the slithy toves
Did gyre and gimble in the wabe:
All mimsy were the borogroves,
And the mome raths outgrabe.

Fire and Ice
ROBERT FROST

Some say the world will end in fire,
Some say in ice.
From what I've tasted of desire
I hold with those who favor fire.
But if I had to perish twice,
I think I know enough of hate
To say that for destruction ice
Is also great
And would suffice.

Frostbite

CONRAD AIKEN

> Some say the world will end by Fire
> And some by Frost
> > By verse of ice, or vice of verser,
> > (God only knows which were the worser!)
> But, anyway, the world well lost.

Unfortunate Coincidence

DOROTHY PARKER

> By the time you swear you're his,
> Shivering and sighing,
> And he vows his passion is
> Infinite, undying—
> Lady, make a note of this:
> One of you is lying.

The Actress

DOROTHY PARKER

> Her name, cut clear upon this marble cross,
> Shines, as it shone when she was still on earth;
> While tenderly the mild, agreeable moss
> Obscures the figures of her date of birth.

An Austrian Army

ALARIC A. WATTS

> An Austrian army awfully array'd
> Boldly by battery besieged Belgrade.
> Cossack commanders cannonading come
> Dealing destruction's devastating doom:
> Every endeavor engineers essay,
> For fame, for fortune fighting—furious fray!
> Generals 'gainst generals grapple, gracious God!
> How heaven honors heroic hardihood!

Infuriate—indiscriminate in ill—
Kinsmen kill kindred—kindred kinsmen kill:
Labor low levels loftiest, longest lines,
Men march 'mid mounds, 'mid moles, 'mid murderous mines;
Now noisy noxious numbers notice nought
Of outward obstacles, opposing ought—
Poor patriots—partly purchased—partly press'd,
Quite quaking, quickly "Quarter! Quarter!" quest:
Reason returns, religious right redounds,
Suwarrow stops such sanguinary sounds.
Truce to thee, Turkey, triumph to thy train,
Unwise, unjust, unmerciful Ukraine!
Vanish, vain victory! Vanish, victory vain!
Why wish we warfare? Wherefore welcome were
Xerxes, Ximenes, Xanthus, Xavier?
Yield, yield, ye youths, ye yeomen, yield your yell:
Zeno's, Zimmermann's, Zoroaster's zeal,
Again attract; arts against arms appeal!

The Ant

RICHARD ARMOUR

The ant, a prodigy of strength,
Lifts objects twice his weight and length
And never stops or sighs or glowers
Because it's after working hours.
Though underground, he bears the onus
And peril without thought of bonus,
And never once is heard to mention
Retiring on a tax-free pension.
Nor does he frown or look askance
At other, lighter-burdened ants.
Not one to bicker, blame, or sob,
Not angling for a better job,
The ant has but one flaw I see,
To wit, he doesn't work for me.

The Honey Bee
DON MARQUIS

The honey bee is sad and cross
and wicked as a weasel
and when she perches on you boss
she leaves a little measle.

The Termite
OGDEN NASH

Some primal termite knocked on wood
And tasted it, and found it good,
And that is why your Cousin May
Fell through the parlor floor today.

On the Vanity of Earthly Greatness
ARTHUR GUITERMAN

The tusks that clashed in mighty brawls
Of mastodons, are billiard balls.

The sword of Charlemagne the Just
Is ferric oxide, known as rust.

The grizzly bear whose potent hug
Was feared by all, is now a rug.

Great Caesar's bust is on the shelf,
And I don't feel so well myself.

The Difference
BENJAMIN FRANKLIN

When man and woman die, as poets sung,
His heart's the last part moves,—her last, the tongue.

Conversation in Avila

PHYLLIS MC GINLEY

Teresa was God's familiar. She often spoke
To Him informally,
As if together they shared some heavenly joke.
Once, watching stormily
Her heart's ambitions wither to odds and ends,
With all to start anew,
She cried, "If this is the way You treat Your friends,
No wonder You have so few!"

There is no perfect record standing by
Of God's reply.

The Perforated Spirit

MORRIS BISHOP

The fellows up in Personnel,
They have a set of cards on me.
The sprinkled perforations tell
My individuality.

And what am I? I am a chart
Upon the cards of IBM;
The secret places of the heart
Have little secrecy for them.

It matters not how I may prate,
They punch with punishments my scroll.
The files are masters of my fate,
They are the captains of my soul.

THE PERFORATED SPIRIT: *Personnel* = the personnel department; *They are the captains of my soul* = see page 15

LIGHT AND HUMOROUS VERSE

Monday my brain began to buzz;
I was in agony all night.
I found out what the trouble was:
They had my paper clip too tight.

Résumé

DOROTHY PARKER

Razors pain you;
Rivers are damp;
Acids stain you;
And drugs cause cramp.
Guns aren't lawful;
Nooses give;
Gas smells awful;
You might as well live.

Money

RICHARD ARMOUR

Workers earn it,
Spendthrifts burn it,
Bankers lend it,
Women spend it,
Forgers fake it,
Taxes take it,
Dying leave it,
Heirs receive it,
Thrifty save it,
Misers crave it,
Robbers seize it,
Rich increase it,
Gamblers lose it . . .
I could use it.

When I Was a Lad

W. S. GILBERT

When I was a lad I served a term
As office boy to an attorney's firm.
I cleaned the windows and I swept the floor,
And I polished up the handle of the big front door.
CHORUS: He polished up the handle of the big front door.

I polished up the handle so carefullee
That now I am the ruler of the Queen's Navee!
CHORUS: He polished up the handle so carefullee
        That now he is the ruler of the Queen's Navee!

As office boy I made such a mark
That they gave me the post of a junior clerk.
I served the writs with a smile so bland,
And I copied all the letters in a big round hand.

I copied all the letters in a hand so free
That now I am the ruler of the Queen's Navee!

In serving writs I made such a name
That an articled clerk I soon became;
I wore clean collars and a brand-new suit
For the pass examination at the Institute.

That pass examination did so well for me
That now I am the ruler of the Queen's Navee!

Of legal knowledge I acquired such a grip
That they took me into the partnership.
And that junior partnership, I ween,
Was the only ship that I ever had seen.

But that kind of ship so suited me
That now I am the ruler of the Queen's Navee!

I grew so rich that I was sent
By a pocket borough into Parliament.
I always voted at my party's call,
And I never thought of thinking for myself at all.

I thought so little they rewarded me
By making me the ruler of the Queen's Navee!

Now landsmen all, whoever you may be,
If you want to rise to the top of the tree,
If your soul isn't fettered to an office stool,
Be careful to be guided by this golden rule,

Stick close to your desks and never go to sea,
And you all may be rulers of the Queen's Navee!

The Stars Have Not Dealt

A. E. HOUSMAN

The stars have not dealt me the worst they could do:
My pleasures are plenty, my troubles are two.
But oh, my two troubles they reave me of rest,
The brains in my head and the heart in my breast.

O grant me the ease that is granted so free,
The birthright of multitudes, give it to me,
That relish their victuals and rest on their bed
With flint in the bosom and guts in the head.

Till here I am, at last, on top!
With dizzy speed, with haste, chop-chop,
Line over line, word over word,
As swift as any soaring bird,
And therefore up and up I go,
Where writers do. Well, now I know,
(How slowly, too) had they begun
Imagine what they would have done
Who built the ancient pyramid.
Start at the bottom? So men did
Used up in writing prose and rhyme.
The precious months and years of time
To think I might have cut in half
And laugh a bitter little laugh
Not having thought of this before,
And famous now, I but deplore
Is where men started who are rich
I started at the bottom, which
And with my eyes upon my goal,
And so, with all my heart and soul,
Should give this new technique a try,
In need of time, I thought that I

the bottom of the paper and work up.—*News Item.*
ing to the pen company's research, the fastest way is to start from
can work faster if he sees his goal—the top of the page. Accord-
to cut writing time in half. The company theorizes that a person
    A pen company reports that studies have shown a new way

RICHARD ARMOUR

New Technique

FREE VERSE

Just as it is not always possible to draw a sharp, clear line between poetry and prose, it is also not always possible to distinguish formal verse from free verse. But a general definition will help: Free verse is poetry that conforms to no specific pattern of rhythm and has no rhyme scheme. Its lines are not strictly arranged; one line may consist of a few syllables, another of many. While free verse has no formal pattern, it does have a pulse or a cadence. Reading free verse aloud can help a person hear these cadences.

What free verse may lack in formal and regular rhythm and rhyme, it can make up in other ways. Free verse often is highly emotional and oratorical, as in Whitman's lines. It is often crowded with sharp, clear images, as in the poems of Sandburg, Lowell, or Williams. It can, like Crane's short lines, relate surprising, highly ironic events. Free verse can, as so many psalms illustrate, also express stately, dignified reverence for the grandeur of life.

I Hear America Singing

WALT WHITMAN

I hear America singing, the varied carols I hear,
Those of mechanics, each one singing his as it should be blithe
    and strong,
The carpenter singing his as he measures his plank or beam,
The mason singing his as he makes ready for work, or leaves off
    work,
The boatman singing what belongs to him in his boat, the deck-
    hand singing on the steamboat deck,

The shoemaker singing as he sits on his bench, the hatter singing
    as he stands,
The wood-cutter's song, the ploughboy's on his way in the morn-
    ing, or at noon intermission or at sundown,
The delicious singing of the mother, or of the young wife at work,
    or of the girl sewing or washing,
Each singing what belongs to him or her and to none else,
The day what belongs to the day—at night the party of young
    fellows, robust, friendly
Singing with open mouths their strong melodious songs.

Poets To Come

WALT WHITMAN

Poets to come! orators, singers, musicians to come!
Not today is to justify me and answer what I am for,
But you, a new brood, native, athletic, continental, greater than
    before known,
Arouse! for you must justify me.

I myself but write one or two indicative words for the future,
I but advance a moment only to wheel and hurry back in the
    darkness.

I am a man who, sauntering along without fully stopping, turns
    a casual look upon you and then averts his face,
Leaving it to you to prove and define it,
Expecting the main things from you.

The Twenty-third Psalm

DAVID

The Lord is my shepherd; I shall not want.
He maketh me to lie down in green pastures:
He leadeth me beside the still waters.
He restoreth my soul:

He leadeth me in the paths of righteousness for his name's sake.
Yea, though I walk through the valley of the shadow of death,
I will fear no evil: for thou art with me;
Thy rod and thy staff they comfort me.
Thou preparest a table before me in the presence of mine ene-
mies:
Thou anointest my head with oil; my cup runneth over.
Surely goodness and mercy shall follow me all the days of my life:
And I will dwell in the house of the Lord forever.

One's-Self I Sing

WALT WHITMAN

One's-self I sing, a simple separate person,
Yet utter the word Democratic, the word En-Masse.

Of physiology from top to toe I sing,
Not physiognomy alone nor brain alone is worthy for the Muse,
          I say the Form complete is far worthier,
The Female equally with the Male I sing.

Of Life immense in passion, pulse, and power,
Cheerful, for freest action form'd under the laws divine,
The Modern Man I sing.

Cavalry Crossing a Ford

WALT WHITMAN

A line in long array where they wind betwixt green islands,
They take a serpentine course, their arms flash in the sun—hark
    to the musical clank,
Behold the silvery river, in it the splashing horses loitering stop
    to drink,
Behold the brown-faced men, each group, each person a picture,
    the negligent rest on the saddles,
Some emerge on the opposite bank, others are just entering the
    ford—while,
Scarlet and blue and snowy white,
The guidon flags flutter gayly in the wind.

A Sight in Camp

A sight in camp in the daybreak gray and dim,
As from my tent I emerge so early sleepless,
As slow I walk in the cool fresh air the path near by the hospital
tent,
Three forms I see on stretchers lying, brought out there untended
lying,
Over each the blanket spread, ample brownish woolen blanket,
Gray and heavy blanket, folding, covering all.
Curious I halt and silent stand,
Then with light fingers I from the face of the nearest the first just
lift the blanket;
Who are you elderly man so gaunt and grim, with well-gray'd
hair, and flesh all sunken about the eyes?
Who are you my dear comrade?

Then to the second I step—and who are you my child and darling?
Who are you sweet boy with cheeks yet blooming?

Then to the third—a face nor child nor old, very calm, as of
beautiful yellow-white ivory;
Young man I think I know you—I think this face is the face of the
Christ himself,
Dead and divine and brother of all, and here again he lies.

When Lilacs Last in the Dooryard Bloom'd

WALT WHITMAN

I

When lilacs last in the dooryard bloom'd
And the great star early droop'd in the western sky in the night,
I mourn'd, and yet shall mourn with ever-returning spring.
Ever-returning spring, trinity sure to me you bring,

Lilac blooming perennial and drooping star in the west,
And thought of him I love.

II

O powerful western fallen star!
O shades of night—O moody, tearful night!
O great star disappear'd—O the black murk that hides the star!
O cruel hands that hold me powerless—O helpless soul of me!
O harsh surrounding cloud that will not free my soul.

III

In the dooryard fronting an old farm-house near the white-
    wash'd palings,
Stands the lilac-bush tall-growing with heart-shaped leaves of
    rich green,
With many a pointed blossom rising delicate, with the perfume
    strong I love,
With every leaf a miracle—and from this bush in the dooryard,
With delicate-color'd blossom and heart-shaped leaves of rich
    green,
A sprig with its flower I break.

IV

In the swamp in secluded recesses,
A shy and hidden bird is warbling a song.
Solitary the thrush,
The hermit withdrawn to himself, avoiding the settlements,
Sings by himself a song.
Song of the bleeding throat,
Death's outlet song of life, (for well dear brother I know,
If thou wast not granted to sing thou would'st surely die.)

V

Over the breast of the spring, the land, amid cities,
Amid lanes and through old woods, where lately the violets
    peep'd from the ground, spotting the gray debris,
Amid the grass in the fields each side of the lanes, passing the
    endless grass,

Passing the yellow-spear'd wheat, every grain from its shroud in
the dark-brown fields uprisen,
Passing the apple-tree blows of white and pink in the orchards,
Carrying a corpse to where it shall rest in the grave,
Night and day journeys a coffin.

VI

Coffin that passes through lanes and streets,
Through day and night with the great cloud darkening the land,
With the pomp of the inloop'd flags with the cities draped in
black,
With the show of the States themselves as of crape-veil'd women
standing,
With processions long and winding and the flambeaus of the
night,
With the countless torches lit, with the silent sea of faces and
unbared heads,
With the waiting depot, the arriving coffin, and the sombre faces,
With dirges through the night, with the thousand voices rising,
strong and solemn,
With all the mournful voices of the dirges pour'd around the
coffin,
The dim-lit churches and the shuddering organs—where amid
these you journey,
With the tolling tolling bells' perpetual clang,
I give you my sprig of lilac.

I Stood Upon a High Place
STEPHEN CRANE

> I stood upon a high place
> And saw, below, many devils
> Running, leaping,
> And carousing in sin.
> One looked up, grinning
> And said, "Comrade! Brother!"

A Man Saw a Ball of Gold in the Sky

STEPHEN CRANE

A man saw a ball of gold in the sky;
He climbed for it,
And eventually he achieved it—
It was clay.

Now this is the strange part:
When the man went to the earth
And looked again,
Lo, there was the ball of gold.
Now this is the strange part:
It was a ball of gold.
Ay, by the heavens, it was a ball of gold.

The Blade of Grass

STEPHEN CRANE

In heaven
Some little blades of grass
Stood before God.
"What did you do?"
Then all save one of the little blades
Began eagerly to relate
The merits of their lives.
This one stayed a small way behind,
Ashamed.
Presently, God said,
"And what did you do?"
The little blade answered, "Oh, my Lord,
Memory is bitter to me,
For, if I did good deeds,
I know not of them."
Then God, in all his splendor,
Arose from his throne.
"Oh, best little blade of grass!" he said.

The Eye

ROBINSON JEFFERS

The Atlantic is a stormy moat, and the Mediterranean,
The blue pool in the old garden,
More than five thousand years has drunk sacrifice
Of ships and blood and shines in the sun; but here the Pacific:
The ships, planes, wars are perfectly irrelevant.
Neither our present blood-feud with the brave dwarfs
Nor any future world-quarrel of westering
and eastering man, the bloody migrations, greed of power, battle-
   falcons,
Are a mote of dust in the great scale-pan.
Here from this mountain shore, headland beyond stormy headland
   plunging like dolphins through the gray sea-smoke
Into pale sea, look west at the hill of water: it is half the
   planet: this dome, this half-globe, this bulging
Eyeball of water, arched over to Asia,
Australia and white Antarctica: those are the eyelids that
   never close; this is the staring unsleeping
Eye of the earth, and what it watches is not our wars.

Hurt Hawks

ROBINSON JEFFERS

The broken pillar of the wing jags from the clotted shoulder,
The wing trails like a banner in defeat,
No more to use the sky forever but live with famine
And pain a few days: cat nor coyote
Will shorten the week of waiting for death, there is game without
   talons.

He stands under the oak-bush and waits
The lame feet of salvation; at night he remembers freedom

THE EYE: *blood feud with the brave dwarfs* = World War II, refers to
the short stature of the Japanese

And flies in a dream, the dawn ruins it.
He is strong and pain is worse to the strong, incapacity is worse.
The curs of the day come and torment him
At distance, no one but death the redeemer will humble that
head,
The intrepid readiness, the terrible eyes.
The wild God of the world is sometimes merciful to those
That ask mercy, not often to the arrogant.
You do not know him, you communal people, or you have for-
gotten him;
Beautiful and wild, the hawks, and men that are dying remember
him.
I'd sooner, except the penalties, kill a man than a hawk; but the
great redtail
Had nothing left but unable misery
From the bone too shattered for mending, the wing that trailed
under his talons when he moved.
We had fed him six weeks, I gave him freedom,
He wandered over the foreland hill and returned in the evening,
asking for death,
Not like a beggar, still eyed with the old
Implacable arrogance. I gave him the lead gift in the twilight.
                    What fell was relaxed,
Owl-downy, soft feminine feathers; but what
Soared: the fierce rush: the night-herons by the flooded river
cried fear at its rising
Before it was quite unsheathed from reality.

Lost

CARL SANDBURG

            Desolate and lone
            All night long on the lake
            Where fog trails and mist creeps,
            The whistle of a boat
            Calls and cries unendingly,

Like some lost child
In tears and trouble
Hunting the harbor's breast
And the harbor's eyes.

The Hammer
CARL SANDBURG

I have seen
The old gods go
And the new gods come.

Day by day
And year by year
The idols fall
And the idols rise.

Today
I worship the hammer.

Grass
CARL SANDBURG

Pile the bodies high at Austerlitz and Waterloo.
Shovel them under and let me work—
    I am the grass; I cover all.

And pile them high at Gettysburg
And pile them high at Ypres and Verdun.
Shovel them under and let me work.
Two years, ten years, and passengers ask the conductor:
    What place is this?
    Where are we now?

    I am the grass.
    Let me work.

GRASS: *Austerlitz* = scene of a major battle of the Napoleonic wars;
Ypres, Verdun = World War I battlegrounds

Cool Tombs

CARL SANDBURG

When Abraham Lincoln was shoveled into the tombs,
    he forgot the copperheads and the assassin ...
    in the dust, in the cool tombs.

And Ulysses Grant lost all thought of con men and Wall
    Street, cash and collateral turned ashes ... in the
    dust, in the cool tombs.

Pocahontas' body, lovely as a poplar, sweet as a red haw
    in November or a pawpaw in May, did she wonder?
    does she remember? ... in the dust, in the cool
    tombs?

Take any streetful of people buying clothes and gro-
    ceries, cheering a hero or throwing confetti and blowing
    tin horns ... tell me if the lovers are losers ...
    tell me if any get more than the lovers ... in the
    dust ... in the cool tombs.

I Am the People, the Mob

CARL SANDBURG

I am the people—the mob—the crowd—the mass.
Do you know that all the great work of the world is done through
    me?
I am the workingman, the inventor, the maker of the world's
    food and clothes.
I am the audience that witnesses history. The Napoleons came
    from me and the Lincolns. They die. And then I send forth
    more Napoleons and Lincolns.
I am the seed ground. I am a prairie that will stand for much
    plowing. Terrible storms pass over me. I forget. The best
    of me is sucked out and wasted. I forget. Everything but

COOL TOMBS: *copperheads* = a northerner who sympathized with the
South during the Civil War

ath comes to me and makes me work and give up what I
    ave. And I forget.
metimes I growl, shake myself and spatter a few red drops
    for history to remember. Then—I forget.
When I, the People, learn to remember, when I, the People,
    use the lessons of yesterday and no longer forget who robbed
    me last year, and who played me for a fool—then there will
    be no speaker in all the world say the name: "The People,"
    with any fleck of a sneer in his voice or any far-off
    smile of derision.
The mob—the crowd—the mass—will arrive then.

Under a Telephone Pole
CARL SANDBURG

I am a copper wire slung in the air,
Slim against the sun I make not even a clear line of shadow.
Night and day I keep singing—humming and thrumming:
It is love and war and money; it is the fighting and the tears,
    the work and want,
Death and laughter of men and women passing through me,
    carrier of your speech,
In the rain and the wet dripping, in the dawn and the shine
    drying,
        A copper wire.

Night Clouds
AMY LOWELL

The white mares of the moon rush along the sky
Beating their golden hoofs upon the glass heavens;
The white mares of the moon are all standing on their hind legs
Pawing at the green porcelain doors of the remote heavens.
Fly, mares!
Strain your utmost,
Scatter the milky dust of stars,
Or the tiger sun will leap upon you and destroy you
With one lick of his vermilion tongue.

FREE VERSE

Silence

MARIANNE MOORE

My father used to say,
"Superior people never make long visits,
have to be shown Longfellow's grave
or the glass flowers at Harvard.
Self-reliant like the cat—
that takes its prey to privacy,
the mouse's limp tail hanging like a shoelace from its mouth—
they sometimes enjoy solitude,
and can be robbed of speech
by speech that has delighted them.
The deepest feeling always shows itself in silence;
not in silence, but restraint."
Nor was he insincere in saying, "Make my house your inn."
Inns are not residences.

Heat

H. D.

> O wind, rend open the heat,
> cut apart the heat,
> rend it to tatters.
>
> Fruit cannot drop
> through this thick air—
> fruit cannot fall into heat
> that presses up and blunts
> the points of pears
> and rounds the grapes.
>
> Cut through the heat—
> plow through it,
> turning it on either side
> of your path.

The Term

WILLIAM CARLOS WILLIAMS

A rumpled sheet
of brown paper
about the length

and apparent bulk
of a man was
rolling with the

wind slowly over
and over in
the street as

a car drove down
upon it and
crushed it to

the ground. Unlike
a man it rose
again rolling

with the wind over
and over to be as
it was before.

From "Irradiations"

JOHN GOULD FLETCHER

O seeded grass, you army of little men
Crawling up the long slope with quivering, quick blades of steel:
You who storm millions of graves, tiny green tentacles of Earth,
Interlace yourselves tightly over my heart,
And do not let me go:
For I would lie here forever and watch with one eye
The pilgrimaging ants in your dull, savage jungles,
The while with the other I see the stiff lines of the slope
Break in mid-air, a wave surprisingly arrested,—
And above them, wavering, dancing, bodiless, colorless, unreal,
The long thin lazy fingers of the heat.

Exit

JOHN GOULD FLETCHER

Thus would I have it:
So should it be for me,
The scene of my departure.
Cliffs ringed with scarlet,

And the sea pounding
The pale brown sand
Mile after mile;
And then, afar off,
White on the horizon,
One ship with sails full-set
Passing slowly and serenely,
Like a proud burst of music,
To fortunate islands.

The Main-Deep
JAMES STEPHENS

The long, rolling,
Steady-pouring,
Deep-trenchèd
Green billow:

The wide-topped,
Unbroken,
Green-glacid,
Slow-sliding,
Cold-flushing,
On—on—on—
Chill-rushing,
Hush-hushing,

Hush—hushing . . .

The Old Bridge
HILDA CONKLING

The old bridge has a wrinkled face.
He bends his back
For us to go over.
He moans and weeps

But we do not hear.
Sorrow stands in his face
For the heavy weight and worry
Of people passing.
The trees drop their leaves into the water;
The sky nods to him.
The leaves float down like small ships
On the blue surface
Which is the sky.
He is not always sad:
He smiles to see the ships go down
And the little children
Playing on the river banks.

Signpost

ROBINSON JEFFERS

Civilized, crying how to be human again: this will tell you how.
Turn outward, love things, not men, turn right away from hu-
    manity,
Let that doll lie. Consider if you like how the lilies grow,
Lean on the silent rock until you feel its divinity
Make your veins cold, look at the silent stars, let your eyes
Climb the great ladder out of the pit of yourself and man.
Things are so beautiful, your love will follow your eyes;
Things are the God, you will love God, and not in vain,
For what we love, we grow to it, we share its nature. At length
You will look back along the stars' rays and see that even
The poor doll humanity has a place under heaven.
Its qualities repair their mosaic around you, the chips of strength
And sickness; but now you are free, even to become human,
But born of the rock and the air, not of a woman.

FREE VERSE

CHARACTER POEMS

Characters may be presented as dramatically and as unforgettably in poems as they are in novels, short stories, and plays. The character may be an historical figure like Abraham Lincoln or Robert E. Lee, or he may be a fictitious figure. But always what is most important is the inner man. The facial expression, the color of the eyes, the cut of the clothes, the manner of walking and the other details of appearance are important only as they suggest the personality, the inner makeup of the man. Lincoln and Lee are known as great American historical figures, but the poet is interested not so much in their political and military performances as in their thoughts and character.

The poet may present his portrait in a number of ways. He may tell you about the character, he may let the character speak for himself in a dramatic monologue, or he may place the character in some action or dialogue with other characters, just as the short-story writer does. But always the attention is on the character's motives, his conflicts, his ideals, and his past, the wellsprings of his actions.

Abraham Lincoln

WILLIAM CULLEN BRYANT

> Oh, slow to smite and swift to spare,
> Gentle and merciful and just!
> Who, in the fear of God, didst bear
> The sword of power—a nation's trust.
>
> In sorrow by thy bier we stand,
> Amid the awe that hushes all,

And speak the anguish of a land
That shook with horror at thy fall.

Thy task is done—the bonds are free;
We bear thee to an honored grave,
Whose noblest monument shall be
The broken fetters of the slave.

Pure was thy life; its bloody close
Hath placed thee with the sons of light,
Among the noble host of those
Who perished in the cause of right.

Miniver Cheevy
EDWIN ARLINGTON ROBINSON

Miniver Cheevy, child of scorn
Grew lean while he assailed the seasons;
He wept that he was ever born,
And he had reasons.

Miniver loved the days of old
When swords were bright and steeds were prancing;
The vision of a warrior bold
Would set him dancing.

Miniver sighed for what was not,
And dreamed, and rested from his labors;
He dreamed of Thebes and Camelot,
And Priam's neighbors.

Miniver mourned the ripe renown
That made so many a name so fragrant;
He mourned Romance, now on the town,
And Art, a vagrant.

MINIVER CHEEVY: *Medici* = family of merchants, statesmen, and patrons of the arts in the 14th, 15th, and 16th centuries, in Italy

CHARACTER POEMS

Miniver loved the Medici,
Albeit he had never seen one;
He would have sinned incessantly
Could he have been one.

Miniver cursed the commonplace
And eyed a khaki suit with loathing;
He missed the medieval grace
Of iron clothing.

Miniver scorned the gold he sought,
But sore annoyed was he without it;
Miniver thought, and thought, and thought,
And thought about it.

Miniver Cheevy, born too late,
Scratched his head and kept on thinking;
Miniver coughed, and called it fate,
And kept on drinking.

In the Study

THOMAS HARDY

He enters, and mute on the edge of a chair
Sits a thin-faced lady, a stranger there,
A type of decayed gentility;
And by some small signs he well can guess
That she comes to him almost breakfastless.

"I have called—I hope I do not err—
I am looking for a purchaser
Of some score volumes of the works
Of eminent divines I own—
Left by my father—though it irks
My patience to offer them." And she smiles
As if necessity were unknown;

"But the truth of it is that oftenwhiles
I have wished, as I am fond of art,
To make my rooms a little smart,
And these old books are so in the way."
And lightly still she laughs to him,
As if to sell were a mere gay whim,
And that, to be frank, Life were indeed
To her not vinegar and gall,
But fresh and honey-like; and Need
No household skeleton at all.

Mr. Flood's Party

EDWIN ARLINGTON ROBINSON

Old Eben Flood, climbing alone one night
Over the hill between the town below
And the forsaken upland hermitage
That held as much as he should ever know
On earth again of home, paused warily.
The road was his with not a native near;
And Eben, having leisure, said aloud,
For no man else in Tilbury Town to hear.

"Well, Mr. Flood, we have the harvest moon
Again, and we may not have many more;
The bird is on the wing, the poet says,
And you and I have said it here before.
Drink to the bird." He raised up to the light
The jug that he had gone so far to fill,
And answered huskily: "Well, Mr. Flood,
Since you propose it, I believe I will."

Alone, as if enduring to the end
A valiant armor of scarred hopes outworn,
He stood there in the middle of the road
Like Roland's ghost winding a silent horn.
Below him, in the town among the trees,

Where friends of other days had honored him,
A phantom salutation of the dead
Rang thinly till old Eben's eyes were dim.

Then, as a mother lays her sleeping child
Down tenderly, fearing it may awake,
He set the jug down slowly at his feet
With trembling care, knowing that most things break
And only when assured that on firm earth
It stood, as the uncertain lives of men
Assuredly did not, he paced away,
And with his hand extended paused again:

"Well, Mr. Flood, we have not met like this
In a long time; and many a change has come
To both of us, I fear, since last it was
We had a drop together. Welcome home!"
Convivially returning with himself,
Again he raised the jug up to the light;
And with an acquiescent quaver said:
"Well, Mr. Flood, if you insist, I might.

"Only a very little, Mr. Flood—
For auld lang syne. No more, sir; that will do."
So, for the time, apparently it did,
And Eben evidently thought so too;
For soon amid the silver loneliness
Of night he lifted up his voice and sang,
Secure, with only two moons listening,
Until the whole harmonious landscape rang—

"For auld lang syne." The weary throat gave out,
The last word wavered; and the song was done.
He raised again the jug regretfully
And shook his head, and was again alone,
There was not much that was ahead of him,
And there was nothing in the town below—
Where strangers would have shut the many doors
That many friends had opened long ago.

Reuben Bright
EDWIN ARLINGTON ROBINSON

Because he was a butcher and thereby
Did earn an honest living (and did right),
I would not have you think that Reuben Bright
Was any more of a brute than you and I;
For when they told him that his wife must die,
He stared at them, and shook with grief and fright,
And cried like a great baby half that night,
And made the women cry to see him cry.

And after she was dead, and he had paid
The singers and the sexton and the rest,
He packed a lot of things that she had made
Most mournfully away in an old chest
Of hers, and put some chopped-up cedar boughs
In with them, and tore down the slaughter-house.

"Butch" Weldy
EDGAR LEE MASTERS

After I got religion and steadied down
They gave me a job in the canning works,
And every morning I had to fill
The tank in the yard with gasoline,
That fed the blow-fires in the sheds
To heat the soldering irons.
And I mounted a rickety ladder to do it,
Carrying buckets full of the stuff.
One morning, as I stood there pouring,
The air grew still and seemed to heave,
And I shot up as the tank exploded.
And down I came with both legs broken,
And my eyes burned crisp as a couple of eggs.
For someone left a blow-fire going,

And something sucked the flame in the tank.
The Circuit Judge said whoever did it
Was a fellow-servant of mine, and so
Old Rhodes' son didn't have to pay me.
And I sat on the witness stand as blind
As Jack the Fiddler, saying over and over,
"I didn't know him at all."

Meg Merrilies
JOHN KEATS

Old Meg she was a gypsy;
And lived upon the moors:
Her bed it was the brown heath turf,
And her house was out of doors.
Her apples were swart blackberries,
Her currants, pods o' broom;
Her wine was dew of the wild white rose,
Her book a church-yard tomb.

Her brothers were the craggy hills,
Her sisters larchen trees;
Alone with her great family
She lived as she did please.
No breakfast had she many a morn,
No dinner many a noon,
And, 'stead of supper, she would stare
Full hard against the moon.

But every morn, of woodbine fresh
She made her garlanding,
And, every night, the dark glen yew
She wove, and she would sing.
And with her fingers, old and brown,
She plaited mats of rushes,
And she gave them to the cottagers
She met among the bushes.

Old Meg was brave as Margaret Queen,
And tall as Amazon;
An old red blanket cloak she wore,
A chip-hat had she on.
God rest her aged bones somewhere!
She died full long agone!

Sam

WALTER DE LA MARE

When Sam goes back in memory,
It is to where the sea
Breaks on the shingle, emerald-green,
In white foam, endlessly;
He says—with small brown eye on mine—
"I used to keep awake,
And lean from my window in the moon,
Watching those billows break.
And half a million tiny hands,
And eyes, like sparks of frost,
Would dance and come tumbling into the moon,
On every breaker tossed.
And all across from star to star,
I've seen the watery sea,
With not a single ship in sight,
Just ocean there and me;
And heard my father snore. And once,
As sure as I'm alive,
Out of those wallowing, moon-flecked waves
I saw a mermaid dive;
Head and shoulders above the wave,
Plain as I now see you,
Combing her hair, now back, now front,
Her two eyes peeping through;
Calling me, 'Sam!'—quietlike—'Sam—'...
But me...I never went,

Making believe I kind of thought
'Twas someone else she meant . . .
Wonderful lovely there she sat,
Singing the night way,
All in the solitudinous sea
Of that there lonely bay.
P'raps," he'd smooth his hairless mouth,
"P'raps, if 'twere now, my son,
P'raps, if I heard a voice say, 'Sam!'
Morning would find me gone."

Pierrot

SARA TEASDALE

Pierrot stands in the garden
Beneath a waning moon,
And on his lute he fashions
A fragile silver tune.

Pierrot plays in the garden,
He thinks he plays for me,
But I am quite forgotten
Under the cherry tree.

Pierrot plays in the garden,
And all the roses know
That Pierrot loves his music,—
But I love Pierrot.

Abou Ben Adhem

LEIGH HUNT

Abou Ben Adhem (may his tribe increase)
Awoke one night from a deep dream of peace,
And saw, within the moonlight in his room,
Making it rich, and like a lily in bloom,

An angel writing in a book of gold:
Exceeding peace had made Ben Adhem bold,
And to the presence in the room he said,
"What writest thou?"—The vision raised its head.
And with a look made of all sweet accord,
Answered, "The names of those that love the Lord."
"And is mine one?" said Abou. "Nay, not so,"
Replied the angel. Abou spoke more low,
But cheerly still; and said, "I pray thee then,
Write me as one that loves his fellow men."

The angel wrote, and vanished. The next night
It came again with a great wakening light,
And showed the names whom love of God had blessed,
And lo! Ben Adhem's name led all the rest.

A Spring Night

ROBERT BELOOF

His son meant something that he couldn't name.
He had his picture in his wallet,
but never remembered taking out the wallet
for anything but cash, or an address, or a name.

He could have hated him, but didn't,
even though the boy reminded him
how stuck he was because of him.
He could have loved him, too, but didn't.

When Mr. Cuff came home at night
there was reading, or sitting on the stoop till dark,
watching the dead-end street he lived on fade to dark,
so they didn't talk together much at night.

Sitting as usual this April evening
watching an impassively dying sun,

CHARACTER POEMS

he became aware that hesitantly his son
was coming to him out of the evening.

They sat down awhile together, then quietly
the boy asked him, "Do you really like boys?
I'd just like to know that, if you really like boys."
Mr. Cuff was stunned. The sun set quietly.

Communication was a rusted hinge to Cuff.
He sought some way convincingly to say
"There's just the word I've wanted long to say
but couldn't say." " 'Like' is the word," thought Cuff.

"I'm damned," said Mr. Cuff under his breath.
Finally, the boy shuffled off. Cuff went to bed.
"What's that you're mumbling over there in bed?"
asked Mrs. Cuff in the dark. Cuff lay still as death.

The Last Leaf

OLIVER WENDELL HOLMES

I saw him once before,
As he pass'd by the door,
And again
The pavement stones resound,
As he totters o'er the ground
With his cane.

They say that in his prime,
Ere the pruning-knife of Time
Cut him down,
Not a better man was found
By the crier on his round
Through the town.

But now he walks the streets,
And he looks at all he meets
Sad and wan,

And he shakes his feeble head,
That it seems as if he said,
"They are gone."

The mossy marbles rest
On the lips that he has prest
In their bloom,
And the names he loved to hear
Have been carved for many a year
On the tomb.

My grandmamma has said—
Poor old lady, she is dead
Long ago—
That he had a Roman nose,
And his cheek was like a rose
In the snow.

But now his rose is thin,
And it rests upon his chin
Like a staff,
And a crook is in his back,
And a melancholy crack
In his laugh.

I know it is a sin
For me to sit and grin
At him here;
But the old three-corner'd hat,
And the breeches, and all that,
Are so queer!

And if I should live to be
The last leaf upon the tree
In the spring,
Let them smile, as I do now,
At the old forsaken bough
Where I cling.

Ulysses

ALFRED, LORD TENNYSON

It little profits that an idle king,
By this still hearth, among these barren crags,
Match'd with an aged wife, I mete and dole
Unequal laws unto a savage race,
That hoard, and sleep, and feed, and know not me.
I cannot rest from travel: I will drink
Life to the lees: all times I have enjoy'd
Greatly, have suffer'd greatly, both with those
That loved me, and alone; on shore, and when
Thro' scudding drifts the rainy Hyades
Vext the dim sea: I am become a name;
For always roaming with a hungry heart
Much have I seen and known; cities of men,
And manners, climates, councils, governments,
Myself not least, but honor'd of them all;
And drunk delight of battle with my peers,
Far on the ringing plains of windy Troy.
I am a part of all that I have met;
Yet all experience is an arch wherethro'
Gleams that untravell'd world, whose margin fades
For ever and for ever when I move.
How dull it is to pause, to make an end,
To rust unburnish'd, not to shine in use!
As tho' to breathe were life. Life piled on life
Were all too little, and of one to me
Little remains: but every hour is saved
From that eternal silence, something more,
A bringer of new things; and vile it were
For some three suns to store and hoard myself,
And this gray spirit yearning in desire
To follow knowledge like a sinking star,
Beyond the utmost bound of human thought.
    This is my son, mine own Telemachus,
To whom I leave the sceptre and the isle—

Well-beloved of me, discerning to fulfill
This labor, by slow prudence to make mild
A rugged people, and thro' soft degrees
Subdue them to the useful and the good.
Most blameless is he, centred in the sphere
Of common duties, decent not to fail
In offices of tenderness, and pay
Meet adoration to my household gods,
When I am gone. He works his work, I mine.
    There lies the port: the vessel puffs her sail:
There gloom the dark broad seas. My mariners,
Souls that have toil'd, and wrought, and thought
    with me—
That ever with a frolic welcome took
The thunder and the sunshine, and opposed
Free hearts, free foreheads—you and I are old;
Old age hath yet his honor and his toil;
Death closes all: but something ere the end,
Some work of noble note may yet be done,
Not unbecoming men that strove with Gods.
The lights begin to twinkle from the rocks:
The long day wanes: the slow moon climbs: the deep
Moans round with many voices. Come, my friends,
'Tis not too late to seek a newer world.
Push off, and sitting well in order smite
The sounding furrows; for my purpose holds
To sail beyond the sunset, and the baths
Of all the western stars, until I die.
It may be that the gulfs will wash us down:
It may be we shall touch the Happy Isles,
And see the great Achilles whom we knew.
Tho' much is taken, much abides; and tho'
We are not now that strength which in old days
Moved earth and heaven; that which we are, we are;
One equal temper of heroic hearts,
Made weak by time and fate, but strong in will
To strive, to seek, to find, and not to yield.

                                     CHARACTER POEMS

Song of the Old Mother
WILLIAM BUTLER YEATS

> I rise in the dawn, and I kneel and blow
> Till the seed of the fire flicker and glow.
> And then I must scrub, and bake, and sweep,
> Till stars are beginning to blink and peep.
> But the young lie long and dream in their bed
> Of the matching of ribbons, the blue and the red,
> And their day goes over in idleness,
> And they sigh if the wind but lift up a tress.
> While I must work, because I am old
> And the seed of the fire gets feeble and cold.

Gunga Din
RUDYARD KIPLING

> You may talk o' gin an' beer
> When you're quartered safe out 'ere,
> An' you're sent to penny-fights an' Aldershot it;
> But when it comes to slaughter
> You will do your work on water,
> An' you'll lick the bloomin' boots of 'im that's got it.
> Now in Injia's sunny clime,
> Where I used to spend my time
> A-servin' of 'Er Majesty the Queen,
> Of all them black-faced crew
> The finest man I knew
> Was our regimental *bhisti*, Gunga Din.

> > He was "Din! Din! Din!
> > You limping lump o' brick-dust, Gunga Din!
> > Hi! *slippey hitherao!*
> > Water, get it! Panee lao!
> > You squidgy-nosed old idol, Gunga Din!"

GUNGA DIN: *Aldershot* = a military camp in Britain; *Lazarushian* =
army slang for dark-skinned

The uniform 'e wore
Was nothin' much before,
An' rather less than 'arf o' that be'ind,
For a piece o' twisty rag
And a goatskin water-bag
Was all the field-equipment e' could find.
When the sweat' troop-train lay
In a sidin' through the day,
Where the 'eat would make your bloomin' eye-brows crawl,
We shouted "*Harry By!*"
Till our throats were bricky-dry,
Then we wopped 'im 'cause 'e couldn't serve us all.

> It was "Din! Din! Din!
> You 'eathen, where the mischief 'ave you been?
> You put some *juldee* in it,
> Or I'll *marrow* you this minute,
> If you don't fill up my helmet, Gunga Din!"

'E would dot an' carry one
Till the longest day was done;
An' 'e didn't seem to know the use o' fear.
If we charged or broke or cut,
You could bet your bloomin' nut,
'E'd be waitin' fifty paces right flank rear.
With 'is *mussick* on 'is back,
'E would skip with our attack,
An' watch us till the bugles made "Retire."
An' for all 'is dirty 'ide,
'E was white, clear white, inside
When he went to tend the wounded under fire!

> It was "Din! Din! Din!"
> With the bullets kickin' dust-spots on the green.
> When the cartridges ran out,
> You could 'ear the front-files shout,
> "Hi! ammunition-mules an' Gunga Din!"

I sha'n't forgit the night
When I dropped be'ind the fight
With a bullet where my belt-plate should'a' been.
I was chokin' mad with thirst,
An' the man that spied me first
Was our good old grinnin, gruntin' Gunga Din.
'E lifted up my 'ead,
An' 'e plugged me where I bled,
An' 'e guv me 'arf-a-pint o' water—green;
It was crawlin' an' it stunk,
But of all the drinks I've drunk,
I'm gratefullest to one from Gunga Din.

> It was "Din! Din! Din!
> 'Ere's a beggar with a bullet through 'is spleen;
> 'E's chawnin' up the ground,
> An' 'e's kickin' all around:
> For Gawd's sake git the water, Gunga Din!"

'E carried me away
To where a *dooli* lay,
An' a bullet come an' drilled the beggar clean.
'E put me safe inside,
An' just before 'e died:
"I 'ope you liked your drink," sez Gunga Din.
So I'll meet 'im later on
In the place where 'e is gone—
Where it's always double drill and no canteen;
'E'll be squattin' on the coals
Givin' drink to pore damned souls,
An' I'll get a swig in Hell from Gunga Din!

> Yes, Din! Din! Din!
> You Lazarushian-leather Gunga Din!
> Tho' I've belted you an' flayed you,
> By the livin' Gawd that made you,
> You're a better man than I am, Gunga Din!

Columbus

JOAQUIN MILLER

Behind him lay the gray Azores,
Behind, the Gates of Hercules;
Before him not the ghost of shores;
Before him only shoreless seas.
The good mate said: "Now must we pray,
For lo! the very stars are gone.
Brave Admiral, speak, what shall I say?"
"Why, say: 'Sail on! sail on! and on!' "

"My men grow mutinous day by day;
My men grow ghastly, wan and weak."
The stout mate thought of home; a spray
Of salt wave washed his swarthy cheek.
"What shall I say, brave Admiral, say,
If we sight naught but seas at dawn?"
"Why, you shall say at break of day,
'Sail on! sail on! sail on! and on!' "

They sailed and sailed, as winds might blow,
Until at last the blanched mate said:
"Why now not even God would know
Should I and all my men fall dead.
These very winds forget their way,
For God from these dread seas is gone.
Now speak, brave Admiral, speak and say"—
He said: "Sail on! sail on! and on!"

They sailed. They sailed. Then spake the mate:
"This mad sea shows his teeth to-night.
He curls his lip, he lies in wait,
With lifted teeth, as if to bite!
Brave Admiral, say but one good word:
What shall we do when hope is gone?"
The words leapt like a leaping sword:
"Sail on! sail on! sail on! and on!"

Then, pale and worn, he kept his deck,
And peered through darkness. Ah, that night
Of all dark nights! And then a speck—
A light! a light! a light! a light!
It grew, a starlit flag unfurled!
It grew to be Time's burst of dawn.
He gained a world; he gave that world
Its grandest lesson: "On! sail on!"

Father Malloy

EDGAR LEE MASTERS

You are over there, Father Malloy,
Where holy ground is, and the cross marks every grave,
Not here with us on the hill—
Us of wavering faith, and clouded vision
And drifting hope, and unforgiven sins.
You were so human, Father Malloy,
Taking a friendly glass sometimes with us,
Siding with us who would rescue Spoon River
From the coldness and the dreariness of village morality.
You were like a traveler who brings a little box of sand
From the wastes about the pyramids
And makes them real and Egypt real.
You were a part of and related to a great past,
And yet you were so close to many of us.
You believed in the joy of life.
You did not seem to be ashamed of the flesh.
You faced life as it is,
And as it changes.
Some of us almost came to you, Father Malloy,
Seeing how your church had divined the heart,
And provided for it,
Through Peter the Flame,
Peter the Rock.

FATHER MALLOY: *Spoon River* = a fictional town

Lucinda Matlock

EDGAR LEE MASTERS

I went to the dances at Chandlerville,
And played snap-out at Wincester.
One time we changed partners,
Driving home in the moonlight of middle June,
And then I found Davis.
We were married and lived together for seventy years,
Enjoying, working, raising twelve children,
Eight of whom we lost
Ere I had reached the age of sixty.
I spun, I wove, I kept the house, I nursed the sick,
I made the garden, and for holiday
Rambled over the fields where sang the larks,
And by Spoon River gathering many a shell,
And many a flower a medicinal weed—
Shouting to the wooded hills, singing to the green valleys.
At ninety-six I had lived enough, that is all,
And passed to a sweet repose.
What is this I hear of sorrow and weariness,
Anger, discontent, and drooping hopes?
Degenerate sons and daughters,
Life is too strong for you—
It takes life to love Life.

Star-Pudding

ROBERT P. TRISTRAM COFFIN

People wondered what Dan Wholebrook found
To live on, up there on his hungry farm.
His cow was always breaking through her fences
And eating up the neighbors' corn by rows,
The soil was spread too thin between the ledges,
And mostly powdered rock, like tiny stars;
The hardtack crowded the potatoes out;

Dan raised a first-rate crop of goldenrod.
The crows used Daniel's farm to crack their clams on,
There was so much of it bare granite rock.
Wind-pudding was what Daniel had, folks said,
And lucky for the man he had no wife
And children's mouths to find potatoes for.

The neighbors did not know about the stars.
A man can get a lot of life from them
If he knows how to go about it. They came
Closer to Daniel's place than down below,
And being on a hill, he had lots more;
They were as thick as daisies in poor hay.
Seemed so, he always was all tangled up
In stars, he had to hoe so long
And get up out of bed so bright and early.
'Twas nothing for him to find a morning star
Beside his shoulder, or an evening one.
It might do for a breakfast or a supper,
And Daniel showed it in his burning eyes.

GREAT THEMES IN POETRY

In all times, among all nations, in every great religion, love and understanding have been recognized as the means to a full, happy life. Love unifies and gives purpose to life. Where love has been lacking, there has always been strife, bitterness, and cruelty. Love has always led to mutual respect and toleration; it has led to joy and thanksgiving; it has given men and women the strength to endure suffering and hardship.

Poets have sung of the pleasure and the pain of love, of love's gladness and grief, of its happiness and its hazards. But they have never failed to recognize that love is the hope of the world.

The Night Has a Thousand Eyes
FRANCIS BOURDILLON

> The night has a thousand eyes,
> And the day but one;
> Yet the light of the bright world dies
> With the dying sun.
>
> The mind has a thousand eyes,
> And the heart but one;
> Yet the light of a whole life dies
> When love is done.

To Silvia

WILLIAM SHAKESPEARE

Who is Silvia? What is she,
That all our swains commend her?
Holy, fair, and wise is she;
The heaven such grace did lend her,
That she might admired be.

Is she kind as she is fair?
For beauty lives with kindness;
Love doth to her eyes repair,
To help him of his blindness:
And being help'd, inhabits there.

Then to Silvia let us sing,
That Silvia is excelling;
She excels each mortal thing
Upon the dull earth dwelling:
To her let us garlands bring.

To Celia

BEN JONSON

Drink to me only with thine eyes,
And I will pledge with mine;
Or leave a kiss but in the cup
And I'll not look for wine.
The thirst that from the soul doth rise
Doth ask a drink divine;
But might I of Jove's nectar sup,
I would not change for thine.

I sent thee late a rosy wreath,
Not so much honoring thee
As giving it a hope that there

It could not wither'd be;
But thou thereon didst only breathe
And sent'st it back to me;
Since when it grows, and smells, I swear,
Not of itself but thee!

To Althea from Prison
RICHARD LOVELACE

When love with unconfined wings
Hovers within my gates;
And my divine Althea brings
To whisper at the grates;
When I lie tangled in her hair,
And fettered to her eye;
The Gods that wanton in the air,
Know no such liberty.

When flowing cups run swiftly round
With no allaying Thames,
Our careless heads with roses bound,
Our hearts with loyal flames;
When thirsty grief in wine we steep,
When healths and draughts go free,
Fishes that tipple in the deep,
Know no such liberty.

When (like committed linnets) I
With shriller throat shall sing
The sweetness, mercy, majesty,
And glories of my King;
When I shall voice aloud, how good
He is, how great should be;
Enlarged winds that curl the flood,
Know no such liberty.

Stone walls do not a prison make,
Nor iron bars a cage;
Minds innocent and quiet take
That for an hermitage;
If I have freedom in my love
And in my soul am free;
Angels alone that soar above,
Enjoy such liberty!

Outwitted

EDWIN MARKHAM

He drew a circle that shut me out—
Heretic, rebel, a thing to flout.
But love and I had the wit to win:
We drew a circle that took him in!

Music I Heard

CONRAD AIKEN

Music I heard with you was more than music,
And bread I broke with you was more than bread;
Now that I am without you, all is desolate;
All that was once so beautiful is dead.

Your hands once touched this table and this silver,
And I have seen your fingers hold this glass.
These things do not remember you, beloved,
And yet your touch upon them will not pass.

For it was in my heart you moved among them,
And blessed them with your hands and with your eyes;
And in my heart they will remember always,—
They knew you once, O beautiful and wise.

Give All to Love

RALPH WALDO EMERSON

Give all to love;
Obey thy heart;
Friends, kindred, days,
Estate, good-fame,
Plans, credit, and the Muse,—
Nothing refuse.

'Tis a brave master;
Let it have scope:
Follow it utterly,
Hope beyond hope:
High and more high
It dives into noon,
With wing unspent,
Untold intent;
But it is a god,
Knows its own path,
And the outlets of the sky.

It was never for the mean;
It requireth courage stout,
Souls above doubt,
Valor unbending;
It will reward,—
They shall return
More than they were,
And ever ascending.

Leave all for love;
Yet, hear me, yet,
One word more thy heart behoved,
One pulse more of firm endeavor,—

Keep thee to-day
To-morrow, forever,
Free as an Arab
Of thy beloved.

Cling with life to the maid;
But when the surprise,
First vague shadow of surmise
Flits across her bosom young
Of a joy apart from thee,
Free be she, fancy-free;
Nor thou detain her vesture's hem,
Nor the palest rose she flung
From her summer diadem.

Though thou loved her as thyself,
As a self of purer clay,
Though her parting dims the day,
Stealing grace from all alive;
Heartily know,
When half-gods go,
The gods arrive.

A Red, Red Rose
ROBERT BURNS

O, my luve is like a red, red rose,
That's newly sprung in June.
O, my luve is like the melodie
That's sweetly played in tune.

As fair art thou, my bonnie lass,
So deep in luve am I,
And I will luve thee still, my dear,
Till a' the seas gang dry.

Till a' the seas gang dry, my dear,
And the rocks melt wi' the sun!
And I will luve thee still, my dear,
While the sands o' life shall run.

And fare thee weel, my only luve,
And fair thee weel a while!
And I will come again, my love,
Tho' it were ten thousand mile!

I Hear It Was Charged Against Me

WALT WHITMAN

I hear it was charged against me that I sought to destroy institu-
tions,
But really I am neither for nor against institutions,
(What indeed have I in common with them? or what with the
destruction of them?)
Only I will establish in the Mannahatta and in every city of these
States inland and seaboard,
And in the fields and woods, and above every keel little or large
that dents the water,
Without edifices or rules or trustees or any argument,
The institution of the dear love of comrades.

When I Peruse the Conquer'd Fame

WALT WHITMAN

When I peruse the conquer'd fame of heroes and the victories of
mighty generals, I do not envy the generals,
Nor the President in his Presidency, nor the rich in his great
house,
But when I hear of the brotherhood of lovers, how it was with
them,
How together through life, through dangers, odium, unchanging
long and long,

Through youth and through middle and old age, how unfaltering,
   how affectionate and faithful they were,
Then I am pensive—I hastily walk away fill'd with the bitterest
   envy.

Song
WILLIAM BLAKE

> My silks and fine array,
> My smiles and languished air,
> By love are driv'n away;
> And mournful lean Despair
> Brings me yew to deck my grave:
> Such end true lovers have.
>
> Her face is fair as heaven,
> When springing buds unfold;
> O why to him was't given
> Whose heart is wintry cold?
> His breast is love's all-worshiped tomb,
> Where all love's pilgrims come.
>
> Bring me an axe and spade,
> Bring me a winding sheet;
> When I my grave have made
> Let winds and tempests beat:
> Then down I'll lie as cold as clay.
> True love doth pass away!

The Passionate Shepherd to His Love
CHRISTOPHER MARLOWE

> Come live with me and be my love,
> And we will all the pleasures prove
> That hills and valleys, dales and fields,
> Or woods or steepy mountain yields.

THE PASSIONATE SHEPHERD TO HIS LOVE: *kirtle* = tunic or coat

And we will sit upon the rocks,
And see the shepherds feed their flocks
By shallow rivers, to whose falls
Melodious birds sing madrigals.

And I will make thee beds of roses
And a thousand fragrant posies;
A cap of flowers, and a kirtle
Embroidered all with leaves of myrtle;

A gown made of the finest wool
Which from our pretty lambs we pull;
Fair-lined slippers for the cold,
With buckles of the purest gold;

A belt of straw and ivy buds
With coral clasps and amber studs—
And if these pleasures may thee move,
Come live with me and be my love.

The shepherd swains shall dance and swing
For thy delight each May morning—
If these delights thy mind may move,
Then live with me and be my love.

The Nymph's Reply to the Shepherd
SIR WALTER RALEIGH

If all the world and love were young
And truth in every shepherd's tongue,
These pretty pleasures might me move
To live with thee and be thy love.

Time drives the flocks from field to fold
When rivers rage and rocks grow cold,
And Philomel becometh dumb;
The rest complain of cares to come.

The flowers do fade, and wanton fields
To wayward winter reckoning yields;
A honey tongue, a heart of gall,
Is fancy's spring, but sorrow's fall.

Thy gowns, thy shoes, thy beds of roses,
Thy cap, thy kirtle, and thy posies
Soon break, soon wither, soon forgotten,
In folly ripe, in reason rotten.

Thy belt of straw and ivy buds,
Thy coral clasps and amber studs,
All these in me no means can move
To come to thee and be thy love.

But could youth last and love still breed,
Had joys no date nor age no need,
Then these delights my mind might move
To live with thee and be thy love.

Poets have always been quick to speak out against all unjust social conditions and against all of man's inhumanity to his fellow man. Often in history poems and stories have been instrumental in bringing about better laws and in improving intolerable social conditions. Against slavery, against bigotry, against exploitation, against war, against tyranny of every sort, the poet's voice has always been clear and strong. Poets have been, to use the phrase of Percy Bysshe Shelley, the "legislators for all mankind." The following poems will present many voices commenting on various social problems and injustices.

Song to the Men of England

PERCY BYSSHE SHELLEY

Men of England, wherefore plough
For the lords who lay ye low?
Wherefore weave with toil and care
The rich robes your tyrants wear?

Wherefore feed, and clothe, and save,
From the cradle to the grave,
Those drones who would
Drain your sweat—nay, drink your blood?

Wherefore, Bees of England, forge
Many a weapon, chain, and scourge,
That these stingless drones may spoil
The forced produce of your toil.

Have ye leisure, comfort, calm,
Shelter, food, love's gentle balm?
Or what is it ye buy so dear
With your pain and with your fear?

The seed ye sow, another reaps;
The wealth ye find, another keeps;
The robes ye weave, another wears;
The arms ye forge, another bears.

Sow seed,—but let no tyrant reap;
Find wealth,—let no impostor heap;
Weave robes,—let not the idle wear;
Forge arms,—in your defense to bear.

Shrink to your cellars, holes, and cells;
In halls ye deck another dwells.
Why shake the chains ye wrought? Ye see
The steel ye tempered glance on ye.

With plough and spade, and hoe and loom,
Trace your grave, and build your tomb,
And weave your winding-sheet, till fair
England be your sepulchre.

The Man with the Hoe
(Written after seeing Millet's world-famous painting)
EDWIN MARKHAM

Bowed by the weight of centuries he leans
Upon his hoe and gazes on the ground,
The emptiness of ages in his face,
And on his back the burden of the world.
Who made him dead to rapture and despair,
A thing that grieves not and that never hopes,
Stolid and stunned, a brother to the ox?
Who loosened and let down this brutal jaw?
Whose was the hand that slanted back this brow?
Whose breath blew out the light within this brain?

Is this the Thing the Lord God made and gave
To have dominion over sea and land;
To trace the stars and search the heavens for power;
To feel the passion of Eternity?
Is this the dream He dreamed who shaped the suns
And marked their ways upon the ancient deep?
Down all the caverns of Hell to their last gulf
There is no shape more terrible than this—
More tongued with censure of the world's blind greed—
More filled with signs and portents for the soul—
More packt with danger to the universe.

What gulfs between him and the seraphim!
Slave of the wheel of labor, what to him
Are Plato and the swing of Pleiades?
What the long reaches of the peaks of song,
The rift of dawn, the reddening of the rose?
Through this dread shape the suffering ages look;
Time's tragedy is in that aching stoop;
Through this dread shape humanity betrayed,
Plundered, profaned, and disinherited,
Cries protest to the Judges of the World,
A protest that is also prophecy.

O masters, lords and rulers in all lands,
Is this the handiwork you give to God,
This monstrous thing distorted and soul-quenched?
How will you ever straighten up this shape;
Touch it again with immortality;
Give back the upward looking and the light;
Rebuild in it the music and the dream;
Make right the immemorial infamies,
Perfidious wrongs, immedicable woes?

O masters, lords and rulers in all lands,
How will the future reckon with this man?

How answer his brute question in that hour
When whirlwinds of rebellion shake all shores?
How will it be with kingdoms and with kings—
With those who shaped him to the thing he is—
When this dumb Terror shall rise to judge the world,
After the silence of centuries?

The Leaden-Eyed
VACHEL LINDSAY

Let not young souls be smothered out before
They do quaint deeds and fully flaunt their pride.
It is the world's one crime its babes grow dull,
Its poor are ox-like, limp and leaden-eyed.
Not that they starve, but starve so dreamlessly;
Not that they sow, but that they seldom reap;
Not that they serve, but have no gods to serve;
Not that they die, but that they die like sheep.

The Very Rich Man
DOROTHY PARKER

He'd have the best, and that was none too good;
No barrier could hold, before his terms.
He lies below, correct in cypress wood,
And entertains the most exclusive worms.

Arms and the Boy
WILFRED OWEN

Let the boy try along this bayonet-blade
How cold steel is, and keen with hunger of blood;
Blue with all malice, like a madman's flash;
And thinly drawn with famishing for flesh.

Lend him to stroke these blind, blunt bullet-heads
Which long to nuzzle in the hearts of lads,

Or give him cartridges of fine zinc teeth,
Sharp with the sharpness of grief and death.

For his teeth seem for laughing round an apple.
There lurk no claws behind his fingers supple;
And God will grow no talons at his heels,
Nor antlers through the thickness of his curls.

Anthem for Doomed Youth
WILFRED OWEN

What passing-bells for these who die as cattle?
Only the monstrous anger of the guns.
Only the stuttering rifles' rapid rattle
Can patter out their hasty orisons.
No mockeries for them; no prayers nor bells,
Nor any voice of mourning save the choirs,—
The shrill, demented choirs of wailing shells;
And bugles calling for them from sad shires.
What candles may be held to speed them all?
Not in the hands of boys, but in their eyes
Shall shine the holy glimmers of good-byes.
The pallor of girls' brows shall be their pall;
Their flowers the tenderness of patient minds,
And each slow dusk a drawing-down of blinds.

In Flanders Fields
JOHN MC CRAE

In Flanders fields the poppies blow
Between the crosses, row on row,
That mark our place; and in the sky
The larks, still bravely singing, fly
Scarce heard amid the guns below.

We are the Dead. Short days ago
We lived, felt dawn, saw sunset glow,

Loved and were loved, and now we lie
    In Flanders fields.

Take up our quarrel with the foe:
To you from failing hands we throw
The torch; be yours to hold it high.
If you break faith with us who die
We shall not sleep, though poppies grow
    In Flanders fields.

Battle: Hit

WILFRED WILSON GIBSON

Out of the sparkling sea
I drew my tingling body clear, and lay
On a low ledge the livelong summer day,
Basking, and watching lazily
White sails in Falmouth Bay.

My body seemed to burn
Salt in the sun that drenched it through and through,
Till every particle glowed clean and new
And slowly seemed to turn
To lucent amber in a world of blue.

· · · · ·　　· · · · ·　　· · · · ·

I felt a sudden wrench—
A trickle of warm blood—
And found that I was sprawling in the mud
Among the dead men in the trench.

The Unknown Citizen JS/07/M/378
This Marble Monument Is Erected by the State

W. H. AUDEN

He was found by the Bureau of Statistics to be
One against whom there was no official complaint,
And all the reports on his conduct agree

　no individuality　

sarcastic

That, in the modern sense of an old-fashioned word, he was a
    saint,
For in everything he did he served the Greater Community.
Except for the war till the day he retired
He worked in a factory and never got fired,
But satisfied his employers, Fudge Motors Inc.
Yet he wasn't a scab or odd in his views,
For his Union reports that he paid his dues,
(Our report on his Union shows it was sound)
And our Social Psychology workers found
That he was popular with his mates and liked a drink.
The Press are convinced that he bought a paper every day
And that his reactions to poetry were normal in every way.
Policies taken out in his name prove that he was fully insured,
And his Health Card shows he was once in hospital but left it
    cured.
Both Producers Research and High-Grade Living declare
He was fully sensible to the advantages of the Installment Plan
And had everything necessary to the Modern Man,
A gramophone, a radio, a car, and a frigidaire.
Our researchers into public opinion are content
That he held the proper opinions for the time of year.
When there was peace, he was for peace; when there was war, he
    went.
He was married and added five children to the population,
Which our Eugenists say was the right number for a parent of his
    generation,
And our teachers report that he never interfered with their educa-
    tion.
Was he free? Was he happy? The question is absurd:
Had anything been wrong, we certainly should have heard.

GREAT THEMES IN POETRY

*Throughout the centuries mankind has devised many methods
for measuring the passage of time: rope clocks, water clocks,
hourglasses, sundials, mechanical clocks, and electronic clocks.
Time has been divided into neat units: the second, the minute,
the hour, week, month, year, decade, century, and millennium.
Yet time has remained mysterious, relentless, indifferent, and
indescribably vast. One legend about time goes as follows:*

> **High up in the North in the land called Sithjod, there
> stands a rock. It is a hundred miles high and a hun-
> dred miles wide. Once every thousand years a little
> bird comes to this rock to sharpen its beak. When the
> rock has thus been worn away, then a single day of
> eternity will have gone by.**

*Poets, like most human beings, have stood before time, awed and
fascinated.*

Ozymandias

PERCY BYSSHE SHELLEY

I met a traveler from an antique land
Who said: "Two vast and trunkless legs of stone
Stand in the desert. Near them, on the sand,
Half sunk, a shatter'd visage lies, whose frown
And wrinkled lip and sneer of cold command
Tell that its sculptor well those passions read
Which yet survive, stamp'd on these lifeless things,
The hand that mock'd them and the heart that fed;
And on the pedestal these words appear:
'My name is Ozymandias, king of kings:
Look on my works, ye Mighty, and despair!'
Nothing beside remains. Round the decay
Of that colossal wreck, boundless and bare,
The lone and level sands stretch far away."

Cocoon

DAVID MC CORD

The little caterpillar creeps
Awhile before in silk it sleeps.
It sleeps awhile before it flies,
And flies awhile before it dies,
And that's the end of three good tries.

John Anderson

ROBERT BURNS

John Anderson my jo, John,
When we were first acquent
Your locks were like the raven,
Your bonnie brow was brent;
But now your brow is beld, John,
Your locks are like the snow;
But blessings on your frosty pow,
John Anderson my jo.

John Anderson my jo, John,
We clamb the hill thegither,
And mony a canty day, John,
We've had wi' ane anither:
Now we maun totter down, John,
But hand in hand we'll go,
And sleep thegither at the foot,
John Anderson my jo.

The Lost Love

WILLIAM WORDSWORTH

She dwelt among the untrodden ways
Beside the springs of Dove;
A maid whom there were none to praise,
And very few to love:

JOHN ANDERSON: *jo* = sweetheart; *acquent* = acquainted; *beld* =
bald; *pow* = head; *canty* = cheerful

A violet by a mossy stone
Half hidden from the eye!
Fair as a star, when only one
Is shining in the sky.

She lived unknown, and few could know
When Lucy ceased to be;
But she is in her grave, and oh,
The difference to me!

The Seven Ages of Man

WILLIAM SHAKESPEARE

All the world's a stage,
And all the men and women merely players:
They have their exits and their entrances;
And one man in his time plays many parts,
His acts being seven ages. At first the infant,
Mewling and puking in the nurse's arms.
And then the whining school-boy, with his satchel,
And shining morning face, creeping like snail
Unwillingly to school. And then the lover
Sighing like a furnace, with a woeful ballad
Made to his mistress' eyebrow. Then a soldier,
Full of strange oaths, and bearded like the pard,
Jealous in honor, sudden and quick in quarrel,
Seeking the bubble reputation
Even in the cannon's mouth. And then the justice,
In fair round belly with good capon lin'd,
With eyes severe, and beard of formal cut,
Full of wise saws and modern instances;
And so he plays his part. The sixth age shifts
Into the lean and slippered pantaloon,
With spectacles on nose and pouch on side,
His youthful hose well sav'd a world too wide
For his shrunk shank; and his big manly voice,

Turning again toward childish treble, pipes
And whistles in his sound. Last scene of all,
That ends this strange eventful history,
Is second childishness and mere oblivion,
Sans teeth, sans eyes, sans taste, sans everything.

Fidele

WILLIAM SHAKESPEARE

Fear no more the heat o' the sun
Nor the furious winter's rages;
Thou thy worldly task hast done,
Home art gone and ta'en thy wages:
Golden lads and girls all must,
As chimney-sweepers, come to dust.

Fear no more the frown o' the great,
Thou art past the tyrant's stroke;
Care no more to clothe and eat;
To thee the reed is as the oak:
The sceptre, learning, physic, must
All follow this, and come to dust.

Fear no more the lightning-flash
Nor the all-dreaded thunder-stone;
Fear not slander, censure rash;
Thou hast finish'd joy and moan:
All lovers young, all lovers must
Consign to thee, and come to dust.

O Mistress Mine

WILLIAM SHAKESPEARE

O mistress mine, where are you roaming?
O stay and hear! your true love's coming
That can sing both high and low:

Trip no further, pretty sweeting;
Journeys end in lovers' meeting—
Every wise man's son doth know.

What is love? 'tis not hereafter;
Present mirth hath present laughter;
What's to come is still unsure:

In delay there lies no plenty,—
Then come kiss me, sweet-and-twenty,
Youth's a stuff will not endure.

The Human Seasons

JOHN KEATS

Four seasons fill the measure of the year;
There are four seasons in the mind of man:
He has his lusty Spring, when fancy clear
Takes in all beauty with an easy span:
He has his Summer, when luxuriously
Spring's honey'd cud of youthful thought he loves
To ruminate, and by such dreaming nigh
His nearest unto heaven: quiet coves
His soul has in its Autumn, when his wings
He furleth close: contented so to look
On mists in idleness—to let fair things
Pass by unheeded as a threshold brook:
He has his Winter too of pale misfeature,
Or else he would forgo his mortal nature.

Three Haiku

BASHŌ

contrast

people in poem are dead

Old battle field, fresh with Spring flowers again—
All that is left of the dream — *of no more war, glory,*
Of twice ten thousand warriors slain. *to grow old*

* * *

Old men, white-haired, beside the ancestral graves,
All of the household now
Stand lonesome, leaning on their staves.

*　*　*

O cricket, from your cheery cry
No one could ever guess
How quickly you must die.

Mutability

PERCY BYSSHE SHELLEY

The flower that smiles to-day
To-morrow dies;
All that we wish to stay,
Tempts and then flies.
What is this world's delight?
Lightning that mocks the night,
Brief even as bright.

Virtue, how frail it is!
Friendship, how rare!
Love, how it sells poor bliss
For proud despair!
But we, though soon they fail,
Survive their joy, and all
Which ours we call.

Whilst skies are blue and bright,
Whilst flowers are gay,
Whilst eyes that change ere night
Make glad the day;
Whilst yet the calm hours creep,
Dream thou—and from thy sleep
Then wake to weep.

297   GREAT THEMES IN POETRY

Gather Ye Rosebuds While Ye May
ROBERT HERRICK

Gather ye rosebuds while ye may:
Old time is still a-flying;
And this same flower that smiles to-day
To-morrow will be dying.

The glorious lamp of heaven, the Sun,
The higher he's a-getting,
The sooner will his race be run,
And nearer he's to setting.

That age is best which is the first,
When youth and blood are warmer;
But being spent, the worse, and worst
Times still succeed the former.

Then be not coy, but use your time,
And while ye may, go marry;
For, having lost but once your prime,
You may forever tarry.

In Time of "The Breaking of Nations"
THOMAS HARDY

Only a man harrowing clods
In slow silent walk,
With an old horse that stumbles and nods
Half asleep as they stalk.

Only thin smoke without flame
From the heaps of couch-grass:
Yet this will go onward the same
Though Dynasties pass.

Yonder a maid and her wight
Come whispering by;
War's annals will fade into night
Ere their story die.

Waiting Both

THOMAS HARDY

A star looks down at me,
And says: "Here I and you
Stand, each in our degree:
What do you mean to do,—
Mean to do?"

I say: "For all I know,
Wait, and let Time go by,
Till my change come."—"Just so.
So mean I."

Blue Girls

JOHN CROWE RANSOM

Twirling your blue skirts, traveling the sward
Under the towers of your seminary,
Go listen to your teachers old and contrary
Without believing a word.

Tie the white fillets then about your lustrous hair
And think no more of what will come to pass
Than bluebirds that go walking on the grass
And chattering on the air.

Practice your beauty, blue girls, before it fail;
And I will cry with my loud lips and publish
Beauty which all our power shall never establish,
It is so frail.

GREAT THEMES IN POETRY

For I could tell you a story which is true:
I know a lady with a terrible tongue,
Blear eyes fallen from blue,
All her perfections tarnished—yet it is not long
Since she was lovelier than any of you.

A Lament

PERCY BYSSHE SHELLEY

O world! O life! O time!
On whose last steps I climb,
Trembling at that where I had stood before;
When will return the glory of your prime?
No more—Oh, never more!

Out of the day and night
A joy has taken flight;
Fresh spring, and summer, and winter hoar,
Move my faint heart with grief, but with delight
No more—Oh, never more!

I Strove with None

WALTER SAVAGE LANDOR

I strove with none; for none was worth my strife;
Nature I loved, and next to Nature, Art;
I warmed both hands before the fire of life;
It sinks, and I am ready to depart.

Many of the great religious teachers of the world—Christian, as well as Mohammedan, Judaic, Buddhist, Confucian—have been poets, and many of the most important religious writings are poetry. But all people of all times and places have wondered about the questions that religious thinkers and poets have pondered. What is life? How did it begin? What is its highest purpose? What is the meaning of death? How important is man in what seems an endless universe of time and space?

The following poems deal with these themes; they are attempts by poets to deal with the eternal and unanswerable questions of life.

The Twenty-fourth Psalm

DAVID

Give unto the Lord, O ye mighty, give unto the Lord glory and
    strength.
Give unto the Lord the glory due unto his name; worship the
    Lord in the beauty of holiness.
The voice of the Lord is upon the waters: the God of glory
    thundereth: the Lord is upon many waters.
The voice of the Lord is powerful; the voice of the Lord is full
    of majesty.
The voice of the Lord breaketh the cedars; yea, the Lord break-
    eth the cedars of Lebanon.
He maketh them also to skip like a calf; Lebanon and Sirion like
    a young unicorn.
The voice of the Lord divideth the flames of fire.
The voice of the Lord shaketh the wilderness; the Lord shaketh
    the wilderness of Kadesh.
The Lord will give strength unto his people; the Lord will bless
    his people with peace.

Sir Walter Raleigh the Night Before His Death

SIR WALTER RALEIGH

Even such is time, that takes in trust
Our youth, our joys, our all we have,
And pays us but with earth and dust;
Who, in the dark and silent grave,
When we have wandered all our ways,
Shuts up the story of our days.
But from this earth, this grave, this dust,
My God shall raise me up, I trust!

Holy Sonnet 10

JOHN DONNE

Death be not proud, though some have called thee
Mighty and dreadful, for thou art not so,
For those whom thou think'st thou dost overthrow,
Die not, poor death, nor yet canst thou kill me;
From rest and sleep, which but thy pictures be,
Much pleasure; then from thee, much more must flow,
And soonest our best men with thee do go,
Rest of their bones, and souls' delivery.
Thou art slave to Fate, Chance, kings, and desperate men,
And doth with poison, war and sickness dwell,
And poppy or charms can make us sleep as well
And better than thy stroke; why swell'st thou then?
One short sleep past, we wake eternally,
And death shall be no more. Death, thou shalt die.

The Tiger

WILLIAM BLAKE

Tiger, tiger, burning bright
In the forests of the night,
What immortal hand or eye
Could frame thy fearful symmetry?

In what distant deeps or skies
Burnt the fire of thine eyes?
On what wings dare he aspire?
What the hand dare seize the fire?

And what shoulder and what art
Could twist the sinews of thy heart?
And, when thy heart began to beat,
What dread hand and what dread feet?

What the hammer? What the chain?
In what furnace was thy brain?
What the anvil? What dread grasp
Dare its deadly terrors clasp?

When the stars threw down their spears,
And water'd heaven with their tears,
Did He smile His work to see?
Did He who made the lamb make thee?

Tiger, tiger, burning bright
In the forest of the night,
What immortal hand or eye
Dare frame thy fearful symmetry?

As I Sat on a Sunny Bank

ANONYMOUS

As I sat on a sunny bank,
A sunny bank, a sunny bank,
As I sat on a sunny bank
On Christmas Day in the morning.

I saw three ships come sailing by,
Come sailing by, come sailing by,
I saw three ships come sailing by,
On Christmas Day in the morning.

And who d'you think were on the ships,
Were on the ships, were on the ships,
And who d'you think were on the ships
But Joseph and his Fair Lady.

O he did whistle and she did sing,
And all the bells on earth did ring
For joy our Savior Christ was born
On Christmas Day in the morning.

God's Grandeur

GERARD MANLEY HOPKINS

The world is charged with the grandeur of God.
It will flame out, like shining from shook foil;
It gathers to a greatness, like the ooze of oil
Crushed. Why do men then now not reck his rod?
Generations have trod, have trod, have trod;
And all is seared with trade; bleared, smeared with toil;
And wears man's smudge and shares man's smell: the soil
Is bare now, nor can foot feel, being shod.
And for all this, nature is never spent;
There lives the dearest freshness deep down things;
And though the last lights off the black west went
Oh, morning, at the brown brink eastward, springs—
Because the Holy Ghost over the bent
World broods with warm breast and with ah! bright wings.

Pied Beauty

GERARD MANLEY HOPKINS

Glory be to God for dappled things—
For skies of couple color as a brinded cow;
For rose-moles all in stipple upon trout that swim;

GOD'S GRANDEUR: *Reck* = to pay heed to, care for

Fresh-firecoal chestnut-falls; finches' wings;
Landscape plotted and pieced—fold, fallow, and plough;
And áll trádes, their gear and tackle and trim.

All things counter, original, spare, strange;
Whatever is fickle, freckled (who knows how?)
With swift, slow; sweet, sour; adazzle, dim;
He fathers-forth whose beauty is past change:
                                        Praise him.

Mercy and Love
ROBERT HERRICK

God hath two wings, which he doth ever move,
The one is Mercy, and the next is Love:
Under the first the sinners ever trust;
And with the last he still directs the Just.

Brahma
RALPH WALDO EMERSON

If the red slayer thinks he slays,
Or if the slain think he is slain,
They know not well the subtle ways
I keep, and pass, and turn again.

Far or forgot to me is near;
Shadow and sunlight are the same;
The vanished gods to me appear;
And one to me are shame and fame.

They reckon ill who leave me out;
When me they fly, I am the wings;
I am the doubter and the doubt,
And I the hymn the Brahmin sings.

GREAT THEMES IN POETRY

The strong gods pine for my abode,
And pine in vain the sacred Seven;
But thou, meek lover of the good!
Find me, and turn thy back on heaven.

The Village Atheist

EDGAR LEE MASTERS

Ye young debaters over the doctrine
Of the soul's immortality.
I who lie here was the village atheist,
Talkative, contentious, versed in the arguments
Of the infidels.
But through a long sickness
Coughing myself to death
I read the Upanishads and the poetry of Jesus.
And they lighted a torch of hope and intuition
And desire which the Shadow,
Leading me through the caverns of darkness,
Could not extinguish.
Listen to me, ye who live in the senses
And think through the senses only:
Immortality is not a gift,
Immortality is an achievement:
And only those who strive mightily
Shall possess it.

I Never Saw a Moor

EMILY DICKINSON

I never saw a moor,
I never saw the sea;
Yet know I how the heather looks,
And what a wave must be.

THE VILLAGE ATHEIST: *Upanishads* = an ancient book treating philo-
sophic problems

r spoke with God,
r visited in heaven;
Yet certain am I of the spot
As if the chart were given.

Journey of the Magi

T. S. ELIOT

"A cold coming we had of it,
Just the worst time of the year
For a journey, and such a long journey:
The ways deep and the weather sharp,
The very dead of winter."
And the camels galled, sore-footed, refractory,
Lying down in the melting snow.
There were times we regretted
The summer palaces on slopes, the terraces,
And the silken girls bringing sherbet.
Then the camel men cursing and grumbling
And running away, and wanting their liquor and women,
And the night-fires going out, and the lack of shelters.
And the cities hostile and the towns unfriendly
And the villages dirty and charging high prices:
A hard time we had of it.
At the end we preferred to travel all night,
Sleeping in snatches,
With the voices singing in our ears, saying
That this was all folly.

Then at dawn we came down to a temperate valley,
Wet, below the snow line, smelling of vegetation;
With a running stream and a water-mill beating the darkness,
And three trees on the low sky,
And an old white horse galloped away in the meadow.
Then we came to a tavern with vine leaves over the lintel,
Six hands at an open door dicing for pieces of silver,

307   GREAT THEMES IN POETRY

And feet kicking the empty wine-skins.
But there was no information, and so we continued
And arrived at evening, not a moment too soon
Finding the place; it was (you may say) satisfactory.
All this was a long time ago, I remember,
And I would do it again, but set down
This set down
This: were we led all that way for
Birth or Death? There was a Birth, certainly,
We had evidence and no doubt. I had seen birth and death,
But had thought they were different; this Birth was
Hard and bitter agony for us, like death, our death.
We returned to our places, these Kingdoms,
But no longer at ease here, in the old dispensation,
With an alien people clutching their gods.
I should be glad of another death.

To a Waterfowl

WILLIAM CULLEN BRYANT

Whither, midst falling dew,
While glow the heavens with the last steps of day,
Far, through their rosy depths, dost thou pursue
Thy solitary way?

Vainly the fowler's eye
Might mark thy distant flight to do thee wrong,
As, darkly seen against the crimson sky,
Thy figure floats along.

Seek'st thou the plashy brink
Of weedy lake, or marge of river wide,
Or where the rocking billows rise and sink
On the chafed ocean-side?

There is a Power whose care
Teaches thy way along the pathless coast—
The desert and illimitable air—
Lone wandering, but not lost.

All day thy wings have fanned,
At that far height, the cold, thin atmosphere,
Yet stoop not, weary, to the welcome land,
Though the dark night is near.

And soon that toil shall end;
Soon shalt thou find a summer home, and rest,
And scream among thy fellows; reeds shall bend,
Soon, o'er thy sheltered nest.

Thou'rt gone, the abyss of heaven
Hath swallowed up thy form; yet, on my heart
Deeply has sunk the lesson thou hast given,
And shall not soon depart.

He who, from zone to zone,
Guides through the boundless sky thy certain flight,
In the long way that I must tread alone,
Will lead my steps aright.

A Hymne to God the Father

JOHN DONNE

Wilt thou forgive that sinne where I begunne,
Which is my sin, though it were done before?
Wilt thou forgive those sinnes, through which I runne,
And do run still: though still I do deplore?
When thou hast done, thou hast not done,
For I have more.

A HYMNE TO GOD THE FATHER: *done* = note that the poet is punning
on his name

Wilt thou forgive that sinne which I have wonne
Others to sinne? and, made my sinne their door?
Wilt thou forgive that sinne which I did shunne
A yeare, or two: but wallowed in, a score?
When thou hast done, thou hast not done,
For, I have more.

I have a sinne of feare, that when I have spunne
My last thread, I shall perish on the shore;
But sweare by thy selfe, that at my death thy sonne
Shall shine as he shines now, and heretofore;
And having done that, Thou hast done,
I fear no more.

Are there eternal truths? If so, what are they? What is the value of loyalty, of perseverance, of justice, of tolerance, of stoicism? How can one distinguish the cheap from the valuable, the ugly from the beautiful, the false from the true, the evil from the good? What are the highest purposes of life? How can a person know whether his life is meaningless or meaningful?

Are there answers for such questions? Philosophers, leaders of men and nations, wise men of all times have thought so, and for centuries they have offered the world their answers. Many of the most profound and enduring answers have come from the poets.

The Right Kind of People
EDWIN MARKHAM

Gone is the city, gone the day,
Yet still the story and the meaning stay:
Once where a prophet in the palm shade basked
A traveler chanced at noon to rest his mules.
"What sort of people may they be," he asked,
"In this proud city on the plains o'erspread?"
"Well, friend, what sort of people whence you came?"
"What sort?" the packman scowled; "why, knaves and fools."
"You'll find the people here the same," the wise man said.

Another stranger in the dusk drew near,
And pausing, cried, "What sort of people here
In your bright city where yon towers arise?"
"Well, friend, what sort of people whence you came?"
"What sort?" the pilgrim smiled with lifted head;
"Good, true, and wise."
"You'll find the people here the same,"
The wise man said.

Sir Patrick Spence

ANONYMOUS

The king sits in Dumferling toune,
Drinking the blude-reid wine:
"O whar will I get guid sailor,
To sail this ship of mine?"

Up and spak an eldern knicht,
Sat at the kings richt knee:
"Sir Patrick Spence is the best sailor,
That sails upon the sea."

The king has written a braid letter,
And signd it wi his hand,
And sent it to Sir Patrick Spence,
Was walking on the sand.

The first line that Sir Patrick red,
A loud lauch lauched he;
The next line that Sir Patrick red,
The teir blinded his ee.

"O wha is this has don this deid,
This ill deid don to me,
To send me out this time o' the yeir,
To sail upon the se!

"Mak haste, mak haste, my mirry men all
Our guid schip sails the morn:"
"O say na sae, my master deir,
For I feir a deadlie storme.

"Late, late yestreen I saw the new moone,
Wi the auld moone in hir arme,

SIR PATRICK SPENCE: *blude-reid* = blood-red; *guid* = good; *braid* =
broad; *cork-heild schoone* = cork-heeled shoes; *lang* = long; *kems* =
combs

And I feir, I feir, my deir master,
That we will cum to harme."

O our Scots nobles wer richt laith
To weet their cork-heild schoone;
Bot lang owre a' the play wer playd,
Thair hats they swam aboone.

O lang, lang may their ladies sit,
Wi thair fans into their hand,
Or eir they se Sir Patrick Spence
Cum sailing to the land.

O lang, lang may the ladies stand,
Wi thair gold kems in their hair
Waiting for thar ain deir lords,
For they'll se thame na mair.

Haf owre, half owre to Aberdour,
It's fiftie fadom deip,
And thair lies guid Sir Patrick Spence,
With the Scots lords at his feit.

The Old Stoic

EMILY BRONTË

Riches I hold in light esteem,
And love I laugh to scorn;
And lust of fame was but a dream
That vanish'd with the morn:

And, if I pray, the only prayer
That moves my lips for me
Is, "Leave the heart that now I bear,
And give me liberty!"

Yea, as my swift days near their goal,
'Tis all that I implore:
In life and death a chainless soul,
With courage to endure.

The Noble Nature

BEN JONSON

It is not growing like a tree
In bulk, doth make Man better be;
Or standing long an oak, three hundred year,
To fall a log at last, dry, bald, and sere:
A lily of a day
Is fairer far in May,
Although it fall and die that night;
It was the plant and flower of Light.
In small proportions we just beauties see;
And in short measures life may perfect be.

The Quiet Life

ALEXANDER POPE

Happy the man, whose wish and care
A few paternal acres bound,
Content to breathe his native air
In his own ground.

Whose herds with milk, whose fields with bread,
Whose flocks supply him with attire;
Whose trees in summer yield him shade,
In winter fire.

Blest, who can unconcern'dly find
Hours, days, and years slide soft away
In health of body, peace of mind,
Quiet by day,

Sound sleep by night; study and ease
Together mix'd; sweet recreation,
And innocence, which most does please
    With meditation.

Thus let me live, unseen, unknown;
Thus unlamented let me die;
Steal from the world, and not a stone
    Tell where I lie.

Character of a Happy Life

SIR HENRY WOTTON

How happy is he born or taught
That serveth not another's will;
Whose armor is his honest thought,
And simple truth his highest skill!

Whose passions not his masters are
Whose soul is still prepared for death;
Untied unto the world with care
Of princely love or vulgar breath;

Who hath his life from rumors freed,
Whose conscience is his strong retreat
Whose state can neither flatterers feed,
Nor ruin make accusers great;

Who envieth none whom chance doth raise
Or vice; who never understood
How deepest wounds are given with praise;
Nor rules of state, but rules of good:

Who God doth late and early pray
More of his grace than gifts to lend;
Who entertains the harmless day
With a well-chosen book or friend;

—This man is free from servile bands
Of hope to rise, or fear to fall;
Lord of himself, though not of lands;
And having nothing, he hath all.

Ode on a Grecian Urn

JOHN KEATS

Thou still unravished bride of quietness
Thou foster-child of silence and slow time,
Sylvan historian, who canst thus express
A flowery tale more sweetly than our rime:
What leaf-fringed legend haunts about thy shape
Of deities or mortals, or of both,
In Tempe or the dales of Arcady?
What men or gods are these? What maidens loth?
What mad pursuit? What struggle to escape?
What pipes and timbrels? What wild ecstasy?

Heard melodies are sweet, but those unheard
Are sweeter; therefore, ye soft pipes, play on;
Not to the sensual ear, but, more endeared,
Pipe to the spirit ditties of no tone:
Fair youth, beneath the trees, thou canst not leave
Thy song, nor ever can those trees be bare;
Bold Lover, never, never canst thou kiss,
Though winning near the goal—yet, do not grieve;
She cannot fade, though thou hast not thy bliss,
Forever wilt thou love, and she be fair!

Ah, happy, happy boughs! That cannot shed
Your leaves, nor ever bid the Spring adieu:
And, happy melodist, unwearied,
Forever piping songs forever new;

ODE ON A GRECIAN URN: *Tempe* = a beautiful valley in Greece; *Attic*
= Grecian, marked by simplicity

More happy love! more happy, happy love!
Forever warm and still to be enjoy'd,
Forever panting, and forever young;
All breathing human passion far above,
That leaves a heart high-sorrowful and cloyed,
A burning forehead, and a parching tongue.

Who are these coming to the sacrifice?
To what green altar, O mysterious priest,
Lead'st thou that heifer lowing at the skies,
And all her silken flanks with garlands drest?
What little town by river or sea shore,
Or mountain-built with peaceful citadel,
Is emptied of this folk, this pious morn?
And, little town, thy streets for evermore
Will silent be; and not a soul to tell
Why thou are desolate, can e'er return.

O Attic shape! Fair Attitude! with brede
Of marble men and maidens overwrought,
With forest branches and the trodden weed;
Thou, silent form, dost tease us out of thought
As doth eternity: Cold Pastoral!
When old age shall this generation waste,
Thou shalt remain, in midst of other woe
Than ours, a friend to man, to whom thou sayst,
Beauty is Truth,—Truth Beauty,—that is all
Ye know on earth, and all ye need to know.

Stars

SARA TEASDALE

> Alone in the night
> On a dark hill
> With pines around me
> Spicy and still,

And a heaven full of stars
Over my head,
White and topaz
And misty-red;

Myriads with beating
Hearts of fire
That aeons
Cannot vex or tire;

Up the dome of heaven
Like a great hill,
I watch them marching
Stately and still,

And I know that I
Am honored to be
Witness
Of so much majesty.

I Died for Beauty

EMILY DICKINSON

I died for beauty, but was scarce
Adjusted in the tomb,
When one who died for truth was lain
In an adjoining room.

He questioned softly why I failed?
"For beauty," I replied.
"And I for truth,—the two are one;
We brethren are," he said.

And so, as kinsmen met a night,
We talked between the rooms,
Until the moss had reached our lips,
And covered up our names.

Fame and Friendship

HENRY AUSTIN DOBSON

Fame is a food that dead men eat,—
I have no stomach for such meat.
In little light and narrow room,
They eat it in the silent tomb,
With no kind voice of comrade near
To bid the feaster be of cheer.

But Friendship is a nobler thing,—
Of Friendship it is good to sing.
For truly, when a man shall end,
He lives in memory of his friend,
Who does his better part recall
And of his fault make funeral.

Beauty Is Not Caused,—It Is

EMILY DICKINSON

Beauty is not caused,—it is;
Chase it and it ceases,
Chase it not and it abides,
Overtake the creases

In the meadow when the wind
Runs his fingers thro' it?
Deity will see to it
That you never do it.

Tell All the Truth

EMILY DICKINSON

Tell all the truth but tell it slant,
Success in circuit lies,
Too bright for our infirm delight
The truth's superb surprise;

As lightning to the children eased
With explanation kind,
The truth must dazzle gradually
Or every man be blind.

Plays
WALTER SAVAGE LANDOR

Alas, how soon the hours are over,
Counted us out to play the lover!
And how much narrower is the stage,
Allotted us to play the sage!

But when we play the fool, how wide
The theatre expands! beside,
How long the audience sits before us!
How many prompters! what a chorus!

A Man's a Man for A' That
ROBERT BURNS

Is there, for honest poverty,
That hings his head, an' a' that?
The coward slave, we pass him by,
We dare be poor for a' that!
For a' that, an' a' that,
Our toils obscure, an' a' that;
The rank is but the guinea's stamp;
The man's the gowd for a' that.

What tho' on hamely fare we dine,
Wear hodden-gray, an' a' that;

A MAN'S A MAN FOR A' THAT: *hings* = hangs; *guinea stamp* = British
currency; *hamely* = homely; *birkie* = young fellow; *coof* = fool;
aboon = above; *mauna fa'* = must not claim or get; *bear the gree* =
have the prize

AN ANTHOLOGY OF POEMS

Gie fools their silks, and knaves their wine,
A man's a man for a' that.
For a' that, an' a' that.
Their tinsel show, an' a' that;
The honest man, though e'er sae poor,
Is king o' men for a' that.

Ye see yon birkie, ca'd a lord,
Wha struts, an' stares, an' a' that;
Tho' hundreds worship at his word,
He's but a coof for a' that.
For a' that, an' a' that,
His riband, star, an' a' that,
The man o' independent mind,
He looks and laughs at a' that.

A prince can mak' a belted knight,
A marquis, duke, an' a' that;
But an honest man's aboon his might,
Guid faith he mauna fa' that!
For a' that, an' a' that,
Their dignities, an' a' that,
The pith o' sense, an' pride o' worth,
Are higher rank than a' that.

Then let us pray that come it may,
As come it will for a' that,
That sense and worth, o'er a' the earth,
May bear the gree, an' a' that.
For a' that, an' a' that,
It's coming yet, for a' that,
That man to man, the warld o'er,
Shall brothers be for a' that.

SONNETS

Invented by the Italian poet Petrarch and first practiced in English during the 16th century by the poets Wyatt and Surrey, the sonnet remains today an appealing, vigorous form. Almost every poet has at one time or another written in this compressed and challenging form. Shakespeare's sonnets are among the very best ever written, Milton's are bold and original, and Wordsworth's have become an immortal part of literature. Shelley, Byron, Keats, Poe, Arnold, and in more recent times Frost, Auden, MacLeish, Millay, and countless others have all composed sonnets of very high quality.

In its simplest terms a sonnet is a fourteen-line poem written entirely in iambic pentameter and employing a rather strict rhyme scheme. Three rhyme schemes have been most used: the Petrarchan, the Shakespearean, and the Spenserian. These rhyme schemes are as follows:

Petrarchan:　　　abba abba cdcdcd (or cde cde)
Shakespearean: abab cdcd efef gg
Spenserian:　　 abab bcbc cdcd ee

The sonnet is traditionally divided into two parts. The first part presents some problem or some rising emotion, and the second part gives a resolution or suggests a hope. In most sonnets the first part consists of eight lines (the octave) and the second consists of six lines (the sestet). But some of the greatest writers of the sonnet do not use this eight-six division. Shakespeare's sonnets, for instance, delay the resolution until the final two lines; they have a twelve-two line division. Milton's sonnets have no strict thought division and hence no line division. Most of the sonnets on the following pages, as you will see, begin with the octave and end with the sestet.

Nuns Fret Not at Their Convent's Narrow Room

WILLIAM WORDSWORTH

Nuns fret not at their convent's narrow room,
And hermits are contented with their cells,
And students with their pensive citadels;
Maids at the wheel, the weaver at his loom,
Sit blithe and happy; bees that soar for bloom,
High as the highest peak of Furness fells,
Will murmur by the hour in foxglove bells:
In truth the prison unto which we doom
Ourselves no prison is: and hence for me,
In sundry moods, 'twas pastime to be bound
Within the Sonnet's scanty plot of ground;
Pleased if some souls (for such there needs must be)
Who have felt the weight of too much liberty,
Should find brief solace there, as I have found.

Sonnet 18

WILLIAM SHAKESPEARE

Shall I compare thee to a summer's day? A
Thou art more lovely and more temperate: B
Rough winds do shake the darling buds of May, A
And summer's lease hath all too short a date. B
Sometimes too hot the eye of heaven shines, C
And often is his gold complexion dimm'd; D
And every fair from fair sometimes declines, C
By chance, or nature's changing course untrimm'd; D
But thy eternal summer shall not fade, E
Nor lose possession of that fair thou owest; F
Nor shall Death brag thou wander'st in his shade, E
When in eternal lines to time thou growest: F
So long as men can breathe, or eyes can see, G
So long lives this, and this gives life to thee. G

NUNS FRET NOT AT THEIR CONVENT'S NARROW ROOM: *Furness fells* =
in a rural area of England

323

SONNETS

Sonnet 116

WILLIAM SHAKESPEARE

Let me not to the marriage of true minds
Admit impediments. Love is not love
Which alters when it alteration finds,
Or bends with the remover to remove:
O, no! it is an ever-fixed mark
That looks on tempests and is never shaken;
It is the star to every wandering bark,
Whose worth's unknown, although his height be taken.
Love's not Time's fool, though rosy lips and cheeks
Within his bending sickle's compass come;
Love alters not with his brief hours and weeks,
But bears it out even to the edge of doom.
    If this be error, and upon me proved,
    I never writ, nor no man ever loved.

Sonnet 106

WILLIAM SHAKESPEARE

When in the chronicle of wasted time
I see descriptions of the fairest wights,
And beauty making beautiful old rhyme
In praise of ladies dead, and lovely knights;
Then in the blazon of sweet beauty's best
Of hand, of foot, of lip, of eye, of brow,
I see their antique pen would have exprest
Ev'n such a beauty as you master now.
So all their praises are but prophecies
Of this our time, all, you prefiguring.
And for they look'd but with divining eyes,
They had not skill enough your worth to sing:
    For we, which now behold these present days,
    Have eyes to wonder, but lack tongues to praise.

SONNET 116: *bark* = boat, ship; *sickle's compass* = scythe's sweep

✷ half-rhymes

Sonnet 30

WILLIAM SHAKESPEARE

When to the sessions of sweet silent thought
I summon up remembrance of things past,
I sigh the lack of many a thing I sought,
And with old woes new wail my dear time's waste:
Then can I drown an eye, unused to flow,
For precious friends hid in death's dateless night,
And weep afresh love's long-since-cancell'd woe,
And moan th' expense of many a vanish'd sight:
Then can I grieve at grievances foregone,
And heavily from woe to woe tell o'er
The sad account of fore-bemoaned moan,
Which I new pay as if not paid before.
But if a while I think on thee, dear friend,
All losses are restored and sorrows end.

Sonnet 29

WILLIAM SHAKESPEARE

When, in disgrace with Fortune and men's eyes,
I all alone beweep my outcast state,
And trouble deaf heaven with my bootless cries,
And look upon myself, and curse my fate,
Wishing me like to one more rich in hope,
Featured like him, like him with friends possest,
Desiring this man's art and that man's scope,
With what I most enjoy contented least;
Yet in these thoughts myself almost despising—
Haply I think on thee: and then my state,
Like to a lark at break of day arising
From sullen earth, sings hymns at Heaven's gate;
For thy sweet love rememb'red such wealth brings
That then I scorn to change my state with Kings.

Sonnet 64

WILLIAM SHAKESPEARE

When I have seen by Time's fell hand defaced
The rich proud cost of out-worn buried age;
When sometime lofty towers I see down-razed,
And brass eternal slave to mortal rage;
When I have seen the hungry ocean gain
Advantage on the kingdom of the shore,
And the firm soil win of the watery main,
Increasing store with loss, and loss with store;
When I have seen such interchange of state,
Or state itself confounded to decay,
Ruin hath taught me thus to ruminate—
That Time will come and take my love away:
  —This thought is as a death, which cannot choose
  But weep to have that which it fears to lose.

Sonnet 55

WILLIAM SHAKESPEARE

Not marble, nor the gilded monuments
Of princes, shall outlive this powerful rime;
But you shall shine more bright in these contents
Than unswept stone, besmeared with sluttish time.
When wasteful war shall statues overturn,
And broils root out the work of masonry,
Nor Mars his sword nor war's quick fire shall burn
The living record of your memory.
'Gainst death and all-oblivious enmity
Shall you pace forth; your praise shall still find room
Even in the eyes of all posterity
That wears this world out to the ending doom.
  So, till the judgment that yourself arise,
  You live in this, and dwell in lovers' eyes.

On His Blindness

JOHN MILTON

When I consider how my light is spent
Ere half my days, in this dark world and wide,
And that one talent which is death to hide
Lodged with me useless, though my soul more bent
To serve therewith my Maker, and present
My true account, lest He returning chide;
"Doth God exact day labor, light denied?"
I fondly ask. But Patience, to prevent
That murmur, soon replies, "God doth not need
Either man's work or his own gifts. Who best
Bear his mild yoke, they serve him best. His state
Is kingly: thousands at his bidding speed,
And post o'er land and ocean without rest;
They also serve who only stand and wait."

Sonnet

WILLIAM BLAKE

Thou Fair-haired Angel of the Evening,
Now, whilst the sun rests on the mountains, light
Thy bright torch of light; thy radiant crown
Put on, and smile upon our evening bed!
Smile on our loves; and whilst thou drawest the
Blue curtains of the sky, scatter thy silver dew
On every flower that shuts its sweet eyes
In timely sleep. Let thy West Wind sleep on
The lake; speak silence with thy glimmering eyes,
And wash the dusk with silver. Soon, full soon,
Dost thou withdraw; then the wolf rages wide,
And the lion glares through the dun forest:
The fleeces of the flock are covered with
Thy sacred dew: protect them with thine influence.

London, 1802

WILLIAM WORDSWORTH

Milton! thou should'st be living at this hour;
England hath need of thee; she is a fen
Of stagnant waters; altar, sword, and pen,
Fireside, the heroic wealth of hall and bower,
Have forfeited their ancient English dower
Of inward happiness. We are selfish men;
Oh! raise us up, return to us again;
And give us manners, virtue, freedom, power.
Thy soul was like a Star, and dwelt apart;
Thou hadst a voice whose sound was like the sea;
Pure as the naked heavens, majestic, free,
So didst thou travel on life's common way,
In cheerful godliness; and yet thy heart
The lowliest duties on herself did lay.

In London, September, 1802

WILLIAM WORDSWORTH

O friend! I know not which way I must look
For comfort, being, as I am, opprest
To think that now our life is only drest
For show; mean handy-work of craftsman, cook,
Or groom!—We must run glittering like a brook
In the open sunshine, or we are unblest;
The wealthiest man among us is the best:
No grandeur now in nature or in book
Delights us. Rapine, avarice, expense,
This is idolatry; and these we adore:
Plain living and high thinking are no more:
The homely beauty of the good old cause
Is gone; our peace, our fearful innocence,
And pure religion breathing household laws.

It Is a Beauteous Evening
WILLIAM WORDSWORTH

It is a beauteous evening, calm and free;
The holy time is quiet as a Nun
Breathless with adoration; the broad sun
Is sinking down in its tranquillity;
The gentleness of heaven broods o'er the Sea:
Listen! the mighty Being is awake,
And doth with his eternal motion make
A sound like thunder—everlastingly.
Dear Child! dear Girl! that walkest with me here,
If thou appear untouch'd by solemn thought,
Thy nature is not therefore less divine:
Thou liest in Abraham's bosom all the year,
And worship'st at the Temple's inner shrine,
God being with thee when we know it not.

To Wordsworth
PERCY BYSSHE SHELLEY

Poet of Nature, thou hast wept to know
That things depart which never may return;
Childhood and youth, friendship and love's first glow,
Have fled like sweet dreams, leaving thee to mourn.
These common woes I feel. One loss is mine,
Which thou too feel'st, yet I alone deplore;
Thou wert as a lone star whose light did shine
On some frail bark in winter's midnight roar;
Thou hast like to a rock-built refuge stood
Above the blind and battling multitude;
In honored poverty thy voice did weave
Songs consecrate to truth and liberty;—
Deserting these, thou leavest me to grieve,
Thus having been, that thou shouldst cease to be.

Sonnet on Chillon

GEORGE GORDON, LORD BYRON

Eternal Spirit of the chainless Mind!
Brightest in dungeons, Liberty! thou art,
For there thy habitation is the heart—
The heart which love of thee alone can bind;
And when thy sons to fetters are consigned—
To fetters, and the damp vault's dayless gloom,
Their country conquers with their martyrdom,
And Freedom's fame finds wings on every wind.
Chillon! thy prison is a holy place,
And thy sad floor an altar—for 'twas trod
Until his very steps have left a trace
Worn, as if thy cold pavements were a sod,
By Bonnivard!—May none those marks efface!
For they appeal from tyranny to God.

The Poetry of Earth

JOHN KEATS

The poetry of earth is never dead:
When all the birds are faint with the hot sun,
And hide in cooling trees, a voice will run
From hedge to hedge about the new-mown mead;
That is the Grasshopper's—he takes the lead
In summer luxury,—he has never done
With his delights; for when tired out with fun
He rests at ease beneath some pleasant weed.

The poetry of earth is ceasing never:
On a lone winter evening, when the frost
Has wrought a silence, from the stove there shrills
The Cricket's song, in warmth increasing ever,
And seems to one in drowsiness half lost,
The Grasshopper's among some grassy hills.

SONNET ON CHILLON: *Chillon* = a castle in Switzerland; *Bonnivard* =
a freedom fighter, imprisoned in Chillon

AN ANTHOLOGY OF POEMS

When I Have Fears

JOHN KEATS

When I have fears that I may cease to be
Before my pen has gleaned my teeming brain,
Before high-piled books, in charactery,
Hold like rich garners the full ripened grain;
When I behold, upon the night's starred face,
Huge cloudy symbols of a high romance,
And think that I may never live to trace
Their shadows, with the magic hand of chance;
And when I feel, fair creature of an hour,
That I shall never look upon thee more,
Never have relish in the fairy power
Of unreflecting love—then on the shore
Of the wide world I stand alone, and think
Till love and fame to nothingness do sink.

Bright Star! Would I Were Steadfast as Thou Art

JOHN KEATS

Bright star! would I were steadfast as thou art—
Not in lone splendor hung aloft the night
And watching, with eternal lids apart,
Like nature's patient, sleepless Eremite,
The moving waters at their priestlike task
Of pure ablution round earth's human shores,
Or gazing on the new soft-fallen mask
Of snow upon the mountains and the moors—
No—yet still steadfast, still unchangeable,
Pillowed upon my fair love's ripening breast,
To feel forever its soft fall and swell,
Awake forever in a sweet unrest,
Still, still to hear her tender-taken breath,
And so live ever—or else swoon to death.

WHEN I HAVE FEARS: *charactery* = letters of the alphabet
BRIGHT STAR! WOULD I WERE STEADFAST AS THOU ART: *eremite* = a religious hermit

If Thou Must Love Me

ELIZABETH BARRETT BROWNING

If thou must love me, let it be for nought
Except for love's sake only. Do not say,
"I love her for her smile—her look—her way
Of speaking gently—for a trick of thought
That falls in well with mine, and certes brought
A sense of pleasant ease on such a day"—
For these things in themselves, Beloved, may
Be changed, or change for thee—and love, so wrought,
May be unwrought so. Neither love me for
Thine own dear pity's wiping my cheeks dry—
A creature might forget to weep, who bore
Thy comfort long, and lose thy love thereby!
But love me for love's sake, that evermore
Thou may'st love on, through love's eternity.

How Do I Love Thee?

ELIZABETH BARRETT BROWNING

How do I love thee? Let me count the ways.
I love thee to the depth and breadth and height
My soul can reach, when feeling out of sight
For the ends of Being and ideal Grace.
I love thee to the level of every day's
Most quiet need, by sun and candlelight.
I love thee freely, as men strive for Right;
I love thee purely, as they turn from Praise.
I love thee with the passion put to use
In my old griefs, and with my childhood's faith.
I love thee with a love I seemed to lose
With my lost saints—I love thee with the breath,
Smiles, tears, of all my life!—and, if God choose,
I shall but love thee better after death.

The Sound of the Sea
HENRY WADSWORTH LONGFELLOW

The sea awoke at midnight from its sleep,
And round the pebbly beaches far and wide
I heard the first wave of the rising tide
Rush onward with uninterrupted sweep;
A voice out of the silence of the deep,
A sound mysteriously multiplied
As of a cataract from the mountain's side,
Or roar of winds upon a wooded steep.
So comes to us at times, from the unknown
And inaccessible solitudes of being,
The rushing of the sea-tides of the soul;
And inspirations, that we deem our own,
Are some divine foreshadowing and foreseeing
Of things beyond our reason or control.

Lucifer in Starlight
GEORGE MEREDITH

Came up above Earth and looked at it

On a starred night Price Lucifer uprose.
Tired of his dark dominion swung the fiend
Above the rolling ball in cloud part screened,
Where sinners hugged their specter of repose.
Poor prey to his hot fit of pride were those. *— arm*
And now upon his western wing he leaned,
Now his huge bulk o'er Afric's sands careened,
Now the black planet shadowed Arctic snows.
Soaring through wider zones that pricked his scars
With memory of the old revolt from Awe,
He reached a middle height, and at the stars, *left*
Which are the brain of heaven, he looked, and sank.
Around the ancient track marched, rank on rank,
The army of unalterable law.

The things going on day after day turning of earth, etc.

333 SONNETS

Remember

CHRISTINA ROSSETTI

Remember me when I am gone away,
Gone far away into the silent land;
When you can no more hold me by the hand,
Nor I half turn to go, yet turning stay.
Remember me when no more, day by day,
You tell me of our future that you planned;
Only remember me; you understand
It will be late to counsel then or pray.
Yet if you should forget me for a while
And afterward remember, do not grieve;
For if the darkness and corruption leave
A vestige of the thoughts that once I had,
Better by far you should forget and smile
Than that you should remember and be sad.

Listening

AMY LOWELL

'Tis you that are the music, not your song.
The song is but a door which, opening wide,
Lets forth the pent-up melody inside,
Your spirit's harmony, which clear and strong
Sings but of you. Throughout your whole life long
Your songs, your thoughts, your doings, each divide
This perfect beauty; waves within a tide
Or single notes amid a glorious throng.
The song of earth has many different chords;
Ocean has many moods and many tones
Yet always ocean. In damp spring woods
The painted trillium smiles, while crisp pine cones
Autumn alone can ripen. So is this
One music with a thousand cadences.

The Soldier

Saying how to remember him if he dies. [handwritten annotation]

RUPERT BROOKE

If I should die, think only this of me:
That there's some corner of a foreign field
That is forever England. There shall be
In that rich earth a richer dust concealed;
A dust whom England bore, shaped, made aware,
Gave, once, her flowers to love, her ways to roam,
A body of England's, breathing English air,
Washed by the rivers, blest by suns of home.
And think, this heart, all evil shed away,
A pulse in the eternal mind, no less
Gives somewhere back the thought by England given;
Her sights and sounds; dreams happy as her day;
And laughter, learnt of friends; and gentleness,
In hearts at peace, under an English heaven.

praises England [handwritten annotation]

Calvary

EDWIN ARLINGTON ROBINSON

Friendless and faint, with martyred steps and slow,
Faint for the flesh, but for the spirit free,
Stung by the mob that came to see the show,
The Master toiled along to Calvary;
We gibed him, as he went, with houndish glee,
Till his dimmed eyes for us did overflow;
We cursed his vengeless hands thrice wretchedly,—
And this was nineteen hundred years ago.

But after nineteen hundred years the shame
Still clings, and we have not made good the loss
That outraged faith had entered in his name.
Ah, when shall come love's courage to be strong!
Tell me, O Lord—tell me, O Lord, how long
Are we to keep Christ writhing on the cross!

Immortal Love

GEORGE EDWARD WOODBERRY

Immortal love, too high for my possessing,—
Yet, lower than thee, where shall I find repose?
Long in my youth I sang the morning rose,
By earthly things the heavenly pattern guessing!
Long fared I on, beauty and love caressing,
And finding in my heart a place for those
Eternal fugitives; the golden close
Of evening folds me, still their sweetness blessing.

Oh, happy we, the first-born heirs of nature,
For whom the Heavenly Sun delays his light!
He by the sweets of every mortal creature
Tempers eternal beauty to our sight;
And by the glow upon love's earthly feature
Maketh the path of our departure bright.

West London

MATTHEW ARNOLD

Crouched on the pavement, close by Belgrave Square,
A tramp I saw, ill, moody, and tongue-tied.
A babe was in her arms, and at her side
A girl; their clothes were rags, their feet were bare.

Some laboring men, whose work lay somewhere there,
Pass'd opposite; she touched her girl, who hied
Across, and begg'd, and came back satisfied.
The rich she had let pass with a frozen stare.

Thought I: "Above her state this spirit towers;
She will not ask of aliens, but of friends,
Of sharers in a common human fate.

"She turns from that cold succor, which attends
The unknown little from the unknowing great,
And points us to a better time than ours."

Quiet Work
MATTHEW ARNOLD

One lesson, Nature, let me learn of thee,
One lesson which in every wind is blown,
One lesson of two duties kept at one
Though the loud world proclaim their enmity—

Of toil unsever'd from tranquillity!
Of labor, that in lasting fruit outgrows
Far noisier schemes, accomplish'd in repose,
Too great for haste, too high for rivalry!

Yes, while on earth a thousand discords ring,
Man's fitful uproar mingling with his toil,
Still do thy sleepless ministers move on,

Their glorious tasks in silence perfecting;
Still working, blaming still our vain turmoil,
Laborers that shall not fail, when man is gone.

Shakespeare
MATTHEW ARNOLD

Others abide our question. Thou art free.
We ask and ask: thou smilest and art still,
Out-topping knowledge. For the loftiest hill,
Who to the stars uncrowns his majesty,

Planting his steadfast footsteps in the sea,
Making the heaven of heavens his dwelling-place,
Spares but the cloudy border of his base
To the foiled searching of mortality;

And thou, who didst the stars and sunbeams know,
Self-schooled, self-scanned, self-honored, self-secure,
Didst tread on earth unguessed at. Better so!

All pains the immortal spirit must endure,
All weakness which impairs, all griefs which bow,
Find their sole speech in that victorious brow.

Who's Who

W. H. AUDEN

A shilling life will give you all the facts:
How Father beat him, how he ran away,
What were the struggles of his youth, what acts
Made him the greatest figure of his day:
Of how he fought, fished, hunted, worked all night,
Though giddy, climbed new mountains; named a sea:
Some of the last researchers even write
Love made him weep his pints like you and me
With all his honors on, he sighed for one
Who, say astonished critics, lived at home;
Did little jobs about the house with skill
And nothing else; could whistle; would sit still
Or potter round the garden; answered some
Of his long marvelous letters but kept none.

Design

ROBERT FROST

I found a dimpled spider, fat and white,
On a white heal-all, holding up a moth
Like a white piece of rigid satin cloth—
Assorted characters of death and blight
Mixed ready to begin the morning right,

who's who: *shilling* = a few cents in British currency

Like the ingredients of a witches' broth—
A snow-drop spider, a flower like froth,
And dead wings carried like a paper kite.
What had that flower to do with being white,
The wayside blue and innocent heal-all?
What brought the kindred spider to that height,
Then steered the white moth thither in the night?
What but design of darkness to appall?—
If design govern in a thing so small.

Once by the Pacific

ROBERT FROST

The shattered water made a misty din.
Great waves looked over others coming in,
And thought of doing something to the shore
That water never did to land before.
The clouds were low and hairy in the skies,
Like locks blown forward in the gleam of eyes.
You could not tell, and yet it looked as if
The shore was lucky in being backed by cliff,
The cliff in being backed by continent;
It looked as if a night of dark intent
Was coming, and not only a night, an age.
Someone had better be prepared for rage.
There would be more than ocean-water broken
Before God's last *Put out the Light* was spoken.

Salem

ROBERT LOWELL

In Salem seasick spindrift drifts or skips
To the canvas flapping on the seaward panes
Until the knitting sailor stabs at ships

SALEM: *Charon's* = in mythology, he who ferried souls across the
underground river Styx

Nosing like sheep or Morpheus through his brain's
Asylum. Seaman, seaman, how the draft
Lashes the oily slick about your head
Beating up whitecaps! Seaman, Charon's raft
Dumps its damned goods into the harbor-bed,
There sewage sickens the rebellious seas.
Remember, seaman, Salem fishermen
Once hung their nimble fleets on the Great Banks.
Where was it that New England bred the men
Who quartered the Leviathan's fat flanks
And fought the British Lion to his knees?

Full Moon: New Guinea

KARL SHAPIRO

These nights we fear the aspects of the moon,
Sleep lightly in the radiance falling clear
On palms and ferns and hills and us; for soon
The small burr of the bombers in our ear
Tickles our rest; we rise as from a nap
And take our helmets absently and meet,
Prepared for any spectacle or mishap,
At trenches fresh and narrow at our feet.

Look up, look up, and wait and breathe. These nights
We fear Orion and the Cross. The crowd
Of deadly insects caught in our long lights
Glitter and seek to burrow in a cloud
Soft-mined with high explosive. Breathe and wait,
The bombs are falling darkly for our fate.

FULL MOON: NEW GUINEA: *bombers* = air force planes in World War
II

The End of the World

ARCHIBALD MAC LEISH

Quite unexpectedly as Vasserot
The armless ambidextrian was lighting
A match between his great and second toe
And Ralph the lion was engaged in biting
The neck of Madame Sossman while the drum
Pointed, and Teeny was about to cough
In waltz-time swinging Jocko by the thumb—
Quite unexpectedly the top blew off:

And there, there overhead, there, there, hung over,
Those thousands of white faces, those dazed eyes,
There in the starless dark the poise, the hover,
There with vast wings across the canceled skies,
There in the sudden blackness the black pall
Of nothing, nothing, nothing,—nothing at all.

A TREASURY OF FINE POEMS:
OLD AND NEW

Winter

WILLIAM SHAKESPEARE

> When icicles hang by the wall
> And Dick the shepherd blows his nail,
> And Tom bears logs into the hall,
> And milk comes frozen home in pail;
> When blood is nipt, and ways be foul,
> Then nightly sings the staring owl
> > Tuwhoo!
> Tuwhit! tuwhoo! A merry note!
> While greasy Joan doth keel the pot.
>
> When all aloud the wind doth blow,
> And coughing drowns the parson's saw,
> And birds sit brooding in the snow,
> And Marian's nose looks red and raw;
> When roasted crabs hiss in the bowl—
> Then nightly sings the staring owl
> > Tuwhoo!
> Tuwhit! tuwhoo! A merry note!
> While greasy Joan doth keel the pot.

WINTER: *blows his nail* = blows on his fingernails to warm them; *keel* = scrub thoroughly

342

Blow, Blow, Thou Winter Wind

WILLIAM SHAKESPEARE

Blow, blow, thou winter wind,
Thou art not so unkind
As man's ingratitude;
Thy tooth is not so keen
Because thou art not seen,
Although thy breath be rude.
Heigh ho! sing heigh ho! unto the green holly:
Most friendship is feigning, most loving mere folly:
Then, heigh ho! the holly!
This life is most jolly.

Freeze, freeze, thou bitter sky,
That dost not bite so nigh
As benefits forgot:
Though thou the waters warp,
Thy sting is not so sharp
As friend remember'd not.
Heigh ho! sing heigh ho! unto the green holly:
Most friendship is feigning, most loving mere folly:
Then, heigh ho! the holly!
This life is most jolly.

The True Beauty

THOMAS CAREW

He that loves a rosy cheek
Or a coral lip admires,
Or from star-like eyes doth seek
Fuel to maintain his fires;
As old Time makes these decay,
So his flames must waste away.

But a smooth and steadfast mind,
Gentle thoughts, and calm desires,

Hearts with equal love combined,
Kindle never-dying fires:—
Where these are not, I despise
Lovely cheeks or lips or eyes.

To Dianeme
ROBERT HERRICK

Sweet, be not proud of those two eyes
Which starlike sparkle in their skies;
Nor be proud, that you can see
All hearts your captives; yours yet free:
Be you not proud of that rich hair
Which wantons with the lovesick air;
Whenas that ruby which you wear,
Sunk from the tip of your soft ear,
Will last to be a precious stone
When all your world of beauty's gone.

To Daffodils
ROBERT HERRICK

Fair daffodils, we weep to see
You haste away so soon:
As yet the early-rising sun
Has not attain'd his noon.
Stay, stay,
Until the hasting day
Has run
But to the even-song;
And, having pray'd together, we
Will go with you along.

We have short time to stay, as you.
We have as short a Spring;

As quick a growth to meet decay,
As you, or any thing.
We die,
As your hours do, and dry
Away,
Like to the Summer's rain;
Or as the pearls of morning's dew
Ne'er to be found again.

Like to the Falling of a Star

HENRY KING

Like to the falling of a star,
Or as the flights of eagles are,
Or like the fresh spring's gaudy hue,
Or silver drops of morning dew,
Or like a wind that chafes the flood,
Or bubbles which on water stood:
Even such is man, whose borrowed light
Is straight called in and paid to night:
The wind blows out, the bubble dies,
The spring intombed in autumn lies:
The dew's dried up, the star is shot,
The flight is past, and man forgot.

On Time

JOHN MILTON

Fly envious Time, till thou run out thy race,
Call on the lazy leaden-stepping hours,
Whose speed is but the heavy Plummet's pace;
And glut thyself with what thy womb devours,
Which is no more than what is false and vain,
And merely mortal dross;
So little is our loss,

ON TIME: *Plummet's* = the sun's

So little is thy gain.
For when as each thing bad thou hast entomb'd,
And last of all, thy greedy self consum'd,
Then long Eternity shall greet our bliss
With an individual kiss;
And Joy shall overtake us as a flood,
When every thing that is sincerely good
And perfectly divine,
With Truth, and Peace, and Love shall ever shine
About the supreme Throne
Of him, t'whose happy-making sight alone,
When once our heav'nly-guided soul shall climb,
Then all this Earthy grossness quit,
Attir'd with Stars, we shall for ever sit,
Triumphing over Death, and Chance, and thee O Time.

Vital Spark of Heavenly Flame

ALEXANDER POPE

Vital spark of heavenly flame!
Quit, O quit this mortal frame:
Trembling, hoping, lingering, flying,
O the pain, the bliss of dying!
Cease, fond Nature, cease thy strife,
And let me languish into life.

Hark! they whisper; angels say,
Sister Spirit, come away!
What is this absorbs me quite?
Steals my senses, shuts my sight,
Drowns my spirits, draws my breath?
Tell me, my soul, can this be Death?

The world recedes; it disappears!
Heav'n opens on my eyes! my ears
With sounds seraphic ring!

Lend, lend your wings! I mount! I fly!
O Grave! where is thy victory?
O Death! where is thy sting?

Elegy Written in a Country Churchyard
THOMAS GRAY

The curfew tolls the knell of parting day,
The lowing herd winds slowly o'er the lea,
The plowman homeward plods his weary way,
And leaves the world to darkness and to me.

Now fades the glimmering landscape on the sight,
And all the air a solemn stillness holds,
Save where the beetle wheels his droning flight,
And drowsy tinklings lull the distant folds;

Save that from yonder ivy-mantled tower
The moping owl does to the moon complain
Of such, as wandering near her secret bower,
Molest her ancient solitary reign.

Beneath those rugged elms, that yew tree's shade,
Where heaves the turf in many a moldering heap,
Each in his narrow cell forever laid,
The rude forefathers of the hamlet sleep.

The breezy call of incense-breathing morn,
The swallow twittering from the straw-built shed,
The cock's shrill clarion, or the echoing horn,
No more shall rouse them from their lowly bed.

For them no more the blazing hearth shall burn,
Or busy housewife ply her evening care:

ELEGY WRITTEN IN A COUNTRY CHURCHYARD: *glebe* = ground; *her-aldry* = study of families and coats of arms; *Hampden* = a landowner who resisted land taxes of Charles I

No children run to lisp their sire's return,
Or climb his knee the envied kiss to share.

Oft did the harvest to their sickle yield,
Their furrow oft the stubborn glebe has broke;
How jocund did they drive their team afield!
How bowed the woods beneath their sturdy stroke!

Let not ambition mock their useful toil,
Their homely joys, and destiny obscure;
Nor grandeur hear with a disdainful smile,
The short and simple annals of the poor.

The boast of heraldry, the pomp of power,
And all that beauty, all that wealth e'er gave,
Awaits alike the inevitable hour.
The paths of glory lead but to the grave.

Nor you, ye proud, impute to these the fault,
If memory o'er their tomb no trophies raise,
Where through the long-drawn aisle and fretted vault
The pealing anthem swells the note of praise.

Can storied urn or animated bust
Back to its mansion call the fleeting breath?
Can honor's voice provoke the silent dust,
Or flatt'ry soothe the dull cold ear of Death?

Perhaps in this neglected spot is laid
Some heart once pregnant with celestial fire;
Hands, that the rod of empire might have swayed,
Or waked to ecstasy the living lyre.

But knowledge to their eyes her ample page
Rich with the spoils of time did ne'er unroll;
Chill penury repressed their noble rage,
And froze the genial current of the soul.

Full many a gem of purest ray serene,
The dark unfathomed caves of ocean bear;
Full many a flower is born to blush unseen,
And waste its sweetness on the desert air.

Some village Hampden that with dauntless breast
The little tyrant of his fields withstood,
Some mute inglorious Milton here may rest,
Some Cromwell guiltless of his country's blood.

The applause of listening senates to command,
The threats of pain and ruin to despise,
To scatter plenty o'er a smiling land,
And read their history in a nation's eyes,

Their lot forbade: nor circumscribed alone
Their growing virtues, but their crimes confined;
Forbade to wade through slaughter to a throne,
And shut the gates of mercy on mankind,

The struggling pangs of conscious truth to hide,
To quench the blushes of ingenuous shame,
Or heap the shrine of luxury and pride
With incense kindled at the Muse's flame.

Far from the madding crowd's ignoble strife,
Their sober wishes never learned to stray;
Along the cool sequestered vale of life
They kept the noiseless tenor of their way.

Yet ev'n these bones from insult to protect,
Some frail memorial still erected nigh,
With uncouth rhymes and shapeless sculpture decked,
Implores the passing tribute of a sigh.

Their name, their years, spelt by the unlettered Muse,
The flame of fame and elegy supply;

And many a holy text around she strews,
That teach the rustic moralist to die.

For who to dumb forgetfulness a prey,
This pleasing anxious being e'er resigned,
Left the warm precincts of the cheerful day,
Nor cast one longing lingering look behind?

On some fond breast the parting soul relies,
Some pious drops the closing eye requires;
Ev'n from the tomb the voice of nature cries,
Ev'n in our ashes live their wonted fires.

For thee, who mindful of the unhonored dead
Dost in these lines their artless tale relate;
If chance, by lonely contemplation led,
Some kindred spirit shall inquire thy fate,

Haply some hoary-headed swain may say,
"Oft have we seen him at the peep of dawn
Brushing with hasty steps the dews away,
To meet the sun upon the upland lawn.

"There at the foot of yonder nodding beech
That wreathes its old fantastic roots so high,
His listless length at noontide would he stretch,
And pore upon the brook that babbles by.

"Hard by yon wood, now smiling as in scorn,
Muttering his wayward fancies he would rove,
Now drooping, woeful wan, like one forlorn,
Or crazed with care, or crossed in hopeless love.

"One morn I missed him on the customed hill,
Along the heath and near his favorite tree,
Another came; nor yet beside the rill,
Nor up the lawn, nor at the wood was he;

"The next, with dirges due in sad array
Slow through the church-way path we saw him borne.
Approach and read (for thou canst read) the lay,
Graved on the stone beneath yon aged thorn."

The Epitaph

Here rests his head upon a lap of earth
A youth to fortune and to fame unknown.
Fair science frowned not on his humble birth,
And melancholy marked him for her own.

Large was his bounty, and his soul sincere,
Heaven did a recompense as largely send;
He gave to misery all he had, a tear;
He gained from Heaven ('twas all he wished) a friend.

No farther seek his merits to disclose,
Or draw his frailties from their dread abode,
(There they alike in trembling hope repose)
The bosom of his Father and his God.

The Lamb
WILLIAM BLAKE

Little Lamb, who made thee?
Dost thou know who made thee?
Gave thee life, and bid thee feed,
By the stream and o'er the mead;
Gave thee clothing of delight,
Softest clothing, woolly, bright;
Gave thee such a tender voice,
Making all the vales rejoice?
Little Lamb, who made thee?
Dost thou know who made thee?

Little Lamb, I'll tell thee,
Little Lamb, I'll tell thee:
He is callèd by thy name,
For He calls Himself a Lamb,
He is meek, and He is mild;
He became a little child.
I a child, and thou a lamb,
We are callèd by His name.
Little Lamb, God bless thee!
Little Lamb, God bless thee!

Bannockburn

ROBERT BURNS

At Bannockburn the English lay,—
The Scots they were na far away,
But waited for the break o' day
That glinted in the east.

But soon the sun broke through the heath
And lighted up that field o' death,
When Bruce, wi' soul-inspiring breath,
His heralds thus addressed:—

Scots, wha hae wi' Wallace bled,
Scots, wham Bruce has aften led;
Welcome to your gory bed,
Or to victorie.

Now's the day, and now's the hour
See the front o' battle lour:
See approach proud Edward's power,—
Chains and slaverie!

Wha will be a traitor knave?
Wha can fill a coward's grave?

Wha sae base as be a slave?
Let him turn and flee!

Wha for Scotland's king and law
Freedom's sword will strongly draw,
Freeman stand, or freeman fa'?
Let him follow me!

By Oppression's woes and pains!
By your sons in servile chains,
We will drain our dearest veins,
But they shall be free!

Lay the proud usurpers low!
Tyrants fall in every foe!
Liberty's in every blow!
Let us do, or die!

I Wandered Lonely as a Cloud
WILLIAM WORDSWORTH

I wandered lonely as a cloud
That floats on high o'er vales and hills,
When all at once I saw a crowd,
A host of golden daffodils;
Beside the lake, beneath the trees,
Fluttering and dancing in the breeze.

Continuous as the stars that shine
And twinkle on the milky way,
They stretched in never-ending line
Along the margin of the bay:
Ten thousand saw I at a glance,
Tossing their heads in sprightly dance.

The waves beside them danced, but they
Outdid the sparkling waves in glee:—

A poet could not but be gay
In such a jocund company:
I gazed—and gazed—but little thought
What wealth the show to me had brought.

For oft when on my couch I lie
In vacant or in pensive mood,
They flash upon that inward eye
Which is the bliss of solitude,
And then my heart with pleasure fills,
And dances with the daffodils.

Lines Written in Early Spring
WILLIAM WORDSWORTH

I heard a thousand blended notes
While in a grove I sate reclined,
In that sweet mood when pleasant thoughts
Bring sad thoughts to the mind.

To her fair works did Nature link
The human soul that through me ran;
And much it grieved my heart to think
What man has made of man.

Through primrose tufts, in that sweet bower,
The periwinkle trailed its wreaths;
And 'tis my faith that every flower
Enjoys the air it breathes.

The birds around me hopped and played,
Their thoughts I cannot measure,—
But the least motion which they made,
It seemed a thrill of pleasure.

The budding twigs spread out their fan
To catch the breezy air;
And I must think, do all I can,
That there was pleasure there.

If this belief from heaven be sent,
If such be Nature's holy plan,
Have I not reason to lament
What man has made of man?

To Autumn

JOHN KEATS

Season of mists and mellow fruitfulness,
Close bosom-friend of the maturing sun;
Conspiring with him how to load and bless
With fruit the vines that round the thatch eaves run;
To bend with apples the mossed cottage-trees,
And fill all fruit with ripeness to the core;
To swell the gourd, and plump the hazel shells
With a sweet kernel; to set budding more,
And still more, later flowers for the bees,
Until they think warm days will never cease,
For summer has o'er-brimmed their clammy cells.

Who hath not seen thee oft amid thy store?
Sometimes whoever seeks abroad may find
Thee sitting careless on a granary floor,
Thy hair soft-lifted by the winnowing wind;
Or on a half-reaped furrow sound asleep,
Drowsed with the fume of poppies, while thy hook
Spares the next swath and all its twined flowers:
And sometimes like a gleaner thou dost keep
Steady thy laden head across a brook;
Or by a cider-press, with patient look,
Thou watchest the last oozings, hours by hours.

Where are the songs of Spring? Ay, where are they?
Think not of them, thou hast thy music too,—
While barred clouds bloom the soft-dying day,
And touch the stubble-plains with rosy hue;
Then in a wailful choir the small gnats mourn
Among the silver sallows, bourne aloft
Or sinking as the light wind lives or dies;
And full-grown lambs loud bleat from hilly bourn;
Hedge-crickets sing; and now with treble soft
The redbreast whistles from a garden-croft,
And gathering swallows twitter in the skies.

Ode to a Nightingale

JOHN KEATS

My heart aches, and a drowsy numbness pains
My sense, as though of hemlock I had drunk,
Or emptied some dull opiate to the drains
One minute past, and Lethe-wards had sunk:
'Tis not through envy of thy happy lot,
But being too happy in thine happiness,—
That thou, lighted-winged Dryad of the trees,
In some melodious plot
Of beechen green, and shadows numberless,
Singest of summer in full-throated ease.

O for a draught of vintage! that hath been
Cool'd a long age in the deep-delvèd earth,
Tasting of Flora and the country green,
Dance, and Provençal song, and sunburnt mirth!
O for a beaker full of the warm South,
Full of the true, the blushing Hippocrene,
With beaded bubbles winking at the brim,
And purple-stained mouth;
That I might drink, and leave the world unseen,
And with thee fade away into the forest dim:

Fade far away, dissolve, and quite forget
What thou among the leaves has never known,
The weariness, the fever, and the fret
Here, where men sit and hear each other groan;
Where palsy shakes a few, sad, last grey hairs,
Where youth grows pale, and spectre-thin, and dies;
Where but to think is to be full of sorrow
And leaden-eyed despairs;
Where Beauty cannot keep her lustrous eyes,
Or new Love pine at them beyond to-morrow.

Away! away! for I will fly to thee,
Not charioted by Bacchus and his pards,
But on the viewless wings of Poesy,
Though the dull brain perplexes and retards:
Already with thee! tender is the night,
And haply the Queen-Moon is on her throne,
Cluster'd around by all her starry Fays;
But here there is no light,
Save what from heaven is with the breezes blown
Through verdurous glooms and winding mossy ways.

I cannot see what flowers are at my feet,
Nor what soft incense hangs upon the boughs,
But, in embalmed darkness, guess each sweet
Wherewith the seasonable month endows
The grass, the thicket, and the fruit tree wild;
White hawthorn, and the pastoral eglantine;
Fast-fading violets cover'd up in leaves;
And mid-May's eldest child
The coming musk-rose, full of dewy wine,
The murmurous haunt of flies on summer eves.

Darkling I listen; and, for many a time,
I have been half in love with easeful Death,
Call'd him soft names in many a mused rhyme,

To take into the air my quiet breath;
Now more than ever seems it rich to die,
To cease upon the midnight with no pain,
While thou art pouring forth thy soul abroad
In such an ecstasy!
Still wouldst thou sing, and I have ears in vain—
To thy high requiem become a sod.

Thou wast not born for death, immortal Bird!
No hungry generations tread thee down;
The voice I heard this passing night was heard
In ancient days by emperor and clown:
Perhaps the self-same song that found a path
Through the sad heart of Ruth, when, sick for home,
She stood in tears amid the alien corn;
The same that oft-times hath
Charm'd magic casements, opening on the foam
Of perilous seas, in faery lands forlorn.

Forlorn! the very word is like a bell
To toll me back from thee to my sole self!
Adieu! the fancy cannot cheat so well
As she is famed to do, deceiving elf.
Adieu! Adieu! thy plaintive anthem fades
Past the near meadows, over the still stream,
Up the hill-side; and now 'tis buried deep
In the next valley-glades:
Was it a vision, or a waking dream?
Fled is that music:—do I wake or sleep?

Ode to the West Wind
PERCY BYSSHE SHELLEY

O wild west wind, thou breath of autumn's being,
Thou, from whose unseen presence the leaves dead
Are driven, like ghosts from an enchanter fleeing,

Yellow, and black, and pale, and hectic red,
Pestilence-stricken multitudes! O thou
Who chariotest to their dark wintry bed

The winged seeds, where they lie cold and low,
Each like a corpse with its grave, until
Thine azure sister of the spring shall blow

Her clarion o'er the dreaming earth, and fill
(Driving sweet buds like flocks to feed in air)
With living hues and odors plain and hill:

Wild spirit, which art moving everywhere;
Destroyer and preserver; hear, oh hear!

2

Thou on whose stream, 'mid the steep sky's commotion,
Loose clouds like earth's decaying leaves are shed,
Shook from the tangled boughs of heaven and ocean,

Angels of rain and lightning! there are spread
On the blue surface of thine airy surge,
Like the bright hair uplifted from the head

Of some fierce Maenad, even from the dim verge
Of the horizon to the zenith's height,
The locks of the approaching storm. Thou dirge

Of the dying year, to which this closing night
Will be the dome of a vast sepulchre,
Vaulted with all thy congregated might

Of vapors, from whose solid atmosphere
Black rain, and fire, and hail, will burst: Oh hear!

3

Thou who didst waken from his summer-dreams
The blue Mediterranean, where he lay,
Lulled by the coil of his crystalline streams,

Beside a pumice isle in Baiae's bay,
And saw in sleep old palaces and towers
Quivering within the wave's intenser day,

All overgrown with azure moss and flowers
So sweet, the sense faints picturing them! Thou
From whose path the Atlantic's level powers

Cleave themselves into chasms, while far below
The sea-blooms and the oozy woods which wear
The sapless foliage of the ocean know

Thy voice, and suddenly grow gray with fear
And tremble and despoil themselves: Oh hear!

4

If I were a dead leaf thou mightest bear;
If I were a swift cloud to fly with thee;
A wave to pant beneath thy power, and share

The impulse of thy strength, only less free
Than thou, O uncontrollable! If even
I were as in my boyhood, and could be

The comrade of thy wanderings over heaven,
As then, when to outstrip thy skyey speed
Scarce seemed a vision; I would ne'er have striven

As thus with thee in prayer in my sore need.
Oh! lift me as a wave, a leaf, a cloud!
I fall upon the thorns of life! I bleed!

A heavy weight of hours has chained and bowed
One too like thee—tameless, swift, and proud.

5

Make me thy lyre, ev'n as the forest is:
What if my leaves are falling like its own!
The tumult of thy mighty harmonies

Will take from both a deep, autumnal tone,
Sweet though in sadness. Be thou, spirit fierce,
My spirit! be thou me, impetuous one!

Drive my dead thoughts over the universe,
Like withered leaves, to quicken a new birth!
And by the incantations of this verse,

Scatter, as from an unextinguished hearth
Ashes and sparks, my words among mankind!
Be through my lips to unawakened earth

The trumpet of a prophecy! O wind,
If winter comes, can spring be far behind?

She Walks in Beauty
GEORGE GORDON, LORD BYRON

She walks in beauty, like the night
Of cloudless climes and starry skies;
And all that's best of dark and bright
Meet in her aspect and her eyes:
Thus mellowed to that tender light
Which heaven to gaudy day denies.

One shade the more, one ray the less,
Had half-impaired the nameless grace
Which waves in every raven tress,

Or softly lightens o'er her face;
Where thoughts serenely sweet express
How pure, how dear their dwelling place.

And on that cheek, and o'er that brow,
So soft, so calm, so eloquent,
The smiles that win, the tints that glow,
But tell of days in goodness spent,
A mind at peace with all below,
A heart whose love is innocent!

All for Love

GEORGE GORDON, LORD BYRON

O talk not to me of a name great in glory;
The days of our youth are the days of our glory;
And the myrtle and ivy of sweet two-and-twenty
Are worth all your laurels, though ever so plenty.

What are garlands and crowns to the brow that is wrinkled?
'Tis but as a dead flower with May-dew besprinkled:
Then away with all such from the head that is hoary—
What care I for the wreaths that can only give glory?

O Fame!—If I e'er took delight in thy praises,
'Twas less for the sake of thy high-sounding phrases,
Than to see the bright eyes of the dear one discover
She thought that I was not unworthy to love her.

There chiefly I sought thee, there only I found thee;
Her glance was the best of the rays that surround thee;
When it sparkled o'er aught that was bright in my story,
I knew it was love, and I felt it was glory.

Margaritae Sorori

WILLIAM ERNEST HENLEY

A late lark twitters from the quiet skies;
And from the west,
Where the sun, his day's work ended,
Lingers as in content,
There falls on the old, gray city
An influence luminous and serene,
A shining peace.

The smoke ascends
In a rosy-and-golden haze. The spires
Shine, and are changed. In the valley
Shadows rise. The lark sings on. The sun,
Closing his benediction,
Sinks, and the darkening air
Thrills with a sense of the triumphing night—
Night with her train of stars
And her great gift of sleep.

So be my passing!
My task accomplished and the long day done,
My wages taken, and in my heart
Some late lark singing,
Let me be gathered to the quiet west,
The sundown splendid and serene,
Death.

Tears, Idle Tears

ALFRED, LORD TENNYSON

Tears, idle tears, I know not what they mean,
Tears from the depth of some divine despair
Rise in the heart, and gather to the eyes,
In looking on the happy autumn-fields,
And thinking of the days that are no more.

Fresh as the first beam glittering on a sail,
That brings our friends up from the under-world,
Sad as the last which reddens over one
That sinks with all we love below the verge;
So sad, so fresh, the days that are no more.

Ah, sad and strange as in dark summer dawns
The earliest pipe of half-awakened birds
To dying ears, when unto dying eyes
The casement slowly grows a glimmering square;
So sad, so strange, the days that are no more.

Dear as remembered kisses after death,
And sweet as those by hopeless fancy feigned
On lips that are for others; deep as love,
Deep as first love, and wild with all regret;
O Death in Life, the days that are no more!

A Bird Came Down the Walk
EMILY DICKINSON

A bird came down the walk:
He did not know I saw;
He bit an angle-worm in halves
And ate the fellow, raw.

And then he drank a dew
From a convenient grass,
And then hopped sidewise to the wall
To let a beetle pass.

He glanced with rapid eyes
That hurried all abroad,—
They looked like frightened beads, I thought
He stirred his velvet head

Like one in danger; cautious,
I offered him a crumb,

And he unrolled his feathers
And rowed him softer home

Than oars divide the ocean,
Too silver for a seam,
Or butterflies, off banks of noon,
Leap, plashless, as they swim.

Success Is Counted Sweetest
EMILY DICKINSON

Success is counted sweetest
By those who ne'er succeed.
To comprehend a nectar
Requires sorest need.

Not one of all the purple host
Who took the flag to-day
Can tell the definition,
So clear, of victory,

As he, defeated, dying,
On whose forbidden ear
The distant strains of triumph
Break, agonized and clear.

Because I Could Not Stop for Death
EMILY DICKINSON

Because I could not stop for Death,
He kindly stopped for me;
The carriage held but just ourselves
And Immortality.

We slowly drove, we knew no haste,
And I had put away
My labor, and my leisure too,
For his civility.

We passed the school where children played
Their lessons scarcely done;
We passed the fields of gazing grain,
We passed the setting sun.

We paused before a house that seemed
A swelling on the ground;
The roof was scarcely visible,
The cornice but a mound.

Since then 'tis centuries; but each
Feels shorter than the day
I first surmised the horses' heads
Were toward eternity.

How the Waters Come Down at Lodore
ROBERT SOUTHEY

"How does the Water
Come down at Lodore?"
   From its sources which well
      In the tarn on the fell;
         From its fountains,
         In the mountains,
      Its rills and its gills,—
Through moss and through brake
      It runs and it creeps
      For awhile, till it sleeps
         In its own little lake.
   And thence at departing,
   Awakening and starting,
   It runs through the reeds,
      And away it proceeds
Through meadow and glade,
      In sun and in shade,
And through the wood-shelter,

Among crags in its flurry,
Helter-skelter,
Hurry-skurry.
Here it comes sparkling,
And there it lies darkling;
Now smoking and frothing
Its tumult and wrath in,
Till, in this rapid race
On which it is bent,
It reaches the place
Of its steep descent.
The cataract strong
Then plunges along,
Striking and raging,
As if a war waging
Its caverns and rocks among;
Rising and leaping,
Sinking and creeping,
Swelling and sweeping,
Showering and springing,
Flying and flinging,
Writhing and wringing,
Eddying and whisking,
Spouting and frisking,
Turning and twisting,
Around and around
With endless rebound!
Smiting and fighting,
A sight to delight in;
Confounding, astounding,
Dizzying and deafening the ear with its sound.
Dividing and gliding and sliding,
And falling and brawling and sprawling,
And driving and riving and striving,
And prinkling and twinkling and wrinkling,
And sounding and bounding and rounding,

And bubbling and troubling and doubling,
And grumbling and rumbling and tumbling,
And clattering and battering and shattering:

Retreating and beating and meeting and sheeting,
Delaying and straying and playing and spraying,
Advancing and prancing and glancing and dancing,
Recoiling, turmoiling, toiling and boiling,
And gleaming and streaming and steaming and beaming,
And rushing and flushing and brushing and gushing,
And flapping and rapping and clapping and slapping,
And curling and whirling and purling and twirling,
And thumping and plumping and bumping and jumping,
And dashing and flashing and splashing and clashing:
And so never ending, but always descending,
Sounds and motions for ever and ever are blending,
All at once and all o'er, with a mighty uproar;
And this way the water comes down at Lodore.

The Snow-Storm

RALPH WALDO EMERSON

Announced by all the trumpets of the sky,
Arrives the snow, and, driving o'er the fields,
Seems nowhere to alight: the whited air
Hides hills and woods, the river, and the heaven,
And veils the farmhouse at the garden's end.
The sled and traveller stopped, the courier's feet
Delayed, all friends shut out, the housemates sit
Around the radiant fireplace, enclosed
In a tumultuous privacy of storm.

Come see the north wind's masonry.
Out of an unseen quarry evermore

THE SNOW-STORM: *Parian* = Parian marble, a dazzling white stone
used in ancient Greece

Furnished with tile, the fierce artificer
Curves his white bastions with projected roof
Round every windward stake, or tree, or door.
Speeding, the myriad-handed, his wild work
So fanciful, so savage, nought cares he
For number or proportion. Mockingly,
On coop or kennel he hangs Parian wreaths;
A swan-like form invests the hidden thorn;
Fills up the farmer's lane from wall to wall,
Maugre the farmer's sighs; and, at the gate,
A tapering turret overtops the work:
And when his hours are numbered, and the world
Is all his own, retiring, as he were not,
Leaves, when the sun appears, astonished Art
To mimic in slow structures, stone by stone,
Built in an age, the mad wind's night-work,
The frolic architecture of the snow.

Voluntaries

RALPH WALDO EMERSON

In an age of fops and toys,
Wanting wisdom, void of right,
Who shall nerve heroic boys
To hazard all in Freedom's fight—
Break sharply off their jolly games,
Forsake their comrades gay
And quit proud homes and youthful dames
For famine, toil, and fray?
Yet on the nimble air benign
Speed nimbler messages,
That waft the breath of grace divine
To hearts in sloth and ease.
So nigh is grandeur to our dust,
So near is God to man,
When Duty whispers low, *Thou must,*
The youth replies, *I can.*

I Heard a Linnet Courting

ROBERT BRIDGES

I heard a linnet courting
His lady in the spring:
His mates were idly sporting,
Nor stayed to hear him sing
His song of love.—
I fear my speech distorting
His tender love.

The phrases of his pleading
Were full of young delight;
And she that gave him heeding
Interpreted aright
His gay, sweet notes,—
So sadly marred in the reading,—
His tender notes.

And when he ceased, the hearer
Awaited the refrain,
Till swiftly perching nearer
He sang his song again,
His pretty song:—
Would that my verse spake clearer
His tender song!

Ye happy, airy creatures!
That in the merry spring
Think not of what misfeatures
Or cares the year may bring;
But unto love
Resign your simple natures
To tender love.

Cargoes

JOHN MASEFIELD

Quinquireme of Nineveh from distant Ophir
Rowing home to haven in sunny Palestine,
With a cargo of ivory,
And apes and peacocks,
Sandalwood, cedarwood, and sweet white wine.

Stately Spanish galleon coming from the Isthmus,
Dipping through the Tropics by the palm-green shores,
With a cargo of diamonds,
Emeralds, amethysts,
Topazes, and cinnamon, and gold moidores.

Dirty British coaster with a salt-caked smoke stack
Butting through the Channel in the mad March days,
With a cargo of Tyne coal,
Road-rail, pig-lead,
Firewood, iron-ware, and cheap tin trays.

The Song of the Shirt

THOMAS HOOD

With fingers weary and worn,
With eyelids heavy and red,
A woman sat, in unwomanly rags,
Plying her needle and thread—
Stitch! Stitch! Stitch!
In poverty, hunger, and dirt,
And still with a voice of dolorous pitch
She sang the "Song of the Shirt."

"Work! work! work!
While the cock is crowing aloof!

CARGOES: *quinquireme* = an ancient fifty-oared vessel

And work—work—work,
Till the stars shine through the roof!
It's Oh! to be a slave
Along with the barbarous Turk,
Where woman has never a soul to save,
If this is Christian work.

"Work—work—work,
Till the brain begins to swim;
Work—work—work,
Till the eyes are heavy and dim!
Seam, and gusset, and band,
Band, and gusset, and seam,
Till over the buttons I fall asleep,
And sew them on in a dream!

"Oh, men, with sisters dear!
Oh, men, with mothers and wives!
It is not linen you're wearing out
But human creatures' lives!
Stitch—stitch—stitch,
In poverty, hunger, and dirt,
Sewing at once, with a double thread,
A Shroud as well as a Shirt.

"But why do I talk of Death?
That phantom of grisly bone,
I hardly fear its terrible shape,
It seems so like my own—
It seems so like my own,
Because of the fasts I keep;
Oh, God! that bread should be so dear,
And flesh and blood so cheap!

"Work—work—work!
My labor never flags;

And what are its wages? A bed of straw,
A crust of bread—and rags.
That shattered roof—this naked floor—
A table—a broken chair—
And a wall so blank, my shadow I thank
For sometimes falling there!

"Work—work—work!
From weary chime to chime,
Work—work—work,
As prisoners work for crime!
Band, and gusset, and seam,
Seam, and gusset, and band,
Till the heart is sick, and the brain benumbed,
As well as the weary hand.

"Work—work—work,
In the dull December light,
And work—work—work,
When the weather is warm and bright—
While underneath the eaves
The brooding swallows cling
As if to show me their sunny backs
And twit me with the spring.

"Oh! but to breathe the breath
Of the cowslip and primrose sweet—
With the sky above my head,
And the grass beneath my feet;
For only one short hour
To feel as I used to feel,
Before I knew the woes of want
And the walk that costs a meal.

"Oh! but for one short hour!
A respite however brief!

No blessed leisure for love or hope,
But only time for grief!
A little weeping would ease my heart,
But in their briny bed
My tears must stop, for every drop
Hinders needle and thread!"

Seam, and gusset, and band,
Band, and gusset, and seam,
Work—work—work,
Like the engine that works by steam!
A mere machine of iron and wood
That toils for Mammon's sake,
Without a brain to ponder and craze
Or a heart to feel—and break!

With fingers weary and worn,
With eyelids heavy and red,
A woman sat, in unwomanly rags,
Plying her needle and thread—
Stitch—stitch—stitch!
In poverty, hunger, and dirt,
And still with a voice of dolorous pitch—
Would that its tone could reach the rich!—
She sang this "Song of the Shirt!"

Binsey Poplars, Felled 1879

GERARD MANLEY HOPKINS

My aspens dear, whose airy cages quelled,
Quelled or quenched in leaves the leaping sun,
Are felled, felled, are all felled;
Of a fresh and following and folded rank
Not spared, not one

BINSEY POPLARS, FELLED 1879: *dandled* = pamper; *unselve the* . . .
scene = cut away its fringe of trees

That dandled a sandalled
Shadow that swam or sank
On meadow and river and wind-wandering weed-winding bank.

O if we but knew what we do
When we delve or hew—
Hack and rack the growing green!
Since country is so tender

To touch, her being só slender,
That, like this sleek and seeing ball
But a prick will make no eye at all,
Where we, even where we mean
To mend her we end her,
When we hew or delve:
After-comers cannot guess the beauty been.
Ten or twelve, only ten or twelve

Strokes of havoc únselve
The sweet especial scene,
Rural scene, a rural scene,
Sweet especial rural scene.

Factory Windows Are Always Broken
VACHEL LINDSAY

Factory windows are always broken.
Somebody's always throwing bricks,
Somebody's always heaving cinders,
Playing ugly Yahoo tricks.

Factory windows are always broken.
Other windows are let alone.
No one throws through the chapel-window.
The bitter, snarling derisive stone.

Factory windows are always broken.
Something or other is going wrong.
Something is rotten—I think, in Denmark.
End of factory-window song.

Abraham Lincoln Walks at Midnight
(*In Springfield, Illinois*)
VACHEL LINDSAY

It is portentous, and a thing of state
That here at midnight, in our little town
A mourning figure walks, and will not rest,
Near the old court-house pacing up and down,

Or by his homestead, or in shadowed yards
He lingers where his children used to play,
Or through the market, on the well-worn stones
He stalks until the dawn-stars burn away.

A bronzed, lank man! His suit of ancient black,
A famous high top-hat and plain worn shawl
Make him the quaint great figure that men love,
The prairie-lawyer, master of us all.

He cannot sleep upon his hillside now.
He is among us:—as in times before!
And we who toss and lie awake for long,
Breathe deep, and start, to see him pass the door.

His head is bowed. He thinks of men and kings.
Yea, when the sick world cries, how can he sleep?
Too many peasants fight, they know not why;
Too many homesteads in black terror weep.

The sins of all the war-lords burn his heart.
He sees the dreadnaughts scouring every main.

He carries on his shawl-wrapped shoulders now
The bitterness, the folly and the pain.

He cannot rest until a spirit-dawn
Shall come;—the shining hope of Europe free:
A league of sober folk, the Workers' Earth,
Bringing long peace to Cornland, Alp and Sea.

It breaks his heart that kings must murder still,
That all his hours of travail here for men
Seem yet in vain. And who will bring white peace
That he may sleep upon his hill again?

Caliban in the Coal Mines
LOUIS UNTERMEYER

God, we don't like to complain;
We know that the mine is no lark.
But—there's the pools from the rain;
But—there's the cold and the dark.

God, You don't know what it is—
You, in Your well-lighted sky,
Watching the meteors whizz;
Warm, with the sun always by.

God, if You had but the moon
Stuck in Your cap for a lamp,
Even You'd tire of it soon,
Down in the dark and the damp.

Nothing but blackness above,
And nothing that moves but the cars ...
God, if You wish for our love,
Fling us a handful of stars!

Roadways

JOHN MASEFIELD

One road leads to London,
One road runs to Wales,
My road leads me seawards
To the white dipping sails.

One road leads to the river,
As it goes singing slow;
My road leads to shipping,
Where the bronzed sailors go.

Leads me, lures me, calls me
To salt green tossing sea;
A road without earth's road-dust
Is the right road for me.

A wet road heaving, shining,
And wild with seagulls' cries,
A mad salt sea-wind blowing
The salt spray in my eyes.

My road calls me, lures me
West, east, south, and north;
Most roads lead men homewards,
My road leads me forth

To add more miles to the tally
Of grey miles left behind,
In quest of that one beauty
God put me here to find.

The Vagabond

ROBERT LOUIS STEVENSON

Give to me the life I love,
Let the lave go by me,
Give the jolly heaven above
And the byway nigh me.

Bed in the bush with stars to see,
Bread I dip in the river—
There's the life for a man like me,
There's the life for ever.

Let the blow fall soon or late,
Let what will be o'er me;
Give the face of earth around
And the road before me.
Wealth I seek not, hope nor love,
Nor a friend to know me;
All I seek, the heaven above
And the road below me.

Or let the autumn fall on me
Where afield I linger,
Silencing the bird on tree,
Biting the blue finger:
White as meal the frosty field—
Warm the fireside haven—
Not to autumn will I yield,
Not to winter even!

Let the blow fall soon or late,
Let what will be o'er me;
Give the face of earth around
And the road before me.
Wealth I ask not, hope nor love,
Nor a friend to know me;
All I ask, the heaven above,
And the road below me.

Autumn

RAINER MARIA RILKE

The dry leaves fall, as if from far away,
fall from distant gardens in the skies,
fall with an air of resignation.

And in the night this heavy Earth falls down,
down from the stars, into a loneliness.

All of us fall. This hand must fall.
And look around you: it will all go the same way.

Yet there is One who holds all falling things,
gently, eternally, within His hands.

At the Aquarium

MAX EASTMAN

Serene the silver fishes glide,
Stern-lipped, and pale, and wonder-eyed!
As, through the aged deeps of ocean,
They have no pathway where they go,
They flow like water to and fro,
They watch with never winking eyes,
They watch with staring, cold surprise,
The level people in the air,
The people peering, peering there:
Who wander also to and fro,
And know not why or where they go,
Yet have a wonder in their eyes,
Sometimes a pale and cold surprise.

Shiloh
A Requiem (April, 1862)

HERMAN MELVILLE

Skimming lightly, wheeling still,
The swallows fly low
Over the field in clouded days,
The forest-field of Shiloh—
Over the field where April rain
Solaced the parched one stretched in pain
Through the pause of night
That followed the Sunday fight
Around the church of Shiloh—

The church so lone, the log-built one,
That echoed to many a parting groan
And natural prayer
Of dying foemen mingled there—
Foemen at morn, but friends at eve—
Fame or country least their care:
(What like a bullet can undeceive!)
But now they lie low,
While over them the swallows skim,
And all is hushed at Shiloh.

The Man He Killed

THOMAS HARDY

Had he and I but met
By some old ancient inn,
We should have sat us down to wet
Right many a nipperkin!

But ranged as infantry,
And staring face to face,
I shot at him as he at me,
And killed him in his place.

I shot him dead because—
Because he was my foe,
Just so: my foe of course he was;
That's clear enough; although

He thought he'd 'list, perhaps,
Off-hand like—just as I—
Was out of work—had sold his traps—
No other reason why.

Yes; quaint and curious war is!
You shoot a fellow down
You'd treat if met where any bar is,
Or help to half-a-crown.

THE MAN HE KILLED: *nipperkin* = a liquor container

By Her Aunt's Grave

THOMAS HARDY

"Sixpence a week," says the girl to her lover,
"Aunt used to bring me, for she could confide
In me alone, she vowed. 'Twas to cover
The cost of her headstone when she died.
And that was a year ago last June;
I've not fixed it yet. But I must soon."
"And where is the money now, my dear?"
"O, snug in my purse . . . Aunt was so slow
In saving it—eighty weeks, or near . . ."
"Let's spend it," he hints. "For she won't know.
There's a dance tonight at the Load of Hay."
She passively nods. And they go that way.

Dover Beach

MATTHEW ARNOLD

The sea is calm tonight.
The tide is full, the moon lies fair
Upon the straits; on the French coast the light
Gleams and is gone; the cliffs of England stand
Glimmering and vast, out in the tranquil bay.
Come to the window, sweet is the night air!
Only, from the long line of spray
Where the sea meets the moon-blanch'd land,
Listen! you hear the grating roar
Of pebbles which the waves draw back, and fling,
At their return, up the high strand,
Begin, and cease, and then again begin,
With tremulous cadence slow, and bring
The eternal note of sadness in.

Sophocles long ago
Heard it on the Aegean, and it brought
Into his mind the turbid ebb and flow

DOVER BEACH: *Sophocles* = a Greek tragedian, 5th century B.C.

Of human misery; we
Find also in the sound a thought,
Hearing it by this distant northern sea.

The Sea of Faith
Was once, too, at the full, and round earth's shore
Lay like the folds of a bright girdle furl'd.
But now I only hear
Its melancholy, long, withdrawing roar;
Retreating, to the breath
Of the night-wind, down the vast edges drear
And naked shingles of the world.

Ah, love, let us be true
To one another! for the world, which seems
To lie before us like a land of dreams,
So various, so beautiful, so new,
Hath really neither joy, nor love, nor light,
Not certitude, nor peace, nor help for pain;
And we are here as on a darkling plain
Swept with confused alarms of struggle and flight,
Where ignorant armies clash by night.

Euclid

VACHEL LINDSAY

Old Euclid drew a circle
On a sand-beach long ago.
He bounded and enclosed it
With angles thus and so.
His set of solemn graybeards
Nodded and argued much
Of arc and of circumference,
Diameter and such.
A silent child stood by them
From morning until noon
Because they drew such charming
Round pictures of the moon.

Preludes

T. S. ELIOT

I

The winter evening settles down
With smell of steaks in passageways.
Six o'clock.
The burnt-out ends of smoky days.
And now a gusty shower wraps
The grimy scraps
Of withered leaves about your feet
And newspapers from vacant lots;
The showers beat
On broken blinds and chimney-pots,
And at the corner of the street
A lonely cab-horse steams and stamps.
And then the lighting of the lamps.

II

The morning comes to consciousness
Of faint stale smells of beer
From the sawdust-trampled street
With all its muddy feet that press
To early coffee-stands.
With the other masquerades
That time resumes,
One thinks of all the hands
That are raising dingy shades
In a thousand furnished rooms.

The Stone

WILFRED WILSON GIBSON

"And will you cut a stone for him,
To set above his head?
And will you cut a stone for him—
A stone for him?" she said.

[handwritten marginal notes: "true painting of city, after atmosphere, mostly after atmosphere of life"; "realistic, pessimistic, mostly after atmosphere"; "things go on the same all the time, ofyr discomfort"; "moor noticable"; "people belong nowhere, have nothing"]

Three days before, a splintered rock
Had struck her lover dead—
Had struck him in the quarry dead,
Where, careless of the warning call,
He loitered, while the shot was fired—
A lively stripling, brave and tall,
And sure of all his heart desired . . .
A flash, a shock,
A rumbling fall . . .
And, broken 'neath the broken rock,
A lifeless heap, with face of clay;
And still as any stone he lay,
With eyes that saw the end of all.

I went to break the news to her;
And I could hear my own heart beat
With dread of what my lips might say
But, some poor fool had sped before;
And flinging wide her father's door
Had blurted out the news to her,
Had struck her lover dead for her,
Had struck the girl's heart dead in her,
Had struck life lifeless at a word,
And dropped it at her feet:
Then hurried on his witless way,
Scarce knowing she had heard.

And when I came, she stood alone,
A woman turned to stone:
And, though no word at all she said,
I knew that all was known.
Because her heart was dead,
She did not sigh nor moan,
His mother wept:
She could not weep.
Her lover slept:
She could not sleep.

Three days, three nights,
She did not stir:
Three days, three nights,
Were one to her,
Who never closed her eyes
From sunset to sunrise,
From dawn to evenfall:
Her tearless, staring eyes,
That seeing naught, saw all.

The fourth night when I came from work,
I found her at my door.
"And will you cut a stone for him?"
She said: and spoke no more:
But followed me, as I went in,
And sank upon a chair;
And fixed her grey eyes on my face,
With still, unseeing stare.
And, as she waited patiently,
I could not bear to feel
Those still, gray eyes that followed me,
Those eyes that plucked the heart from me,
Those eyes that sucked the breath from me
And curdled the warm blood in me,
Those eyes that cut me to the bone,
And pierced my marrow like cold steel.

And so I rose, and sought a stone;
And cut it, smooth and square:
And, as I worked, she sat and watched,
Beside me, in her chair.
Night after night, by candlelight,
I cut her lover's name:
Night after night, so still and white,
And like a ghost she came;
And sat beside me in her chair;

And watched with eyes aflame.
She eyed each stroke;
And hardly stirred:
She never spoke
A single word:
And not a sound or murmur broke
The quiet, save the mallet-stroke.
With still eyes ever on my hands,
She watched, with bloodless lips apart,
And silent, indrawn breath:
And every stroke my chisel cut,
Death cut still deeper in her heart:
The two of us were chiseling,
Together, I and death.

And when at length the job was done,
And I had laid the mallet by,
As if, at last, her peace were won,
She breathed his name; and, with a sigh,
Passed slowly through the open door:
And never crossed my threshold more.

Next night I labored late, alone,
To cut her name upon the stone.

The Donkey
G. K. CHESTERTON

When fishes flew and forests walked
And figs grew upon thorn,
Some moment when the moon was blood,
Then surely I was born;

With monstrous head and sickening cry
And ears like errant wings,
The devil's walking parody
On all four-footed things.

The tattered outlaw of the earth,
Of ancient crooked will;
Starve, scourge, deride me: I am dumb,
I keep my secret still.

Fools! For I also had my hour;
One far fierce hour and sweet:
There was a shout about my ears,
And palms before my feet.

Lament

EDNA ST. VINCENT MILLAY

Listen, children:
Your father is dead.
From his old coats
I'll make you little jackets;
I'll make you little trousers
From his old pants.
There'll be in his pockets
Things he used to put there,
Keys and pennies,
Covered with tobacco;
Dan shall have the pennies
To save in his bank;
Anne shall have the keys
To make a pretty noise with.
Life must go on,
And the dead be forgotten;
Life must go on,
Though good men die.
Anne, eat your breakfast;
Dan, take your medicine.
Life must go on;
I forget just why.

Janet Waking

JOHN CROWE RANSOM

Beautifully Janet slept
Till it was deeply morning. She woke then
And thought about her dainty-feathered hen,
To see how it had kept.

One kiss she gave her mother,
Only a small one gave she to her daddy
Who would have kissed each curl of his shining baby;
No kiss at all for her brother.

"Old Chucky, old Chucky!" she cried,
Running across the world upon the grass
To Chucky's house, and listening. But alas,
Her Chucky had died.

It was a transmogrifying bee
Came droning down on Chucky's old bald head
And sat and put the poison. It scarcely bled,
But how exceedingly

And purply did the knot
Swell with the venom and communicate
Its rigor! Now the poor comb stood up straight
But Chucky did not.

So there was Janet
Kneeling on the wet grass, crying her brown hen
(Translated far beyond the daughters of men)
To rise and walk upon it.

And weeping fast as she had breath
Janet implored us, "Wake her from her sleep!"
And would not be instructed in how deep
Was the forgetful kingdom of death.

JANET WAKING: *transmogrifying* = a humorous coinage from trans-
mogrify, meaning to transform

Bells for John Whiteside's Daughter
JOHN CROWE RANSOM

There was such speed in her little body,
And such lightness in her footfall,
It is no wonder her brown study
Astonishes us all.

Her wars were bruited in our high window.
We looked among orchard trees and beyond,
Where she took arms against her shadow,
Or harried unto the pond

The lazy geese, like a snow cloud
Dripping their snow on the green grass,
Tricking and stopping, sleepy and proud,
Who cried in goose, Alas,

For the tireless heart within the little
Lady with rod that made them rise
From their noon apple-dreams and scuttle
Goose-fashion under the skies!

But now go the bells, and we are ready,
In one house we are sternly stopped
To say we are vexed at her brown study,
Lying so primly propped.

The Eagle and the Mole
ELINOR WYLIE

Avoid the reeking herd,
Shun the polluted flock, *worker in assembly line*
Live like that stoic bird,
The eagle of the rock.

BELLS FOR JOHN WHITESIDE'S DAUGHTER: *brown study* = usually, a
revery or state of deep thought; here, a metaphor for death

The huddled warmth of crowds
Begets and fosters hate;
He keeps, above the clouds,
His cliff inviolate.

When flocks are folded warm,
And herds to shelter run,
He sails above the storm,
He stares into the sun.

If in the eagle's track
Your sinews cannot leap,
Avoid the lathered pack,
Turn from the steaming sheep.

If you would keep your soul
From spotted sight or sound,
Live like the velvet mole; Learn it non researcher
Go burrow underground.

And there hold intercourse
With roots of trees and stones,
With rivers at their source,
And disembodied bones.

One Star Fell and Another
CONRAD AIKEN

One star fell and another as we walked.
Lifting his hand toward the west, he said—
—How prodigal that sky is of its stars!
They fall and fall, and still the sky is sky.
Two more have gone, but heaven is heaven still.

Then let us not be precious of our thought,
Nor of our words, nor hoard them up as though

ONE STAR FELL AND ANOTHER: *foplings* = a little fop, a foolish silly
person

We thought our minds a heaven which might change
And lose its virtue when the word had fallen.
Let us be prodigal, as heaven is;
Lose what we lose, and give what we may give,—
Ourselves are still the same. Lost you a planet—?
Is Saturn gone? Then let him take his rings
Into the Limbo of forgotten things.

O little foplings of the pride of mind,
Who wrap the phrase in lavender, and keep it
In order to display it: and you, who save our loves
As if we had not worlds of love enough—!

Let us be reckless of our words and worlds,
And spend them freely as the tree his leaves;
And give them where the giving is most blest.
What should we save them for,—a night of frost? . . .
All lost for nothing, and ourselves a ghost.

The Day
THEODORE SPENCER

The day was a year at first
When children ran in the garden;
The day shrank down to a month
When the boys played ball.

The day was a week thereafter
When young men walked in the garden;
The day was itself a day
When love grew tall.

The day shrank down to an hour
When old men limped in the garden;
The day will last forever
When it is nothing at all.

King Juke

KENNETH FEARING

The juke box has a big square face,
A majestic face, softly glowing with red and green and purple
    lights.
Have you got a face as bright as that?

BUT IT'S A PROVEN FACT, THAT A JUKE BOX HAS NO
    EARS.

With its throat of brass, the juke box eats live nickels raw;
It can turn itself on or shut itself off;
It has no hangovers, knows no regrets, and it never feels the need
    for sleep.
Can you do that?
What can you do that a juke box can't, and do it ten times better
    than you?

And it hammers at your nerves, and stabs you through the heart,
    and beats upon your soul—
But can you do that to the box?

Its resourceful mind, filled with thoughts that range from love to
    grief, from the gutter to the stars, from pole to pole,
Can seize its thoughts between fingers of steel,
Begin them at the start and follow them through in an orderly
    fashion at the very end.
Can you do that?
And what can you say that a juke box can't, and say it in a
    clearer, louder voice than yours?
What have you got, a juke box hasn't got?

Well, a juke box has no ears, they say.
The box, it is believed, cannot even hear itself.
IT SIMPLY HAS NO EARS AT ALL.

Eight-Cylinder Man

FLORENCE RIPLEY MASTIN

He grinds the clover at its root
with a creaking and enormous foot.
In his circumference vast and dim
no small life has a place for him.
The needlepoint of curious moss
where delicate footprints cross,
the brook composing mountain blues,
the bereaved and cynical yews,
columbines dancing on a wall—
these he has never seen at all.

Speed is the only register
within his mind, and in that blur
of gas and gleaming chromium
he adds the swiftly mounting sum
of miles, a purely abstract space,
and passes summer face to face.

The Fury of Aerial Bombardment

RICHARD EBERHART

You would think the fury of aerial bombardment
Would rouse God to relent; the infinite spaces
Are still silent. He looks on shock-pried faces.
History, even, does not know what is meant.

You would feel that after so many centuries
God would give man to repent; yet he can kill
As Cain could, but with a multitudinous will,
No further advanced than in his ancient furies.

Was man made stupid to see his own stupidity?
Is God by definition indifferent, beyond us all?

THE FURY OF AERIAL BOMBARDMENT: *belt feed lever* and *belt . . . pawl*
= units of a machine gun

Is the eternal truth man's fighting soul
Wherein the Beast ravens in its own avidity?

Of Van Wettering I speak, and Averill,
Names on a list, whose faces I do not recall
But they are gone to early death, who late in school
Distinguished the belt feed lever from the belt holding pawl.

The Death of the Ball Turret Gunner

RANDALL JARRELL

From my mother's sleep I fell into the State,
And I hunched in its belly till my wet fur froze.
Six miles from earth, loosed from its dream of life,
I woke to black flak and the nightmare fighters.
When I died they washed me out of the turret with a hose.

Vale from Carthage

(Spring, 1944)

PETER VIERECK

I, now at Carthage. He, shot dead at Rome.
Shipmates last May. "And what if one of us,"
I asked last May, in fun, in gentleness,
"Wears doom like dungarees, and doesn't know?"
He laughed, *Not see Times Square again?*" The foam
Feathering across that deck a year ago,
Swept those five words—like seeds—beyond the seas

Into his future. There they grew like trees;
And as he passed them there next spring, they laid
Upon his road of fire their sudden shade.
Though he had always scraped his mess-kit pure
And scrubbed redeemingly his barracks floor,
Though all his buttons glowed their ritual-hymn

THE DEATH OF THE BALL TURRET GUNNER: *ball turret* = glass, ball-shaped turret on a plane's fuselage

Like cloudless moons to intercede for him,
No furlough fluttered from the sky. He will
Not see Time Square—he will not see—he will
Not see Times
    change; at Carthage (while my friend,
Living those words at Rome, screamed in the end)
I saw an ancient Roman's tomb and read
Vale in stone. Here two wars mix their dead:
    Roman, my shipmate's dream walks hand in hand
    With yours tonight ("New York again" and "Rome"),
    Like widowed sisters bearing water home
    On tired heads through hot Tunisian sand
    In good cool urns, and says, "I understand."
Roman, you'll see your Forum Square no more;
What's left but this to say of any war?

Auto Wreck

KARL SHAPIRO

Its quick soft silver bell beating, beating,
And down the dark one ruby flare
Pulsing out red light like an artery,
The ambulance at top speed floating down
Past beacons and illuminated clocks
Wings in a heavy curve, dips down,
And brakes speed, entering the crowd.
The doors leap open, emptying light;
Stretchers are laid out, the mangled lifted
And stowed into the little hospital.
Then the bell, breaking the hush, tolls once,
And the ambulance with its terrible cargo
Rocking, slightly rocking, moves away,
As the doors, an afterthought, are closed.

We are deranged, walking among the cops
Who swept glass and are large and composed.

One is still making notes under the light.
One with a bucket douches ponds of blood
Into the street and gutter.
One hangs lanterns on the wrecks that cling,
Empty husks of locusts, to iron poles.

Our throats were tight as tourniquets,
Our feet were bound with splints, but now
Like convalescents intimate and gauche,
We speak through sickly smiles and warn
With the stubborn saw of common sense,
The grim joke and the banal resolution.
The traffic moves around with care,
But we remain, touching a wound
That opens to our richest horror.

Already old, the question Who shall die?
Becomes unspoken Who is innocent?
For death in war is done by hands;
Suicide has cause and stillbirth, logic.
But this invites the occult mind,
Cancels our physics with a sneer,
And spatters all we knew of denouement
Across the expedient and wicked stones.

The Horse Chestnut Tree
RICHARD EBERHART

Boys in sporadic but tenacious droves
Come with sticks, as certainly as Autumn,
To assault the great horse chestnut tree.

There is a law governs their lawlessness.
Desire is in them for a shining amulet
And the best are those that are highest up.

They will not pick them easily from the ground.
With shrill arms they fling to the higher branches,
To hurry the work of nature for their pleasure.

I have seen them trooping down the street
Their pockets stuffed with chestnuts shucked, unshucked.
It is only evening keeps them from their wish.

Sometimes I run out in a kind of rage
To chase the boys away; I catch an arm,
Maybe, and laugh to think of being the lawgiver.

I was once such a young sprout myself
And fingered in my pocket the prize and trophy.
But still I moralize upon the day.

And see that we, outlaws on God's property,
Fling out imagination beyond the skies
Wishing a tangible good from the unknown.

And likewise death will drive us from the scene
With the great flowering world unbroken yet,
Which we held in idea, a little handful.

I May, I Might, I Must
MARIANNE MOORE

If you will tell me why the fen
appears impassable, I then
will tell you why I think that I
can get across it if I try.

The Fish
ELIZABETH BISHOP

I caught a tremendous fish
and held him beside the boat
half out of water, with my hook

fast in a corner of his mouth.
He didn't fight.
He hadn't fought at all.
He hung a grunting weight,
battered and venerable
and homely. Here and there
his grown skin hung in strips
like ancient wall-paper,
and its pattern of darker brown
was like wall-paper:
shapes like full-blown roses
stained and lost through age.
He was speckled with barnacles,
fine rosettes of lime,
and infested
with tiny white sea-lice,
and underneath two or three
rags of green weed hung down.
While his gills were breathing in
the terrible oxygen
—the frightening gills,
fresh and crisp with blood,
that can cut so badly—
I thought of the coarse white flesh
packed in like feathers,
the big bones and the little bones,
the dramatic reds and blacks
of his shiny entrails,
and the pink swim-bladder
like a big peony.
I looked into his eyes
which were far larger than mine
but shallower, and yellowed,
the irises backed and packed
with tarnished tinfoil
seen through the lenses

of old scratched isinglass.
They shifted a little, but not
to return my stare.
—It was more like the tipping
of an object toward the light.
I admired his sullen face,
the mechanism of his jaw,
and then I saw
that from his lower lip
—if you could call it a lip—
grim, wet, and weapon-like,
hung five old pieces of fish-line,
or four and a wire leader
with the swivel still attached,
with all their five big hooks
grown firmly in his mouth.
A green line, frayed at the end
where he broke it, two heavier lines,
and a fine black thread
still crimped from the strain and snap
when it broke and he got away.
Like medals with their ribbons
frayed and wavering,
a five-haired beard of wisdom
trailing from his aching jaw.
I stared and stared
and victory filled up
the little rented boat,
from the pool of bilge
where oil had spread a rainbow
around the rusted engine
to the bailer rusted orange,
the sun-cracked thwarts,
the oarlocks on their strings,
the gunnels—until everything
was rainbow, rainbow, rainbow!
And I let the fish go.

Sky-Writer

VINCENT STARRETT

Today, while thousands stared with captured eyes,
And vaguely wondered how the thing was done,
Across the shifting billboard of the skies
There flashed an aeroplane that whirled and spun
Upward in some fantastical unrest,
Writing in smoke a flippant epithet,
As if to challenge Heaven itself to test
The virtues of that famous cigarette.

Much had I pondered how the world might learn
What wonder and what miracle was mine.
Lo, I have found a vehicle to burn
My boast of happiness from pole to line . . .
Harness your breeze, mad gods, and stand from under,
While I inscribe her name beside the thunder!

Evening

ROBERT WALLACE

Sunly the day streams
into dark,

Sky of ribbed orange and blue
above the park.

In the trees chattering
birds discuss

The strange anarchy of
the populace.

The Bird Fancier

JAMES KIRKUP

Up to his shoulders
In grasses coarse as silk,
The white cat with the yellow eyes

Sits with his paws together,
Tall as a quart of milk.

He hardly moves his head
To touch with neat nose
What his wary whiskers tell him
Is here a weed
And here a rose.

His sleepy eyes are wild with birds.
Every sparrow, thrush, and wren
Widens their furred horizons;
Then their flying song
Narrows them again.

Steam Shovel

CHARLES MALAM

The dinosaurs are not all dead.
I saw one raise its iron head
To watch me walking down the road
Beyond our house today.
Its jaws were dripping with a load
Of earth and grass that it had cropped.
It must have heard me where I stopped,
Snorted white steam my way,
And stretched its long neck out to see,
And chewed, and grinned quite amiably.

The Monkey

VLADISLAV KHODASEVICH

The day was hot. The forests were on fire.
Time dragged. Behind the country house next door
A cock was crowing. The gate swung behind me.

There on a bench, leaning against the fence,
A wandering Serb, lean, swarthy, had dozed off.
A heavy cross, fashioned of silver, hung
On his half-naked breast, down which great drops
Of sweat were rolling. On the fence, close by,
A small red-skirted monkey crouched, and chewed
The dusty leaves of lilac overhead.
A leather collar on a heavy chain
That pulled her back pressed hard against her throat.
The Serb, roused by my step, awoke and wiped
His sweat, and begged some water for the creature.
He tasted it, to test how cold it was,
Then placed the saucer on the bench. At once
The monkey, wetting eager fingers, seized
The saucer in both hands. She leaned her elbows
Upon the bench, and crouching thus, she drank.
Her chin was almost resting on the boards,
And her back arched above her half-bald head.
Even so Darius, centuries ago,
Fleeing the phalanxes of Alexander,
Must have leaned to a puddle in the road.
When she had drunk her water, casually
The monkey brushed the saucer off the bench,
And standing up, with an immortal gesture
She offered me her small black horny hand
The moisture had left cool . . .
Though I have pressed the hands of lovely women,
Of poets, and of men who led a nation,
Yet there was not one hand among them all
Had such a noble shape. Not any hand
Ever touched mine in such full comradeship!
I swear by God that no one ever looked
Into my eyes so wisely and so deeply;
Her soft gaze pierced me. That indigent creature
Revived for me the sweetest lore bequeathed
By far antiquity to human hearts.

And in that moment life appeared so full,
It seemed to me the sun and moon, the waves
Of all the seas, the winds, the heavenly spheres,
Were choiring together, organ music
That rang as wonderfully in my ears
As in the days beyond man's memory.
And then the Serb, knuckling his tambourine,
Went off, the monkey perched on his left shoulder:
A maharajah on an elephant.
And in the heavens, wreathed in opal smoke,
A swollen, raspberry-colored sun was hanging.
Heat, with no hope of thunder, lay upon
The wheat fields that were wilting in the blaze.
That was the very day war was declared.

Country Club Sunday
PHYLLIS MC GINLEY

It is a beauteous morning, calm and free.
The fairways sparkle. Gleam the shaven grasses.
Mirth fills the locker rooms and, hastily,
Stewards fetch ice, fresh towels, and extra glasses.

On terraces the sandaled women freshen
Their lipstick; gather to gossip, poised and cool;
And the shrill adolescent takes possession,
Plunging and splashing, of the swimming pool.

It is a beauteous morn, opinion grants.
Nothing remains of last night's Summer Formal
Save palms and streamers and the wifely glance,
Directed with more watchfulness than normal,
At listless mate who tugs his necktie loose,
Moans, shuns the light, and gulps tomato juice.

COUNTRY CLUB SUNDAY: see page 329

Nebraska

JON SWAN

There, there is no mountain within miles.
The land, slowly rising toward a distant glory,
Is devoid of ornaments or sudden splendor.
It is a land no tourist travels far to see.

Those who ride through it, hurrying to strong streams
Broken and shot across stone, or running to find
Gay palaces to possess the mind, hardly notice as they pass,
Or note with anger, the constant, level wind.

Yet this, the one companion of the land,
Might tell them, though they are always hurrying,
And though they hate that hot and wheat-high wind:
This was the bed of forgotten seas; this wheat its blossoming.

Three Jet Planes

MAY SWENSON

Three jet planes skip above the roofs
    through a tri-square of blue
    tatooed by TV crossbars
    that lean in cryptic concert in their wake.

Like skaters on a lake
    combined into a perfect arrowhead up there
    they sever space with bloodless speed
    and are gone without a clue

but a tiny bead the eye can scarcely find
leaving behind
where they first burst into blue
the invisible boiling wind of sound

As horsemen used to do
As horsemen used to gallop through
a hamlet on hunting morn
and heads and arms were thrust
through windows
leaving behind them the torn
shriek of the hound
and their wrestling dust

Above the roofs three jet planes
leave their hoofs of violence on naive ground.

Hiroshima

MURRAY NOSS

A saucer-valley open oven,
a dish of tea on which the tea leaves
dried and baked into a pattern
of streets and houseplots,
An archeologic study like Pompeii's ruins:
fragile cups and china figurines
lie chipless upon the green-glazed
sand among the shivered bricks;
I mount the little concrete bridge and see
the cross-like shadow burnt thereon
of the unknown little man;
Standing below the spot where forty days before
the light that brought the mushroom-clouded
darkness burst upon the world,

I see a branchless stump of tree,
  two hollowed concrete shells,
  and nothing more
Except a crumbled cross of what might once
  have been a Christian church.

Elegy for Jane
(My student, thrown by a horse)
THEODORE ROETHKE

I remember the neckcurls, limp and damp as tendrils;
And her quick look, a sidelong pickerel smile;
And how, once startled into talk, the light syllables leaped for her,
And she balanced in the delight of her thought,
A wren happy, tail into the wind,
Her song trembling the twigs and small branches.
The shade sang with her;
The leaves, their whispers turned to kissing,
And the mould sang in the bleached valleys under the rose.

Oh, when she was sad, she cast herself down into such a pure
    depth,
Even a father could not find her:
Scraping her cheek against straw,
Stirring the clearest water.

My sparrow, you are not here,
Waiting like a fern, making a spiney shadow.
The sides of wet stones cannot console me,
Nor the moss, wound with the last light.

If only I could nudge you from this sleep,
My maimed darling, my skittery pigeon.

Over the damp grave I speak the words of my love:
I, with no rights in this matter,
Neither father nor lover.

Poetry

MARIANNE MOORE

I, too, dislike it: there are things that are important beyond all
    this fiddle.
  Reading it, however, with a perfect contempt for it, one dis-
    covers in
  it after all, a place for the genuine.
    Hands that can grasp, eyes
    that can dilate, hair that can rise
      if it must, these things are important not because a

high-sounding interpretation can be put upon them but because
    they are
  useful. When they become so derivative as to become unintel-
    ligible,
  the same thing may be said for all of us, that we
    do not admire what
    we cannot understand: the bat
      holding on upside down or in quest of something to

eat, elephants pushing, a wild horse taking a roll, a tireless wolf
    under
  a tree, the immovable critic twitching his skin like a horse that
    feels a flea, the base-
  ball fan, the statistician—
    nor is it valid
      to discriminate against 'business documents and

school-books'; all these phenomena are important. One must make
        a distinction
however: when dragged into prominence by half poets, the re-
        sult is not poetry,
nor till the poets among us can be
    'literalists of
    the imagination'—above
        insolence and triviality and can present

for inspection, 'imaginary gardens with real toads in them,' shall
        we have
it. In the meantime, if you demand on the one hand,
the raw material of poetry in
    all its rawness and
    that which is on the other hand
        genuine, you are interested in poetry.

Ars Poetica

ARCHIBALD MAC LEISH

    A poem should be palpable and mute
    As a globed fruit

    Dumb
    As old medallions to the thumb

    Silent as the sleeve-worn stone
    Of casement ledges where the moss has grown—

    A poem should be wordless
    As the flight of birds

A poem should be motionless in time
As the moon climbs

Leaving, as the moon releases
Twig by twig the night-entangled trees,

Leaving, as the moon behind the winter leaves,
Memory by memory the mind—

A poem should be motionless in time
As the moon climbs

A poem should be equal to
Not true

For all the history of grief
An empty doorway and a maple leaf

For love
The leaning grasses and two lights above the sea—

A poem should not mean
But be.

The Composer

W. H. AUDEN

All the others translate: the painter sketches
A visible world to love or reject;
Rummaging into his living, the poet fetches
The images out that hurt and connect.

From Life to Art by painstaking adaption,
Relying on us to cover the rift;

Only your notes are pure contraption,
Only your song is an absolute gift.

Pour out your presence, O delight, cascading
The falls of the knee and the weirs of the spine,
Our climate of silence and doubt invading;

You alone, alone, O imaginary song,
Are unable to say an existence is wrong,
And pour out your forgiveness like a wine.

ANSWER KEY

CHAPTER 1

Exercise: Identifying Poems
Selections 1, 2, 3, and 5 are poems.
Selection 4 is a passage from Joseph Conrad's novel *Typhoon*.

CHAPTER 2

Exercise: Discovering Meter
1. iambic tetrameter   *2.* trocaic dimeter with an extra accent
3. anapestic trimeter   *4.* trocaic tetrameter   *5.* iambic pentameter
6. iambic pentameter   *7.* dactylic trimeter with an extra accent
8. iambic hexameter   *9.* anapestic tetrameter   *10.* spondaic dimeter   *11.* iambic pentameter   *12.* trochaic tetrameter

Exercise: Hearing Rhythm and Rhyme
1. b   *2.* c   *3.* c   *4.* a   *5.* a

Exercise: The Sound of a Poem
A. 1. aabbccdd
   2. trochaic, iambic
   3. sweet violets sicken/ beloved's bed/ thy thoughts when thou art.
   4. Live within the sense they quicken/ when sweet violets sicken/ beloved's bed.
   5. itself shall slumber

412

Index of Titles

INDEX OF TITLES

Index of Authors and Titles

INDEX OF AUTHORS AND TITLES

INDEX OF AUTHORS AND TITLES